Introduction to financial investment

KEITH REDHEAD
Principal Lecturer
Coventry University Business School

PRENTICE HALL
WOODHEAD-FAULKNER

LONDON NEW YORK TORONTO SYDNEY TOKYO
SINGAPORE MADRID MEXICO CITY MUNICH

First published 1995 by
Prentice Hall/Woodhead-Faulkner Limited

Campus 400, Maylands Avenue
Hemel Hempstead
Hertfordshire, HP2 7EZ

A division of
Simon & Schuster International Group

Typeset in 10 on $12\frac{1}{2}$pt Sabon
by MHL Typesetting Ltd, Coventry

Printed and bound in Great Britain by
T.J. Press (Padstow) Ltd

British Library Cataloguing in Publication Data

A catalogue record for this book is available from
the British Library

ISBN 0-13-355686-7 (pbk)

1 2 3 4 5 99 98 97 96 95

Contents

Preface

Financial investment is now one of the essential decisions taken by a large proportion, probably a majority, of the adult populations of developed countries. Although direct holding of stocks and bonds remains a minority (albeit a significant minority) activity, many more people have collective investments in forms such as pension funds and insurance funds. Indeed with demographic trends increasing the proportion of pensioners in the population governments are signalling their reduced future provision in the form of state pensions. Reduced government provision requires increased investment by individuals in their preparations for retirement.

This need for increased personal investment arises against a background of increasing volatility in financial markets. In the early 1970s the Bretton Woods system of fixed exchange rates broke down. As exchange rates began to fluctuate governments resorted to the manipulation of interest rates in an attempt to control exchange rate movements. So interest rates also became more volatile. Since interest rates are a major determinant of stock and bond prices the increased volatility of interest rates made stock market prices more unstable. So the early 1970s saw the beginning of much increased financial instability. This increased instability was accompanied by a rapid development of derivative instruments whose purpose is the provision of means to manage the risks arising from the instability of financial markets.

This book is written for three types of reader. There is the retail investor (individual investor) who needs to make the decision on how best to invest for good returns whilst avoiding excessive risk. Secondly, there is the professional investment manager who makes investment decisions on behalf of retail investors. Thirdly, there are students of finance, whether on professional or academic courses. The increasing importance of investment and finance in unversity courses reflects the growing importance of financial investment in the lives of most people.

Financial investment is a rapidly growing industry. Within that industry probably the most rapidly growing dimension is that of financial derivatives. Options, futures, forwards and swaps have greatly increased the ability to manage the risks and returns on investments. A feature of this book is that it puts the contribution of derivatives into sharp focus, both in the role of the management of other investments and in the role of a distinct class of asset in their own right.

Last but not least, a word of thanks is due to Chandrika, Lin, and Sandra whose word-processing skills have made up for my lack of them.

1

Introduction: risk and return

Investment returns

It is important to be clear as to what is meant when investment returns are being referred to. In particular, a number of important distinctions need to be made.

INTEREST YIELD VERSUS TOTAL RETURN

When money is deposited in a bank account it leads to a flow of interest payments, and these payments are the only source of return on the deposit. Other investments have two sources of return: not only are there income flows such as interest payments but there are also capital gains or losses. Taking the example of bonds Figure 1.1 illustrates the interest yield (alternatively known as the coupon yield, flat yield or running yield). Bonds typically pay a fixed sum, the coupon, at specified intervals: for example, every six months. The interest yield is calculated as the annual coupon payments divided by the current bond price.

Figure 1.2 illustrates the calculation of the redemption yield, which is the total return on a bond. The redemption yield incorporates both the coupon yield and the prospective capital gain. The example in Figure 1.2 uses a bond maturing in one year. For a bond with a more distant maturity the redemption yield would be calculated as the rate of discount that equates the future cash flows (coupon payments and principal repayment) with the present bond price. When a bond

---

Interest yield (flat yield) $= \dfrac{\text{Coupon}}{\text{Bond price}}$

Example
- Coupon   £10 p.a.
- Bond price   £98

Therefore, interest yield $= \dfrac{£10}{£98} \times 100 = 10.2\%$ p.a.

Note: Interest yield ignores capital gains or losses

Figure 1.1 Illustration of the interest yield on bonds

1

Redemption yield incorporates coupon and capital gain or loss

Example

- Coupon £10 p.a.
- Bond price £98
- Bond matures in 1 year

Therefore: Interest yield $= \dfrac{£10}{£98} \times 100 = 10.2\%$

Capital gain $= \dfrac{£2}{£98} \times 100 = 2.04\%$

Redemption yield $= \dfrac{£12}{£98} \times 100 = 12.24\%$

Figure 1.2 Calculation of the redemption yield on a bond

has a maturity that lies beyond the date at which an investor is likely to sell the bond it is necessary to estimate the expected selling price in order to calculate the total return over the holding period. In this case the difference between the present and future bond prices might be divided by the number of years for which the bond is expected to be held in order to ascertain prospective capital gain (or loss) per year. This would then be added to the annual coupon payments when estimating the total rate of return on the bond.

RATES OF INTEREST VERSUS RATES OF DISCOUNT

Some investments, such as Treasury bills and zero coupon bonds, pay no interest or coupon. Capital gain is the only source of return on such securities. Figure 1.3 compares interest basis and discount basis. It can be seen that a 10 per cent rate of discount is equivalent to a rate of interest of 11.1 per cent. Bills promise the payment of a specific sum of money at maturity (redemption) and provide a return to investors by selling at a lower price (at a discount). The percentage rate of discount on bills is expressed relative to the sum payable at redemption whereas the interest on deposits is expressed relative to the sum invested. As a result a particular rate of discount (e.g. 10 per cent) is worth more than the rate of interest of the same percentage.

Exercise 1.1

Question
If the current rate of discount on Treasury bills is 11 per cent p.a., calculate the price of a £50,000 ninety-one-day bill with sixty days to redemption. What will its price be in four weeks' time if interest rates remain unchanged? What assumptions need to be made in order to make these calculations?

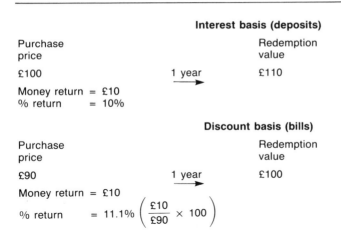

Interest basis (deposits)

Purchase price		Redemption value

£100   1 year ⟶   £110

Money return = £10
% return = 10%

Discount basis (bills)

Purchase price   Redemption value

£90   1 year ⟶   £100

Money return = £10

% return = 11.1% $\left(\dfrac{£10}{£90} \times 100 \right)$

Figure 1.3 Comparison of interest basis and discount basis

Answer

The sixty-day rate of discount is:

$(60/365) \times 11\% = 1.81\%$

So the price of the Treasury bill is

$(100 - 1.81) \times £50,000 = £49,096.$

After four weeks there would be $60 - 28 = 32$ days to redemption.

The thirty-two-day rate of discount is:

$(32/365) \times 11\% = 0.96\%$

So the price of the Treasury bill would be:

$(100 - 0.96) \times £50,000 = £49,518.$

It has been necessary to assume a flat yield curve over the one- to ninety-one-day period.

NOMINAL VERSUS REAL RATES OF RETURN

Figure 1.4 illustrates the distinction between nominal and real rates of return. The nominal rate of return is made up of an income flow (interest, coupon or dividend payments) and the capital gain or loss. If there is a prospect of inflation, then some return is required simply to compensate for the rise in prices. The real return is the yield net of compensation for inflation. The real return measures the receipts from investment in terms of enhanced purchasing power.

3

Nominal rate of return = $\dfrac{\text{Income flow + Capital gain}}{\text{Cost of investment}}$

$R_N = R_R + I_P + (R_R \times I_P)$

where

R_N = Nominal rate of return
R_R = Real rate of return
I_P = Rate of inflation

$(1 + R_N) = (1 + R_R)(1 + I_P)$
$(1 + R_R) = (1 + R_N)/(1 + I_P)$

Figure 1.4 The distinction between the nominal and real rates of return

SIMPLE RETURNS VERSUS COMPOUND RETURNS

Simple returns are based on dividing the return over a period by the number of years in that period. However, such an approach ignores the fact that cash flows from investments can be reinvested. The compound rate of return is based on receipts being reinvested and hence producing their own returns. The formula is shown in Figure 1.5.

For example, if an investment produces returns of 0, 10, and 20 per cent in successive years the average simple rate of return would be 10 per cent, whereas the average compound rate of return would be $[(1.0)(1.1)(1.2)]^{1/3} - 1 = 0.097$ i.e. 9.7 per cent p.a. When compounding (returns on returns) is allowed for, the underlying rate required for the realisation of a particular sum of money is lower (e.g. 9.7 per cent p.a. as opposed to 10 per cent p.a.). Examples of calculating the average compound rate of return are shown in Figure 1.6.

The average compound rate of return (or geometric mean rate of return)

= [(final value of investment)/(initial investment)]$^{1/N}$ − 1

where N = number of time periods

Figure 1.5 The formula for calculating the average compound rate of return

Average compound rate of return

1. 1st year 5% p.a.
   2nd year 6% p.a.

   Average compound rate of return over two years $= \sqrt{(1.05)(1.06)} - 1$
   $= 0.055$, i.e. 5.5% p.a.

2. 1st year 5% p.a.
   2nd year 6% p.a.
   3rd year 16% p.a.

   Average compound rate of return over three years $= [(1.05)(1.06)(1.16)]^{1/3} - 1$
   $= 0.089$, i.e. 8.9% p.a.

Note: The arithmetic average is reasonably accurate when rates vary little from year to year.

Figure 1.6 Illustration of the average compound rate of return

Exercise 1.2

Question
1. A bank deposit pays 8 per cent one year and 10 per cent the next. Calculate the average compound rate of return.
2. Suppose that the figures in item 1 are nominal interest rates and that inflation in the two years was 5 per cent and 8 per cent. Calculate the average compound real rate of return.
3. If the proceeds of the deposit in items 1 and 2 were reinvested for a further year at 10 per cent while inflation during that third year was 12 per cent, what would the average compound nominal and real rates of return have been over the three-year period?
4. What were the nominal and real values of the investment at the end of each of the three years?

Answer
1. $\sqrt{[(1.08)(1.1)]} - 1 = 0.09$ as a decimal, which as a percentage is 9 per cent p.a.
2. $\sqrt{[(1.08/1.05)(1.1/1.08)]} - 1 = 0.0235$ as a decimal, which as a percentage is 2.35 per cent p.a.
3. The average compound nominal rate of return for the three years would have been $[(1.08)(1.1)(1.1)]^{1/3} - 1 = 0.0933$ as a decimal, which as a percentage is 9.33 per cent p.a. The average compound real rate of return for the three years would have been $[(1.08/1.05)(1.1/1.08)(1.1/1.12)]^{1/3} - 1 = 0.0095$ as a decimal and 0.95 per cent p.a. as a percentage.
4. For each unit of currency deposited the nominal value of the investment at the end of each of the three years was (1) 1.08, (2) $1.08 \times 1.1 = 1.188$, (3) $1.08 \times 1.1 \times 1.1 = 1.307$ and the real values were (1) $1.08/1.05 = 1.029$, (2) $(1.08/1.05)(1.1/1.08) = 1.048$, (3) $(1.08/1.05)(1.1/1.08)(1.1/1.12) = 1.029$.

Investment risk

The risk on financial assets is frequently subdivided between systematic and non-systematic risk. Systematic risk is common to all assets whereas non-systematic risk is specific to individual assets or classes of assets. Figure 1.7 indicates major sources of these types of risk.

SYSTEMATIC RISK

Market risk perhaps typifies sytematic risk. When the stock market as a whole rises individual stock prices tend to rise with it. So one source of price volatility, and hence risk, of an individual stock is the general sentiment that moves the stock market as a whole. That general sentiment would be the result of many influences stemming from economic developments. One aspect of the economy might be of particular note in this context, and that is the level of interest rates. Rising interest rates tend to be associated with falling stock and bond prices, and vice versa (this follows from asset prices being the present values of expected income flows and the rates of discount of these income flows being related to interest rates).

Another general source of risk arises from changes in the rate of inflation

---

Types of investment risk

Systematic (non-diversifiable) risk

Market risk
• interest rate risk

Inflation risk
• purchasing power risk
• interest rate risk
• market risk

Political risk
• tax rate risk

Exchange rate risk

Non-systematic (diversifiable) risk

Industry risk

Specific risk
• management risk
• operating risk
• financial risk
• default risk
• credit risk
• information risk
• liquidity risk
• manipulation risk

Systematic risk + non-systematic risk = total risk

Figure 1.7 Sources of investment risk

(especially when they are not expected). Inflation erodes the purchasing power of money, so that income receipts from investments lose value. Investments that are often regarded as safe, such as bank deposits, government bonds, and national savings are vulnerable to this source of risk whereas investments normally seen as risky such as corporate stocks (company shares) tend to produce dividend flows that rise to compensate for inflation. Although interest rates may adjust so as to incorporate compensation for expected inflation they would not compensate for inflation that is not expected.

Inflation can have indirect influences on the prices of financial assets. When expectations of inflation are incorporated into interest rates the resulting interest rate changes will impact on the prices of stocks, bonds and other financial investments. Changes in the rate of inflation may also move share prices as a whole and hence constitute a source of market risk.

Political risks are also common to a wide range of financial investments, at least within the borders of a particular country. The election of a government that is seen as very left wing may adversely affect stock market prices. International tension often results in market falls. For example, Middle East conflicts may threaten oil supplies and hence the operation of national economies. A specific type of political risk in tax-rate risk. Changes in tax rates affect the attractiveness of investments and hence the prices that people are willing to pay for stocks, bonds and other securities.

Changes in exchange rates affect the international competitiveness and profitability of companies. This is particularly the case when they export, buy imported materials or components, or own foreign subsidiaries. Such currency fluctuations also tend to impact on security prices via an influence on inflation. Since these effects are widespread throughout an economy, exchange rate movements are often regarded as a source of systematic risk.

NON-SYSTEMATIC RISK

Non-systematic risk is specific to a particular security or class of security. Industry risk could be seen as one category of non-systematic risk. At any point in time some industries are doing relatively well and others relatively badly. The pharmaceutical industry may be prospering whilst the construction industry suffers from falling demand. Circumstances that affect individual industries would be reflected in the prices of shares of firms within those industries. The scenario mentioned should be accompanied by the stocks of pharmaceutical firms performing more strongly than those of construction companies.

In addition to industry risk there is risk that is specific to individual corporations. Such specific risk includes management risk, which is the risk that there is a change in the quality of management. Operating risk, which stems from high levels of fixed operating costs having to be met even when sales are low. There is also a financial risk arising from debts that need to be financed irrespective of the level of operating profits.

From the perspective of the investor there is default risk arising from the possibility that the corporation will fail to honour its debt commitments, such as coupon payments and repayment of principal on bonds. Related to this is the credit risk which arises from the possibility of bond prices changing as a result of the corporation suffering a change in its credit rating.

There are sources of specific risk present in the markets in which the securities are traded. Information risk is the risk of investors taking inaccurate views of the value of the company. Liquidity risk arises when there are few investors buying and selling shares in the firm and as a result holders of stock are not able to sell quickly without accepting excessively low prices. Manipulation risk is present when large traders intentionally distort stock prices.

RISK AND DIVERSIFICATION

Non-systematic risk can be reduced, and even eliminated, by holding a diversified portfolio. If an investor has a variety of different stocks it is likely that weak performances by some will be offset by strong returns on others. In other words the factors creating non-systematic risk tend to operate in different directions for different stocks with the effect that stock price deviations cancel each other out. The less related the corporations are, the greater will be the effect of diversification. Combining a bank stock with that of an engineering company would produce more risk reduction than adding shares in one bank to a holding of shares in another bank. The risk reduction effect can be enhanced by combining different classes of security, such as holding a mixture of bonds and shares. This effect is further strengthened by international diversification. By holding financial assets from different countries some of the elements of systematic risk in Figure 1.7 can be diversified away (in other words the systematic risk from an international perspective is less than the national systematic risk). However, systematic risk cannot be eliminated by diversification, but could be expected to be compensated for by higher returns.

THE SECURITY MARKET LINE

The security market line is developed from a security pricing model known as the Capital Asset Pricing Model. The expected return on an investment is seen as consisting as the return on risk-free assets (such as Treasury bills or bank deposits) plus an additional element to compensate for systematic risk. The greater the systematic risk, the higher the enhancement of return.

Two points need to be emphasised. One is that return includes both income flows (such as dividends, coupons, and interest) and capital gains or losses. The other is that when referring to expected returns the relevant definition is that of statistical expectation. Figure 1.8 illustrates the calculation of a statistical expectation.

Expected return

= (possible return A)   × (probability of occurrence)

+ (possible return B)   × (probability of occurrence)

+ . . . .

+ (possible return N)   × (probability of occurrence)

Example:

The probability of a   −4% return is 10%

The probability of a   0% return is 20%

The probability of a   +4% return is 40%

The probability of a   +8% return is 20%

The probability of a +12% return is 10%

The expected return

= (−4)(0.1) + (0)(0.2) + (4)(0.4) + (8)(0.2) + (12)(0.1) = 4%

Figure 1.8 The calculation of a statistical expectation

The equation for the security market line is

$$E(Ri) = r_f + B\,[E(Rm) - r_f]$$

where $E(Ri)$ is the expected return on the particular stock (stock i), r_f is the risk-free rate of return, B is the beta of stock i, and $E(Rm)$ is the expected return on the market portfolio (which is a portfolio of shares in every stock with the weighting based on market capitalization).

Beta is a measure of systematic risk. The market portfolio would have a beta of 1. A defensive stock would be less volatile than the market (in terms of systematic risk) and would therefore have a beta less than one. As a result such a conservative stock would have a relatively low expected return. Conversely an aggressive stock has a beta greater than 1, indicating greater volatility and hence risk. This additional risk is compensated for by a relatively high expected rate of return. So the security market line indicates that expected investment returns rise with increasing risk. (The non-systematic risk is not compensated for with a higher return since it can be diversified away).

An important implication of the security market line is that stock prices will be inversely related to systematic risk. A high level of beta leads to a high expected return on the stock. This in turn implies a high rate of discount when calculating the stock price by means of ascertaining the present value of future dividends. A high rate of discount produces a relatively low estimate of the fair stock price.

Exercise 1.3

Question
The risk-free interest rate is 7 per cent p.a. The expected rate of return on the FT All Share index portfolio is 10 per cent p.a. A unit trust portfolio has a beta of 1.67 and an expected rate of dividend yield of 3 per cent p.a. What is the expected rate of capital appreciation on the unit trust portfolio?

Answer
The FT All Share index portfolio provides an expected return 3 per cent p.a. above the risk-free rate. The unit trust portfolio would have an expected return of 1.67 × 3 per cent = 5 per cent p.a. above the risk-free rate, and hence a total return of 7 per cent + 5 per cent p.a. = 12 per cent p.a. Since 3 per cent of that 12 per cent is expected from the dividend yield the remaining 9 per cent p.a. is in the form of expected capital appreciation.

Exercise 1.4

Question
The rate of return on Treasury bills is 5 per cent p.a. over the next three months. The expected rate of return on the FT All Share index portfolio over the same period is 8 per cent p.a. An investment trust portfolio has a beta of 1.2 and an expected rate of dividend yield of 4 per cent p.a. What might be the expected rate of capital growth of the investment trust portfolio?

Answer
The securities market line of the Capital Asset Pricing Model states that

$$E(R_i) = r_f + B\,[E(R_m) - r_f]$$

i.e.

$$E(R_i) = 0.05 + 1.2\,[0.08 - 0.05] = 0.086$$

i.e.   8.6% p.a.

So the expected rate of return on the investment trust portfolio is 8.6 per cent p.a. of which 4 per cent p.a. is in the form of dividend yield. So the expected rate of capital gain on the investment trust portfolio is 8.6 per cent − 4 per cent = 4.6 per cent p.a. (which is 1.15 per cent over the three-month period).

Exercise 1.5

Question
The risk-free interest rate is 4 per cent p.a. and the expected return on the market portfolio is 10 per cent p.a. An investor has a choice between two portfolios, with expected returns of 7 per cent p.a. and 13 per cent p.a. What are the betas of these portfolios? If the investor has a high degree of risk aversion which portfolio should be chosen?

If the investor wanted a portfolio with a beta of 0.25, what investment decisions would be taken and what would be the expected rate of return?

Answer
Using the securities market line,

$$E(R_p) = R_F + B[E(R_M) - R_F]$$

where $E(R_p)$ is the expected portfolio return, R_F is the risk-free rate of return, B is the portfolio beta, and $E(R_M)$ is the expected return on the market portfolio.

In the first case

$$7 = 4 + B[10-4]$$

so

$$3 = 6B$$

hence beta is 0.5.

In the second case

$$13 = 4 + B[10-4]$$

so

$$9 = 6B$$

hence beta is 1.5.

An investor with a high degree of risk aversion would choose the portfolio with the lower beta since the beta is a measure of the systematic risk of the portfolio. High beta portfolios are more sensitive to market movements than low beta portfolios.

If the investor wants a portfolio with a beta of 0.25, an appropriate strategy would be to split the investment equally between the lower beta portfolio and risk-free assets (e.g. Treasury bills or deposits with banks of high credit standing). This new portfolio would have a beta equal to the average of the betas of the constituent investments: $(0+0.5)/2 = 0.25$. The expected return would also be an average of the two expected returns: $(4+7)/2 = 5.5$ per cent p.a.

Bond duration

Beta is a measure of stock price volatility. The corresponding measure of volatility for fixed income investments such as bonds is modified duration. Modified duration is the percentage change in the bond price as a result of a particular change in the rate of interest (redemption yield). The computation

A bond with a final maturity of two years pays a coupon of £6 six monthly. The yield curve is flat at an interest rate of 10% p.a.

The price of the bond is

$$\frac{£6}{(1.05)} + \frac{£6}{(1.05)^2} + \frac{£6}{(1.05)^3} + \frac{£106}{(1.05)^4}$$

$$= £103.54 \ (= £5.71 + £5.44 + £5.18 + £87.21)$$

Duration equals

$$\left(\frac{5.71}{103.54}\right) 0.5 + \left(\frac{5.44}{103.54}\right) + \left(\frac{5.18}{103.54}\right) 1.5 + \left(\frac{87.21}{103.54}\right) 2$$

$$= 0.028 + 0.053 + 0.075 + 1.685$$

$$= 1.841 \text{ years}$$

Figure 1.9 The calculation of duration

of modified duration begins with the calculation of Macauley's duration (frequently referred to simply as duration).

Macauley's duration is the average period of time to the receipt of cash flows. Each time period (to the receipt of a cash flow) is weighted by the proportional contribution of that cash flow to the price of the bond. The calculation of Macauley's duration is illustrated by Figure 1.9. Macauley's duration is transformed into modified duration by means of dividing it by $(1 + r/n)$ where r is the rate of interest (redemption yield) and n is the number of coupon payments per year (see Figure 1.10).

Duration (and hence modified duration) tends to rise with increasing maturity of the bond. This makes intuitive sense since distant cash flows are more affected by changes in the rate of discount, and hence rate of interest (low coupon bonds also exhibit relatively high sensitivity to discount rate changes since the repayment of principal at maturity provides a high proportion of the present value of the future cash flows). So bond volatility, and hence bond risk, increases with lengthening bond maturity. It might be expected that this higher risk would be compensated for by increased expected returns.

The relationship between duration and maturity would suggest the existence

Modified duration

$= \text{duration}/(1 + r/n)$

where n = number of coupon payments per year

$\%\Delta p = -\text{modified duration} \times \Delta r$

Figure 1.10 The calculation of modified duration

of a risk premium in the returns on longer maturity bonds to compensate for increased risk. This is a risk of changes in the capital value of a bond, and is correspondingly referred to as capital risk.

Another type of risk is income risk. This arises from the possibility of fluctuations in the level of cash flows arising from an investment. A bank deposit has no capital risk, the sum deposited will not fall in value, but will have income risk since the interest payments will be variable. On the other hand a long maturity bond provides a constant flow of coupon payments far into the future and hence provides income certainty. So a long maturity bond has low income risk but high capital risk.

If investors dislike income risk they will require a premium on bank deposit interest rates to compensate for income risk, but will accept lower returns on long-term bonds because of the income certainty of such bonds. Whether long-term bonds or short-term deposits exhibit a risk premium in their rates of return depends upon the relative strengths of capital risk aversion and income risk aversion.

One implication of this analysis is that it is a mistake to regard bank deposits (or deposits in other institutions such as building societies or savings and loan associations) as risk free. Such deposits exhibit income risk. Furthermore they suffer from inflation risk if interest rates do not rise sufficiently to compensate for the erosion of the purchasing power of the deposits (even if pre-tax interest rates rise to compensate for inflation it is unlikely that the net of tax rise will be sufficient to offset inflation).

Exercise 1.6

Question
It is 24 November 1992. Treasury 12 per cent 1994 (which has just paid a coupon) has a final maturity date of 24 May 1994. The yield curve is flat at 8 per cent p.a. Calculate (i) the duration, and (ii) the modified duration, of the gilt.

What capital gain or loss would arise from a holding of £1 million nominal of this gilt in the event of a $\frac{1}{4}$ per cent p.a. fall in interest rates (throughout the length of the yield curve). Comment on the accuracy of this estimate of capital gain or loss.

Answer
The price of the bond would be

$$B = £6/(1.04) + £6/(1.04)^2 + £106/(1.04)^3$$
$$= £5.77 + £5.55 + £94.23$$
$$= £105.55$$

The duration of the bond would be

$$D = \left(\frac{£5.77}{£105.55}\right) 0.5 + \left(\frac{£5.55}{£105.55}\right) + \left(\frac{£94.23}{£105.55}\right) 1.5$$

= 0.0273 + 0.0526 + 1.3391 = 1.419
= 1.42 years (to 2 decimal places)

The modified duration would be

M = 1.419/1.04 = 1.3644
= 1.36 years (to 2 decimal places)

The value of £1 million nominal of the gilt would be

£1,000,000 × £105.55/£100 = £1,055,500

The capital gain would be calculated from

% rise in bond price = modified duration × change in redemption yield
= 1.36 × 0.25 = 0.34%

So the capital gain would be 0.0034 × £1,055,500 = £3,588.7. Hence the new value of the bonds would be £1,055,500 + £3,588.7 = £1,059,088.7. It is to be noted that £6/(1.03875) + £6/(1.03875)^2 + £106/(1.03875)^3 = £5.7762 + £5.5607 + £94.5742 = £105.9111. Hence according to the discount model the new value of the bonds would be £1,059,111. So the modified duration approach predicts the new value of the bonds very closely — the error is less than £23.

Modified duration does not priovide a precisely accurate answer since it assumes a linear price—yield relationship, whereas the relationship is actually convex.

Exercise 1.7

Question
A government bond which has just paid a coupon has two years to final maturity. It has a 10 per cent coupon yield. Calculate the price, duration, and modified duration when the two-year interest rate is (a) 10 per cent p.a. and (b) 5 per cent p.a. Comment on the usefulness of modified duration as a means of predicting the bond price changes arising from interest rate changes.

Answer
(a) Price = 5/1.05 + 5/(1.05)^2 + 5/(1.05)^3 + 105/(1.05)^4
= 4.76 + 4.54 + 4.32 + 86.38
= 100

$$\text{Duration} = 0.5 \left(\frac{4.76}{100} \right) + 1 \left(\frac{4.54}{100} \right) + 1.5 \left(\frac{4.32}{100} \right) + 2 \left(\frac{86.38}{100} \right)$$

= 1.86 years

Modified duration = Duration/(1.05)
= 1.77 years

(b) Price = 5/1.025 + 5/(1.025)^2 + 5/(1.025)^3 + 105/(1.025)^4
= 4.88 + 4.76 + 4.64 + 95.12
= 109.4

$$\text{Duration} = 0.5\left(\frac{4.88}{109.4}\right) + 1\left(\frac{4.76}{109.4}\right) + 1.5\left(\frac{4.64}{109.4}\right) + 2\left(\frac{95.12}{109.4}\right)$$

$$= 1.87 \text{ years}$$

$$\text{Modified duration} = \text{Duration}/(1.025)$$
$$= 1.82 \text{ years}$$

Using modified duration to predict bond price changes arising from particular yield changes assumes that the yield/price relationship is linear. However, it is convex. Convexity introduces error and the extent of error increases as interest rate changes become larger.

Stock leverage and stock options

It is possible to buy stock in a leveraged way. This means that part of the cost of the stock is met with borrowed money. The shareholder's equity is the difference between the value of the stock and the outstanding debt. The proportionate changes in the value of the equity exceed the proportionate changes in the stock price.

Leverage = stock value/owner's equity

or

= stock value/(stock value minus debt).

If, for example, the leverage were 2 and the stock price rose by 10 per cent, then the owner's equity would have risen by 20 per cent. If the leverage had been 1.5 the 10 per cent stock price rise would have provided a 15 per cent rise in the owner's equity. So

Leverage = % change in owner's equity/% change in stock price

and

% change in owner's equity = leverage × % change in stock price.

The beta of a leveraged holding of shares is equal to the stock beta multiplied by the leverage. So if the stock beta is 1.2 and the leverage is 1.5 the leveraged shareholding has a beta of 1.2 × 1.5 = 1.8.

An alternative way of obtaining a leveraged position in stock is to buy a call option. A call option gives the right to buy a particular quantity of stock at a particular price during a specified time period. The price of the call option is a fraction of the price of the stock but provides a high level of exposure to changes in the stock price.

The change in the option price per unit rise in the stock price is known as the option delta. If the price at which the option holder has the right to buy shares (the option strike price) is equal to the share price, the option delta will be approximately 0.5. The option delta would rise and fall with the stock price (but not in proportion to changes in the stock price). The elasticity of the option price is the percentage change in the option price divided by the percentage change in the stock price.

$$\text{Option delta} = \text{change in option price} / \text{change in stock price}$$

$$\text{option elasticity} = \% \text{ change in option price} / \% \text{ change in stock price}$$

or

$$\text{option elasticity} = \frac{\text{change in option price}}{\text{option price}} \left/ \frac{\text{change in stock price}}{\text{stock price}} \right.$$

$$\text{option elasticity} = \text{option delta} \times \text{stock price} / \text{option price}.$$

Option elasticity is similar to the leverage mentioned earlier. The leverage of a shareholding bought on margin (i.e. partially financed with borrowed money) can be expressed as

$$\% \text{ change in shareholder's equity} / \% \text{ change in stock price}$$

which is the same as option elasticity if the value of the option is looked upon as the owner's equity.

The beta of a call option can be calculated in a way that is analogous to the derivation of the beta of a leveraged holding of shares. The beta of a call option equals the stock beta multiplied by the elasticity of the option.

MANAGING THE BETA OF A PORTFOLIO

Before the emergence of derivatives markets the beta of a portfolio could be adjusted in two ways. The first was to vary the proportions of equities (common stocks or ordinary shares), fixed interest securities (such as bonds) and deposits in the portfolio. The second was to move between high beta and low beta stocks. These methods are still used, but derivatives (futures and options) provide alternative approaches. Using derivatives is normally quicker and cheaper.

As indicated above, options have beta values. They can be used to increase the beta of a portfolio by means of buying call options (or selling put options). If the wish is to reduce the portfolio beta, put options can be bought or call options sold, in both cases the option position provides a negative beta.

Positions in stock index futures can achieve the same results. A stock index futures contract is a notional commitment to buy or sell a portfolio of stocks at a future date. Although futures contracts never lead to the purchase and sale of stocks their prices move to reflect movements in the corresponding stock market and hence provide profits and losses from such movements. Futures are highly leveraged since only a small fraction of the value of the underlying portfolio need be deposited when the futures position is taken.

Since futures contracts are based on stock indices (e.g. S&P 500, FTSE 100, Nikkei 225, Dax, CAC 40, Hang Seng) their betas can normally be treated as being equal to one. Long futures positions (i.e. buying futures) will increase the portfolio beta, whereas short futures (i.e. selling) will reduce the beta of the portfolio. (A long futures has a beta of one, a short futures has a beta of minus one.)

The following exercise illustrates the use of stock index futures to bring the portfolio beta to approximately zero: that is, to eliminate market exposure. The market exposure of each stock is ascertained by multiplying its market value by its beta (e.g. $10,000 of a stock with a beta of 0.5 is equivalent to $5,000 of a stock with a beta of one). Adding these market exposures gives the market exposure of the portfolio. The market exposure of a futures contract is then calculated. Dividing the portfolio exposure by the exposure of a futures contract indicates the number of futures that need to be sold to bring the total exposure (net beta) to approximately zero.

Exercise 1.8

Question
You are the manager of a stock portfolio. On October 1, your holdings consist of the stocks listed below, which you intend to sell on December 31. You are concerned about a market decline over the next three months. The number of shares, their prices, and the betas are as follows:

Stock	Number of shares	Beta	Price
R.R.Donnelley	10,000	1.00	$27 \frac{3}{8}$
Raytheon	15,800	1.15	$53 \frac{5}{8}$
Maytag	8,900	0.90	$77 \frac{7}{8}$
Kroger	11,000	0.85	$47 \frac{7}{8}$
Comdisco	14,500	1.45	$28 \frac{5}{8}$
Cessna	9,900	1.20	$30 \frac{1}{8}$

On October 1, you decide to execute a hedge using S&P 500 futures. The March contract price is 212.10. On December 31, the March contract price is 202.10. Determine the requisite number of contracts and the futures profit/loss (the contract size is $500 per index point).

Answer
$$10,000 \times 27.375 \times 1.00 = \$273,750.000$$
$$15,800 \times 53.625 \times 1.15 = \$974,366.250$$
$$8,900 \times 77.875 \times 0.90 = \$623,778.750$$
$$11,000 \times 47.875 \times 0.85 = \$447,631.250$$
$$14,500 \times 28.625 \times 1.45 = \$601,840.625$$
$$9,900 \times 30.125 \times 1.20 = \$357,885.000$$

Total market exposure = $3,279,251.875

Exposure covered by one futures contract

$= 212.10 \times \$500 = \$106,050$

Number of contracts to be sold to eliminate total market exposure

$= \$3,279,251.875/\$106,050 = 30.92$

This rounds to 31 contracts.

Profit on futures $= (212.1 - 202.1) \times \$500 \times 31 = \$155,000$

Portfolio management

According to portfolio theory investors are seen as having expectations not of a specific rate of return, or future share price, but of a range or distribution of possible returns or prices. The possibilities are not seen as bearing equal likelihoods. The most likely return (or price) is known as the statistical expectation. This statistical expectation is also the average of the possible outcomes.

However, the most likely outcome, as forecast by the investor, is likely to be deviated from. No one expects their forecasts to turn out to be precisely accurate. Portfolio theorists believe that investors take a view as to the possible extent of deviation of actual results from their forecasts and that they have in mind an average of possible deviations. This average is known as the standard deviation, and is used as a measure of the riskiness of an investment.

Investors are seen as wanting to maximise return whilst minimising risk. Although a trade-off will have to be accepted (higher returns tending to involve higher risk) it is possible to eliminate some risk without sacrificing return. This is achieved by means of diversifying the investor's portfolio with a view to relatively poor performances of some of the securities being offset by better than expected returns on others.

Combining securities, such as shares, into portfolios tends to reduce overall risk. The risk of a portfolio of stocks is much less than the risk of an individual stockholding. This risk reduction becomes increasingly marked as the correlation of returns (inclusive of price movements) between securities falls. The less the extent to which securities perform well or badly together the greater is the likelihood that a poor result from one will be offset by a good outcome on another. The principle underlying Markowitz diversification is that assets with low correlations of returns should be chosen so as to enhance the likelihood of good and bad results offsetting each other and thereby dampening the degree to which the experienced returns (including capital gains or losses) vary.

Ideally, securities with negative correlation should be combined (negative correlation implies that one does well when the other does badly). If it is consistently the case that one does well when the other does badly (so that there is perfect negative correlation), risk can be eliminated completely. This is

Table 1.1 Eliminating portfolio risk by diversification

Circumstances	Probability of occurrence	Return on low-risk share (%)	Return on high-risk share (%)	Return on portfolio (%)
1	$\frac{1}{3}$	4	29	5.25
2	$\frac{1}{3}$	5	10	5.25
3	$\frac{1}{3}$	6	−9	5.25

illustrated in Table 1.1, which shows the risk of each of two shares (one with low risk and one with high risk) and that of a portfolio containing 95 per cent of the low-risk share and 5 per cent of the high-risk share.

It can be seen in Table 1.1 that the portfolio has zero risk since the returns are the same whatever happens. It is to be noted that the addition of a high-risk share (which offers the possibility of losses) to a holding of a very low risk share can reduce risk to less than that of the low-risk share alone.

Negative correlation between returns on assets is rarely, if ever, found. A strong rise in the market tends to involve most, possibly all, share prices rising. Likewise, few, if any, shares would avoid being part of a sharp fall. Certain changes, such as interest rate movements, tend to move all stock prices in the same direction. So some degree of positive correlation is the norm. As a result there is an element of risk that cannot be diversified away. This is known as systematic risk. Systematic risk is the risk associated with movements in the market as a whole rather than with characteristics specific to the firm or its sector (risk specific to a company or industry is referred to as non-systematic risk).

It is possible to reduce portfolio risk to the systematic risk (eliminating all non-systematic risk) by appropriate diversification. Markowitz diversification involves combining securities whose correlations are relatively low. The equation for portfolio variance is

$$V_p = \sum_{j=1}^{n} W_j^2\, S_j^2 + \sum_{\substack{j=1 \\ j \neq k}}^{n} \sum_{k=1}^{n} W_j\, W_k\, S_j\, S_k\, \mathrm{CORR}_{jk}$$

where W_j is the weighting of asset j in the portfolio, S_j is the standard deviation of returns on asset j, and CORR_{jk} is the coefficient of correlation between returns on assets j and k.

The equation for portfolio risk has two components. The first component is based on the risk inherent in the individual securities in the portfolio. It is the square of each stock's proportion in the portfolio multiplied by the square of that stock's standard deviation of returns. So, for example, if a security was 10 per cent of the portfolio and that security had a standard deviation of 5 per cent (that is the average deviation from its expected return was 5 per cent), then the contribution to total risk would be $(0.1)^2 \times 5^2$. Since squaring small decimals produces tiny numbers a large number of shares, each being a very small proportion of the portfolio, would reduce this component of the equation to a negligible amount (for example $(0.01)^2 = 0.0001$ for a share constituting 1 per cent of a portfolio).

The other component of the equation determining portfolio risk involves the correlation between stock returns. For each pair of stocks (every stock being paired with every other stock) the two weightings are multiplied together (the proportion of the portfolio in one of the stocks is multiplied by the proportion in the other) and the result is multiplied by the two standard deviations (one for each of the two stocks) and by the correlation between the returns on the two stocks. Although a portfolio containing a large number of securities would entail a tiny value for this calculation, since multiplying together small proportions produces a tiny number, the number of pairs of securities in such a portfolio would be vast, so that adding together all the resulting terms would produce a number that is not negligible.

From the foregoing description of the calculation the importance of the correlations is apparent. If all correlations were zero the second component of the equation for portfolio risk would equal zero, and since for a large portfolio, with no asset constituting more than a very small proportion, the first term in the equation becomes a negligible number, the result would be virtually zero risk. In other words a well-diversified portfolio with no correlation of returns between its component securities would provide a standard deviation of returns of virtually zero. The desirability of constructing a portfolio with the lowest possible correlations between its component securities is thus apparent.

Unfortunately, some positive correlation between returns on stocks is the normal situation. In other words there is some systematic risk, some tendency for prices and returns to move in the same direction. However, there is evidence to suggest that commodity futures funds display negative correlations with stock portfolios. The incorporation of such funds into portfolios thus serves to reduce the second component of the equation and hence overall risk.

The effects of adding a commodity futures fund to a portfolio can be illustrated by means of a hypothetical example. Suppose an investor holds two securities, A and B, in equal proportions. A has an expected return of 6 per cent p.a. and a standard deviation of returns of 4 per cent p.a. whereas B has an expected return of 8 per cent p.a. and a standard deviation of returns of 10 per cent p.a. The coefficient of correlation between their returns is 0.5. The portfolio variance is

$$V_p = (0.5)^2 (4)^2 + (0.5)^2 (10)^2 + 2(0.5)^2 (4) (10) (0.5)$$
$$= 4 + 25 + 10 = 39$$

Consider an alternative portfolio in which A and B are held in equal proportions with a commodity futures fund, C. Suppose that the coefficient of correlation of returns between the futures fund and each of the other two funds is minus 0.25 whilst the expected return and expected standard deviation of returns of that futures fund are both 7 per cent p.a. The portfolio variance is now

$$V_p = (\tfrac{1}{3})^2 (4)^2 + (\tfrac{1}{3})^2 (10)^2 + (\tfrac{1}{3})^2 (7)^2 + 2 (\tfrac{1}{3})^2 (4) (10) (0.5)$$
$$+ 2 (\tfrac{1}{3})^2 (4) (7) (-0.25) + 2 (\tfrac{1}{3})^2 (10) (7) (-0.25)$$
$$= 1.78 + 11.11 + 5.44 + 4.44 - 1.56 - 3.89$$
$$= 17.32$$

It can thus be seen that the addition of the futures fund has reduced portfolio variance to less than half its original value. Furthermore, given the assumed rates of return, there will have been no overall reduction in the expected return of the portfolio (evidence suggests that returns on commodity futures funds are on average similar to those on stock portfolios). So the addition of a commodity futures fund to a stock portfolio offers the potential of improving the risk–return characteristics of the portfolio.

Exercise 1.9

Questions
1. An investor holds two securities, A and B, in equal proportions. A has an expected return of 6 per cent p.a. and a standard deviation of 2 per cent p.a. B has an expected return of 8 per cent p.a. and a standard deviation of 6 per cent p.a.

    Ascertain the expected portfolio return and risk under the assumptions of:
    (a)   zero correlation of returns;
    (b)   a correlation coefficient of one; and
    (c)   a correlation coefficient of 0.5.
2. An investor has three securities available, A, B and C. Their expected returns are 6, 8 and 10 per cent p.a. respectively and the corresponding standard deviation of returns are 2, 6 and 10 per cent p.a. The correlation coefficient between returns are $CORR_{AB} = 0.8$, $CORR_{AC} = 0.2$, and $CORR_{BC} = 0.4$.

    Ascertain the expected return and risk if these securities are:
    (a)   held in equal proportions; and
    (b)   held in the proportions 50 per cent C, 25 per cent A, 25 per cent B.

Answers
1. (a) $E(R_p) = 0.5 \cdot 6 + 0.5 \cdot 8 = 7\%$ p.a.
    $$V_p = (0.5)^2 \, 2^2 + (0.5)^2 \cdot 6^2 + 2(0.5)^2 \cdot (2)(6)(0)$$
    $$= (0.25) \, 4 + (0.25) \, 36 = 10$$

    (b) $E(R_p) = 7\%$ p.a.
    $$V_p = (0.5)^2 \, 2^2 + (0.5)^2 \cdot 6^2 + 2 \cdot (0.5)^2 \, (2)(6)(1)$$
    $$= 10 + 6 = 16$$

    (c) $E(R_p) = 7\%$ p.a.
    $$V_p = (0.5)^2 \, 2^2 + (0.5)^2 \cdot 6^2 + 2 \cdot (0.5)^2 (2)(6)(0.5)$$
    $$= 10 + 3 = 13$$

2. (a) $E(R_p) = (\frac{1}{3}) 6 + (\frac{1}{3}) 8 + (\frac{1}{3}) 10 = 8$

$V_p = (\frac{1}{3})^2 2^2 + (\frac{1}{3})^2 6^2 + (\frac{1}{3})^2 10^2 + 2(\frac{1}{3})^2 (2)(6)(0.8)$
$+ 2(\frac{1}{3})^2 (2)(10)(0.2) + 2(\frac{1}{3})^2 (6)(10)(0.4)$

$= 15.556 + 2.133 + 0.889 + 5.333$

$= 23.91$

(b) $E(R_p) = (0.5) 10 + (0.25) 6 + (0.25) 8$

$= 8.5$

$V_p = (0.5)^2 10^2 + (0.25)^2 (2)^2 + (0.25)^2 (6)^2 + 2(0.25)^2(2)(6)(0.8)$
$+ 2(0.25)(0.5)(2)(10)(0.2) + 2(0.25)(0.5)(6)(10)(0.4)$

$= 25 + 0.25 + 2.25 + 1.2 + 1.00 + 6.00$

$= 35.70$

Exercise 1.10

Question

Stocks A, B and C have expected rates of return of 6 per cent p.a. and standard deviations of returns of 10 per cent p.a. The coefficients of correlation between the returns are:

A and B	0.9
A and C	0.2
B and C	0.2

1. Calculate the risk of a portfolio of 40 per cent A, 40 per cent B, and 20 per cent C.
2. Suggest a portfolio with lower risk.
3. What practical difficulties would an investment manager face when calculating the risk of a portfolio of stocks?

Answer

1. $V = (0.4)^2(0.1)^2 + (0.4)^2(0.1)^2 + (0.2)^2(0.1)^2 + 2(0.4)^2(0.1)^2(0.9)$
$+ 2(0.4)(0.2)(0.1)^2(0.2) + 2 (0.4)(0.2)(0.1)^2(0.2)$

$= 0.0016 + 0.0016 + 0.0004 + 0.00288 + 0.00032 + 0.00032$

$= 0.00712$

$\therefore$ Standard deviation of portfolio returns $= \sqrt{0.00712}$

$= 8.44$ per cent p.a.

2. Since C has a low correlation with both A and B a higher proportion of C might reduce risk. One possibility could be 30 per cent A, 30 per cent B, and 40 per cent C. In this case the risk would be calculated as:

$V = (0.3)^2(0.1)^2 + (0.3)^2(0.1)^2 + (0.4)^2(0.1)^2 + 2(0.3)^2(0.1)^2(0.9)$
$+ 2(0.3)(0.4)(0.1)^2(0.2) + 2(0.3)(0.4)(0.1)^2(0.2)$

$= 0.00598$

$\therefore$ Standard deviation of portfolio returns $= \sqrt{0.00598}$

$= 7.73$ per cent p.a.

3. The calculations in items 1 and 2 have involved just three stocks. In reality there are thousands of stocks that might be incorporated into a portfolio and calculating

correlation coefficients between each possible pair of stocks would be impossible. Even a portfolio of 50 different shares (not an unusual number) would involve 1,225 correlation coefficients. This very substantial number would require considerable time spent in carrying out calculations. Correlating each stock with a stock index would be a little less accurate but would reduce the number of correlations required to 50.

Another practical difficulty is that past statistical data may not be a reliable guide to future values. Returns, risks, and correlations can change over time so that the past is not always a reliable guide to the future.

2

Deposits and bonds

Deposits (see Figure 2.1) and bonds are forms of loan made by the investor, and correspondingly constitute debt on the part of the borrower. They are to be distinguished from ordinary shares, or common stock, which constitute part ownership of a firm rather than a loan to that firm.

Deposits are short-term investments, normally ranging from overnight, or immediate access, deposits to 12-month deposits. Bonds typically have initial maturities ranging from five to thirty years, with some bonds having no redemption date. In some countries, such as the United States of America, there are also notes whose maturities are longer than those of deposits, but shorter than those of bonds.

Short maturity investments

A variation on the normal deposit is the certificate of deposit (CD). A bank receiving a deposit may issue a CD to the depositor stating that at maturity (which is frequently three months) the deposit plus interest will be paid to the holder (or bearer) of the CD. The advantage of a certificate of deposit to the investor, as compared to a normal three-month deposit, is that it can be sold and hence is more liquid. This greater liquidity leads depositors to accepting rates of interest below the ruling three-month rates. Banks are thus able to

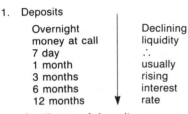

1. Deposits

    | Overnight money at call | Declining liquidity |
    | 7 day | ∴ |
    | 1 month | usually |
    | 3 months | rising |
    | 6 months | interest |
    | 12 months | rate |

2. Certificates of deposit

3. Commercial paper

Figure 2.1 Forms of deposit

Bills

1. Public sector
   Treasury bills
   Local authority bills

2. Private sector
   Bills of exchange
   ↓
   Bank bills

Figure 2.2 Forms of bills

borrow for three months at lower interest rates than would normally be the case. Blue-chip corporates may sell commercial paper, which is similar to the certificate of deposit, with maturities up to one year or more.

The longer the term of a deposit the less accessible the money is. This lower liquidity is usually compensated for by higher interest rates. The tendency for rates of yield to rise with increasing maturity is also normally the case in the market for bonds.

Another form of short-term investment is the bill (see Figure 2.2). Like CDs, bills can be sold prior to maturity. A major difference between bills and deposits is that bills yield no rate of interest. The return that a bill provides to its holder arises from the fact that it is bought at a discount. The issuer of a bill promises to pay a specified sum of money at its maturity date. The investor buying the bill will pay a smaller sum for it and thus obtains a return in the form of a capital gain.

Bills may be issued by central government, in which case they are often known as Treasury bills and typically have maturities of three months. They may also be issued by corporates as a means of short-term borrowing, normally with maturities of 12 months or less. Such private sector bills are often referred to as bills of exchange. If the payment of principal is guaranteed by a bank then the bill is known as a bank bill.

Long-maturity investments

Bonds are used for long-term borrowing by the issuer. Central governments are major issuers of bonds (and in some countries they are called gilt-edged securities, or gilts) (see Figure 2.3). Such government issues are usually for the purpose of long-term borrowing, although they may also be sold as a means of conducting monetary policy.

Bonds are issued in a wide variety of forms. However, most government bonds conform to a conventional format (see Figure 2.4). A conventional government bond pays a fixed sum of money, known as the coupon, every six months. It has a definite redemption date on which the government is obliged to pay the

Government bonds
(gilt-edged securities)

1. Sold for the purpose of long-term borrowing (Treasury bills sold for short-term borrowing).
2. May be bought or sold as a means of conducting monetary policy.

Figure 2.3 The uses of government bonds

The conventional government bond or gilt:

1. Pays a fixed coupon per period (usually six months).
2. Has a definite redemption date.
3. Has a market price expressed as a sum per £100 nominal.

Figure 2.4 The conventional form of government bonds

nominal, or par, value of the bond to its owner. Its market price is expressed in relation to its nominal or par value. For example, pounds per £100 nominal or dollars per $1000 par (so a market price of £96 means that £96 must be paid for every £100 to be repaid at redemption).

Dated bonds (see Figure 2.5) — that is those with a specified redemption date — may be classed as short, medium or long term. This classification is based on their term to maturity when they are first issued: that is, their initial maturity. One possible classification is to treat those with initial maturities of five years or less as being short term (in some countries such short-term bonds are called notes). Medium-term bonds might be those with initial maturities of five to fifteen years and long-term bonds might be those with initial maturities over fifteen years.

Undated bonds have no stated redemption date. The government, or other issuer, is never obliged to repay the nominal value but may simply pay the coupon forever. Such bonds could be redeemed by means of the government buying them back in the market.

1. Dated stocks
   - Short-term: up to 5 years to redemption
   - Medium-term: 5 years to 15 years
   - Long-term: over 15 years
2. Undated stocks
3. Index-linked stocks

Figure 2.5 Types of government bond

Index-linked bonds are a form of investment that protects the investor from inflation. Both the sum to be repaid by the issuer at redemption and the periodic coupon payment are adjusted in line with a price index. Conventional bonds suffer from a fall in their real values (in terms of purchasing power) as a result of inflation. Since the values of index-linked bonds are adjusted upwards in line with an index of prices of goods and services the investor is protected against an erosion of the real value of the bonds.

Corporate bonds

Governments are not the only issuers of bonds. In particular, corporations are major issuers of bonds. As a means of borrowing money, bonds provide an alternative that falls between borrowing from banks and issuing ordinary shares or common stock.

Corporate bonds vary very considerably in terms of their riskiness. Some bonds are secured against property of the company that issues them, whereas other bonds would be unsecured. The fact that unsecured bonds do not provide their holders with a claim on the property of the issuing firm in the event of default is normally compensated for with a higher rate of coupon payments. Often bonds have differing priorities of payment in the event of the issuer becoming insolvent. Bonds with a high priority for repayment are often referred to as being senior debt, whilst those bonds that would be redeemed only after the senior debt (and only if sufficient funds remain) would be termed junior or subordinated debt. The greater risk of non-redemption of junior debt is compensated for by a higher rate of coupon yield.

Issuers of bonds are frequently credit rated. There are credit-rating agencies (such as Moody's and Standard & Poors) that give ratings to issuers and their bonds. A high credit rating indicates a low risk of default, whereas a low rating is suggestive of a high default risk. Low ratings indicate higher risk for the investor and this higher risk tends to be compensated for by a higher rate of coupon yield. Bonds with very low credit ratings and hence subject to very high risk of default are often referred to as junk bonds and tend to pay very high rates of coupon yield (see Figure 2.6).

---

1. Issuers of bonds are credit rated.
2. High-quality borrowers pay the lower interest rates.
3. The bonds of very low rated borrowers are called junk bonds. These bonds pay high interest because of the risk of default.

Figure 2.6 Corporate bonds: credit rating and yields

Deposits and bonds

Eurocurrency deposits and eurobonds

Eurocurrency deposits are bank deposits in a currency held outside the control of the monetary authorities of the country of origin of that currency (see Figure 2.7). This usually means that a eurocurrency deposit is a deposit of one country's currency in a bank in a different country. For example, a dollar deposit in a London bank would be a eurodollar deposit. The prefix euro is misleading since eurocurrency deposits can be held in any major financial centre, not just those in Europe. The eurodollar is the major eurocurrency but eurocurrency deposits exist in all hard currencies, so there are euro-Deutschmarks, euroyen, eurosterling, euro-Swiss francs and so forth.

Eurocurrency markets are wholesale money markets. In other words each deposit or borrowing is for a large sum, typically in millions of dollars (or other currency). The wholesale nature of these markets, together with their relative lack of regulation, allows for fine interest rate quotes. Depositors receive relatively high rates whilst borrowers pay relatively low ones. The bid−offer spread, which is the excess of borrowing rates over deposit rates, tends to be smaller in eurocurrency markets than in the domestic (internal) money markets.

Eurobonds are bonds denominated in a currency which is not the currency of the country in which the bonds are issued (see Figure 2.8). So a bond denominated in sterling but sold in Paris would be a eurosterling bond. Eurobonds are often issued in several financial centres at the same time, so, for example, a US dollar eurobond might be simultaneously issued in London, Paris, Sydney, Hong Kong, and Singapore. Eurobonds are usually bearer bonds.

Eurocurrency is either:

- currency held outside the control of the monetary authorities of the country where the currency originated;

or:

- currency held on deposit outside its country of origin.

Figure 2.7 Eurocurrency

International bond issues

1. Eurobonds, denominated in a currency that is not that of the country in which the bonds are issued.
2. Bonds issued in a country, whose currency is being borrowed, by a foreign organisation (e.g. Yankees, Bulldogs, Samurais, Rembrandts, Matadors).

Figure 2.8 Eurobonds and foreign bonds

This means that coupons and principal are payable to the holder (or bearer) of the bond and bonds are not registered in the names of investors. This allows investors to retain anonymity.

Eurobonds are not the only form of international bond. Bonds may be issued in the country whose currency is being borrowed by a borrower in another country. So a German company might borrow Canadian dollars by issuing Canadian dollar bonds in Canada. Such bonds tend to have names that symbolise the country whose currency is being borrowed. For example bonds issued in the United States of America are called Yankees, bonds issued in Britain are known as Bulldogs, likewise Samurais in Japan, Rembrandts in the Netherlands, Matadors in Spain and so forth.

Bond pricing

As with other financial investments bond prices are based on the present value of expected future cash flows. The general formula for calculating a bond price is

$$P = C/(1+r) + C/(1+r)^2 + C/(1+r)^3 + \ldots + C/(1+r)^n + B/(1+r)^n$$

or

$$P = C \sum_{k=1}^{n} 1/(1+r)^k + B/(1+r)^n$$

where P is the market price of the bond (strictly speaking its dirty price, which includes accrued interest), C is the regular coupon payment per period, B is the nominal value to be paid to the bondholder at redemption, r is the rate of discount per period, and n is the number of periods remaining to redemption.

An important simplification that has been made in the above equation is the use of the same rate of discount for all the future cash flows. This assumes that interest rates are the same irrespective of the term of the investment (i.e. that the yield curve is flat). When valuing a bond an investment analyst would use a different rate of discount for each cash flow in order to take account of the fact that there are different interest rates for different maturities.

Interest rates are not the only determinants of discount rates. Bonds with relatively high default risk need to yield a high expected rate of return to compensate for the risk. The rate of discount might be regarded as the required rate of return on a bond. High risk entails a high required rate of return and hence a high discount rate. It follows that for any particular stream of expected cash flows high-risk bonds would have lower prices than low-risk bonds.

Although rates of discount vary according to the time to the receipt of a cash flow it is possible to calculate a single rate of discount that would equate all future cash flows to the current price of the bond (this would be a form of average of the discount rates). This single discount rate is known as the redemption yield, or yield to maturity, of the bond. The redemption yield indicates the average annual return to be received by an investor holding the bond to maturity.

Two conclusions that can be drawn from this account of bond pricing are, first, that bond prices have an inverse relationship to interest rates, and secondly, that they have an inverse relationship to the risk of default. These relationships can be generalised to all financial investments. High interest rates and high risk will be associated with low prices of securities.

An important distinction to be made when considering bond prices is between the clean and dirty prices. When a bond is purchased the buyer must include in the purchase price a sum corresponding to the seller's share of the next coupon. If the coupon is paid six monthly and the bond is sold three months after the last coupon payment date, the seller would require the price to include half the next coupon so that holding the bond for the previous three months provides an interest yield. The coupon rights accumulated by the seller are referred to as accrued interest. The clean price of a bond excludes accrued interest whereas the dirty price includes it. Quoted prices are often clean prices whereas the price actually to be paid is the dirty price.

Portfolio immunisation

Bond portfolios may be held with a view to the provision of a known flow of income in the future. The investor could be an individual or an institutional investor such as a pension fund with future pension payment commitments. Immunisation of such bond portfolios aims to protect the investor from capital losses that could jeopardise the required cash flows from the portfolio (see Figure 2.9).

One approach to portfolio immunisation is the construction of a dedicated portfolio. A dedicated portfolio entails future cash flow receipts, both of coupons and principal repayments at redemption, that precisely match the cash flow requirements. The matching of receipts with requirements must relate to both amount and timing. Although dedicated portfolios achieve immunisation they are very difficult to construct.

An alternative approach to immunisation is maturity matching. The required

---

Interest rate risk on bond portfolios may be reduced by means of

1. *Dedicated portfolios*   The prospective cash flows from the assets correspond to the future cash flow requirements in both amount and timing.

2. *Maturity matching*   The maturity of the assets matches the time at which the cash flow will be required. This avoids price risk from interest rate changes but is subject to reinvestment risk (the rate of interest on invested coupon receipts is uncertain).

3. *Duration matching*   The modified duration of the assets matches the time at which the cash flow will be required. Asset price changes tend to closely match (and offset) variations in returns from reinvested coupons. This immunisation is less effective if the slope of the yield curve changes.

Figure 2.9 Immunisation strategies for bond portfolios

cash flows from the portfolio, in terms of both amount and timing, are used as the basis for choosing the bonds for the portfolio. By ensuring that bond maturities coincide with cash withdrawals from the portfolio the risk of interest rate changes depressing the market values of bonds is avoided, and the portfolio manager would be sure of receiving the redemption value of a bond. One element of uncertainty does remain with such a strategy. Since interest rates vary over time there is uncertainty as to the rate of return to be obtained from investing coupon receipts. Changes in the rates of return on such reinvested income can have a substantial impact on subsequent values of the portfolio. This reinvestment risk can be reduced by using duration matching instead of maturity matching.

The duration of a bond is the average time to the receipt of cash flows from it. A conventional bond does not, strictly speaking, have a single maturity date. The date of each cash flow, not just that of the final redemption, constitutes a maturity date. (A conventional bond could be seen as a portfolio of zero coupon bonds. A zero coupon bond pays no interest yield but merely a sum at redemption. So each coupon payment, and final redemption, of a conventional bond can be looked upon as belonging to a constituent zero coupon bond.) The duration of a bond is the average of the constituent maturities. In calculating this average the final maturity will tend to have a higher weighting than the times to the receipt of coupons. To be precise, each constituent maturity is weighted by the contribution of the corresponding cash flow to the present value of the bond. This duration is often referred to as Macauley's duration.

Modified duration (see Figures 1.9 and 1.10) is Macauley's duration divided by $(1 + r/n)$ where r is the redemption yield of the bond and n is the number of coupon payments per year. Modified duration can be used to calculate the proportionate, or percentage, change in the bond price resulting from a change in the redemption yield. Duration matching involves choosing bonds whose modified durations correspond to the periods to the anticipated cash payments from the portfolio.

The future cash payments to be made by a portfolio manager are equivalent to a short position in bonds. The modified duration of this short position should equal that of the actual bond portfolio. This is difficult to achieve and maintain, especially since the passage of time and changes in interest rates will tend to destroy such an equality (see Figure 2.10). An easy and cash-efficient means of maintaining the equality is to use government bond futures.

The volatility of a portfolio can be calculated as the current value of the portfolio multiplied by its modified duration. Likewise the volatility of a bond futures contract can be calculated as the value of the futures contract times its modified duration (strictly speaking the modified duration of the 'cheapest to deliver' bond, which is the government bond that would be delivered by the seller of a futures contract). Any difference between the volatilities of the implicit short bond position and the actual bond portfolio can be matched by an offsetting position in government bond futures.

A bond portfolio immunised by matching modified duration to the investment horizon will require frequent rebalancing in order to maintain the matching. This is because:

1. Modified duration declines more slowly than term to maturity, so the passage of a year will reduce modified duration by less than a year. Modified duration would then exceed the investment horizon.

2. The price—yield relationship for bonds is convex. Modified duration therefore changes as interest rates rise or fall.

3. Changes in the slope of the yield curve will affect duration.

Figure 2.10 The effect of time and changes in interest rates on modified duration

Exercise 2.1

Question
A government bond with two years to final maturity has just paid its six-monthly coupon of $6. The yield curve is flat at 10 per cent p.a. What is the duration of the bond? What is its modified duration?

Answer
The cash flows to be received are:

After 0.5 of a year	$6
After 1 year	$6
After 1.5 years	$6
After 2 years	$106

A six-month interest rate of 10 per cent p.a. means that 5 per cent is yielded each six months. The period is six months and the rate of discount is 5 per cent, so the fair price of the bond is calculated as:

$$P = \$6/(1.05) + \$6/(1.05)^2 + \$6/(1.05)^3 + \$106/(1.05)^4$$
$$= \$5.71 + \$5.44 + \$5.18 + \$87.21$$
$$= \$103.54$$

Macauley's duration is calculated as:

$$D = (\$5.71/\$103.54)(0.5) + (\$5.44/\$103.54)(1) + (\$5.18/\$103.54)(1.5)$$
$$+ (\$87.21/\$103.54)(2)$$
$$= 0.0276 + 0.0525 + 0.075 + 1.6846$$
$$= 1.84 \text{ years (to two decimal places)}.$$

Modified duration

$$= D/(1+r/n)$$

Since the redemption yield is 0.1 and there are two coupon payments per year, modified duration

$$= 1.84/(1.05)$$
$$= 1.75 \text{ years (to two decimal places)}.$$

Convertibles

Convertibles are bonds that can be exchanged for ordinary shares (common stock) of the company issuing the convertible. Each bond would be convertible into a specified number of shares at predetermined dates in the future. Such a bond would have an investment value, which would be the value of the bond in the absence of the option to convert. It would also have a conversion value, which is the value of the shares into which it may be converted. Its market value, the price at which it can be bought, would normally be greater than the higher of the investment and conversion values.

Figure 2.11 illustrates these three values. The illustration relates to a bond that can be converted into 20 shares of stock (per £100 nominal of the bond). It is said to have a conversion rate of 20. The convertible bond has an investment value of £90 (per £100 nominal). This would be its value in the absence of the facility to convert, and if it remains unconverted after the final conversion date the investment value will be the market value. Figure 2.11 indicates that at a stock price of £4.50 per share the conversion value (20 × £4.50) equals the investment value. At lower stock prices the investment value exceeds the conversion value, whereas at higher stock prices the conversion value is the greater. The market price of the convertible should be at least equal to the higher of the investment and conversion values.

The market value of a convertible normally exceeds the higher of the investment and conversion values. The reason for this can be seen by focusing

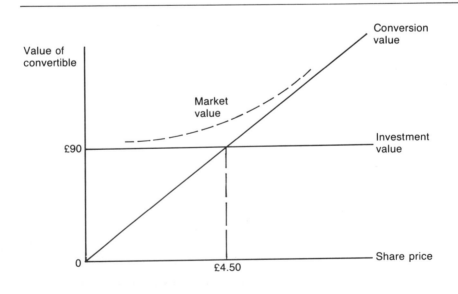

Figure 2.11 The three values of a convertible

on the investment and conversion values in turn. From the perspective of the investment value the convertible can be seen as a straight bond that provides some scope to benefit from an increase in the stock price. This potential to profit from an increase in the stock price is reflected in an excess of the market price over the investment value. From the perspective of the conversion value the convertible bond might be seen as equivalent to a holding of stock with protection against a fall in the value of the shares below the investment value. The excess of the market value over the conversion value could be seen as the price paid for this downside protection.

An investor could regard a convertible either as a bond that gains from a rising stock price or as a holding of stock that is protected against a large fall in the stock price. The periodic income yield is in the form of bond coupons rather than dividends. Although the bond coupons would typically exceed the dividend yield on the corresponding stock (if the dividends were the greater there would be a temptation to convert into shares) the rate of coupon yield would be less than that on a straight bond because of the potential capital gain from a rising stock price. So corporate issuers of convertibles can use them as means of raising capital at a lower cost in terms of coupon payments than would be the case with straight bonds.

Another way of looking at a convertible is to see it as a bond with an attached call option. A call option gives the right to buy a specified number of shares (the conversion rate), at a particular price (£100 nominal of the bond), at a point (or points) of time in the future. The factors that influence the price of a call option will also influence the market value of a convertible. So the market price of a convertible can be expected to rise as a result of an increase in stock price, an increase in the time to the most distant date at which conversion can take place, and an increase in the market expectations of volatility of the price of the stock.

Exercise 2.2

Question
A convertible has a maturity of ten years and pays an annual coupon of £10. It has a conversion rate of 100 and the current share price is £1.10p. Conversion can take place on 1 June of the fifth, sixth, seventh and eighth years. The yield curve is flat at 12 per cent p.a.

1. Calculate the investment and conversion values of the convertible. What would be the significance for the market value of the convertible if conversion could take place in year five only rather than in any of the four years?
2. If at the end of the eighth year one- and two-year interest rates were 5 per cent p.a. what would you expect the price of the convertible to be at that time?

Answer

1. Investment value:

$$= £10/1.12 + £10/(1.12)^2 + £10/(1.12)^3 + £10/(1.12)^4 + £10/(1.12)^5$$
$$+ £10/(1.12)^6 + £10/(1.12)^7 + £10/(1.12)^8 + £10/(1.12)^9 + £10/(1.12)^{10}$$
$$+ £100/(1.12)^{10}$$

$$= £56.5 + £32.2 = £88.70$$

Conversion value:
$$= 100 \times £1.10 = £110$$

The ability to convert in year five only would reduce the time to expiry of the option and hence reduce its value. So the convertible would have a lower market value.

2. $£10/(1.05) + £110/(1.05)^2 = £109.30$

(Strictly speaking it would not be a convertible at the end of the eighth year since the facility to convert would no longer exist.)

Floating rate notes (FRNs)

Unlike conventional bonds, floating rate notes (FRNs) have variable coupons. The coupon would be realigned with market interest rates at predetermined points in time (e.g. every six months). Since at each coupon adjustment date the rate of coupon yield would be equated to the required rate of return, and hence rate of discount, the FRN would equal its par value on that date.

Since the value of an FRN will be equal to par on the coupon adjustment date the valuation of an FRN can be carried out as if there were only two future cash flows. These cash flows are the next coupon payment and the par value on the coupon adjustment date. If the coupon payment date coincides with the coupon adjustment date the equation for the value of an FRN would be

$$P = C/(1+r)^T + B/(1+r)^T$$

where P is the price of the floating rate note, C is the next coupon, B is the par value of the FRN, r is the rate of discount, and T is the period in years (normally a fraction of a year) to the next coupon payment (and adjustment) date.

As the period for discounting (i.e. T) is short, normally less than six months, the price of a floating rate note will have only limited sensitivity to changes in the rate of discount, and hence to changes in the interest rate. This is in contrast to a conventional bond whose fixed coupons involve long discount times and hence high sensitivity to interest rate movements.

The yield curve

Interest rates vary according to the maturity of the investment. The relationship between the length of the investment and the rate of interest is known as the term structure of interest rates and is graphically depicted by a yield curve.

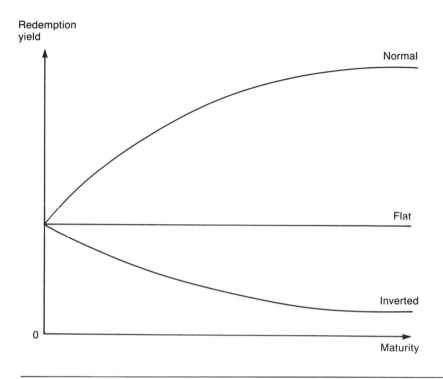

Figure 2.12 The yield curve

Figure 2.12 illustrates three possible yield curve patterns. The most common pattern is for yields (interest rates) to rise with increasing maturity but for the rate of increase to diminish so that for distant maturities increases in maturity entail little or no increment to yields. The yield curve labelled 'normal' illustrates this pattern. The yield curve sometimes exhibits a downward slope, as illustrated by the curve labelled 'inverted'. The flat yield curve illustrates a situation in which interest rates are the same irrespective of the length of time for which money is lent and borrowed; such a situation is extremely unusual.

Explanations of the term structure of interest rates, and hence the shape of the yield curve, can be subdivided into the pure expectations approach, expectations with risk premiums, and market segmentation. Theories based upon expectations are probably the most generally accepted (see Figure 2.13).

According to the pure expectations approach (see Figure 2.14), long-term interest rates can be seen as averages (geometric means) of actual and expected future short-term interest rates. So, for example, the twelve-month interest rate would be an average of the current three-month rate and the expected rates for each of the subsequent three three-month periods. Figure 2.15 illustrates the case in which a current one-year rate of 10 per cent p.a. and an expected

Theories of term structure

1. Pure expectations
2. Expectations with risk premium
3. Market segmentation

Figure 2.13 Theories of the term structure of interest rates

Long-term interest rates are seen as an average of expected future short-term rates (e.g. five-year rate is an average of the next five one-year rates).

This theory assumes:

1. Indifference between a long-term investment or borrowing and succession of short-term investments/borrowings.
2. Perfect substitutability between maturities.

Figure 2.14 The pure expectations theory of term structure

$$(1.1)(1.12) = 1.232$$
$$(1+x)(1+x) = 1.232$$
$$(1+x) = \sqrt{1.232}$$
$$x = \sqrt{1.232} - 1$$
$$= 0.11 \text{ (i.e 11\%)}$$

Figure 2.15 Illustration of pure expectations theory: the two-year interest rate

one-year rate of 12 per cent p.a. for the following year produce a two-year rate of 11 per cent p.a. The two one-year rates compound to 1.232 after two years. The single rate which, when compounded for two years, also produces 1.232 is the two-year rate. This two-year rate, x, is calculated to be 0.11, that is, 11 per cent p.a.

It is possible to infer expected future interest rates from current rates for different maturities. These implied expected future rates are called forward-forward interest rates (or simply forward interest rates). Figure 2.16 shows the case in which a one-year rate of 10 per cent p.a. and a two-year rate of 12 per cent p.a. can be used to infer an expected rate of 14 per cent p.a. for the 12-month period commencing one year from the present. The forward-forward interest rate, y, is the rate which when compounded on the one-year rate of 10 per cent p.a. produces the same sum of 12 per cent p.a. compounded over two years.

$(1.12)(1.12) = 1.254$
$(1.1)(1+y) = 1.254$
$(1+y) = 1.254/1.1$
$y = (1.254/1.1) - 1$
$= 0.14 \text{ (i.e. } 14\%)$

Figure 2.16 Illustration of pure expectations theory: the forward-forward interest rate

Exercise 2.3

Question
1. The current three-month interest rate is 11 per cent p.a. and market expectations of the next seven three-month rates are 11, 11, 10, 10, 10, 9 and 9 per cent. (a) What, according to the pure expectations theory, would the current two-year rate be? (b) What would be the effect of a $\frac{1}{2}$ per cent risk premium on two-year investments?
2. If the two-year interest rate is 10.5 per cent p.a., and the one-year interest rate is 9.5 per cent, what does the market expect the one-year interest rate to be a year from now?

Answer
1. (a) 10.52 per cent p.a. (b) 11.02 per cent p.a.
2. 11.51 per cent p.a. (Expectations will be less than this if the two-year rate contains a risk premium.)

Calculations
1. (a) $(\sqrt{(1.0275)^3 (1.025)^3 (1.0225)^2} - 1) \times 100 = 10.52$ per cent p.a.
   (b) $10.52 + 0.5 = 11.02$ per cent p.a.

2. $\dfrac{(1.105)^2}{(1.095)} = 1.1151$

   $(1.1151 - 1) \times 100 = 11.51$ per cent p.a.

Exercise 2.4

Question
The spot three-month interest rate is 6 per cent p.a. and the subsequent three-month rates are expected to be $5\frac{7}{8}$, $5\frac{1}{2}$, and $5\frac{3}{4}$ per cent p.a.

1. What one-year interest rate is suggested by the pure expectations model?
2. If the spot six-month rate was $6\frac{1}{4}$ per cent p.a. and the one-year rate was $7\frac{1}{16}$ per

cent p.a., what forward-forward rate is implied for the six-month period commencing six months from the present?

3. How would the answers to (1) and (2) change if there was a risk or liquidity premium?
4. In the case of (2) if the price of three-month futures maturing six months from now indicated a futures interest rate of $7\frac{3}{8}$ per cent p.a., what might you expect the three-month interest rate available in nine months time to be?

Answer

1. $[(1.015)(1.0146875)(1.01375)(1.014375)] - 1$
   $= [1.0590775] - 1 = 0.0590775$
   i.e. 5.90775 per cent p.a.

2. $\left\{ \left[\dfrac{1 + 0.070625}{1 + (0.0625)/2} \right] - 1 \right\} \times 2 = 0.07636$

   i.e. 7.636 per cent p.a.

3. The one-year interest rate in 1. would exceed 5.90775 per cent p.a. by the risk or liquidity premium.

   In 2. the one-year rate should be reduced by the risk or liquidity premium in carrying out the calculation. So the implied forward-forward rate would be less than 7.636 per cent p.a.

4. $0.07636/2 = 0.03819$ (return over second six-month period)

   $0.07375/4 = 0.0184375$ (three-month return implied by futures price)

   $[(1.03819/1.0184375) - 1] \times 4 = 0.0775796$

   i.e. 7.75796 per cent p.a.

Exercise 2.5

Question

1. If the spot one-year interest rate is 20 per cent p.a. and the one-year rate expected to be available one year from now is 5 per cent p.a., what would the two-year interest rate be?
2. If the rates in 1. are nominal rates and inflation is expected to be 10 per cent and 3 per cent in years one and two respectively, what is the expected two-year real rate of interest?
3. If the two-year nominal rate is 8 per cent p.a. and the one-year nominal rate is 6 per cent p.a., what one-year rate is expected to be available one year from now?
4. If the two-year rate in 3. contains a 1 per cent risk premium (and the one-year rate contains no risk premium), how would the answer change?

Answer

1. $(1.2)(1.05)$ $= 1.26$
   $\sqrt{1.26}$ $= 1.1225$
   $1.1225 - 1$ $= 0.1225$, i.e. 12.25 per cent p.a.

2. $(1.2/1.1)(1.05/1.03)$ $= 1.1121$
    $\sqrt{1.1121}$ $= 1.0546$
    $1.0546 - 1$ $= 0.0546$, i.e. 5.46 per cent p.a.
3. $(1.06)(1 + x)$ $= (1.08)^2$
    So $(1 + x)$ $= (1.08)^2/(1.06)$
    $= 1.1004$
    Hence x $= 0.1004$, i.e. 10.04 per cent p.a.
4. Remove the risk premium from the two-year rate. Then

    $(1.06)(1 + x)$ $= (1.07)^2$
    $(1 + x)$ $= (1.07)^2/(1.06)$
    $= 1.0801$
    Hence x $= 0.0801$, i.e. 8.01 per cent p.a.

The pure expectations approach assumes that investors are indifferent between investing for a long period on the one hand and investing for a shorter period with a view to reinvesting the principal plus interest on the other hand. For example, an investor would have no preference between making a 12-month deposit and making a six-month deposit with a view to reinvesting the proceeds for a further six months. This is equivalent to saying that the pure expectations approach assumes that investors treat alternative maturities as perfect substitutes for one another.

However, investors may not be indifferent between alternative maturities. In particular, attitudes to liquidity and risk may generate preferences for either short or long maturities. If such is the case the term structure of interest rates will reflect liquidity or risk premiums (see Figure 2.17). Longer-term investments are less liquid than shorter-term investments. By liquidity is meant the ability to turn the investment into cash without the risk of doing so at an unfavourable price. If an investment is close to maturity there is little risk of capital loss arising from interest rate changes; such an investment is liquid since it can be sold with little risk of the sale price being substantially lowered by a rise in interest rates. On the other hand, a bond with a very distant maturity (long duration) would suffer considerable capital loss in the event of a large rise in interest rates; in consequence such an investment might be liquidated at a very unfavourable price.

---

1. *Capital risk aversion*
    - Causes preference for short-term assets
    - Interest premium required on long-term assets

2. *Income risk aversion*
    - Causes preference for long-term assets
    - Interest premium required on short-term assets

Figure 2.17 Preference for short or long maturities: liquidity or risk premiums

To compensate for the risk that capital losses might be realised on long-term investments, investors may require a risk premium on such investments; in other words, investors may require a higher expected rate of return. This in itself would tend to cause the yield curve to be upward sloping. This tendency is likely to be reinforced by the preference of many borrowers to borrow for long periods (rather than borrowing for a succession of short periods). Such borrowers may be willing to pay an interest rate premium for the ability to borrow long-term.

There is a form of risk that would tend to have the opposite effect on the yield curve: this is known as income risk. Some investors may prefer long maturity investments because they provide greater certainty of income flows. For example, a conventional government bond pays a known coupon each period until the bond reaches its redemption date. On the other hand, interest receipts from bank deposits can vary almost continually as market interest rates fluctuate, with the result that the income flows from such a bank deposit are very uncertain. This uncertainty is known as income risk.

If investors prefer certainty of income receipts they may require a higher rate of interest on short-term investments to compensate for the income risk. This would tend to cause the yield curve to be inverted (downward sloping). So income risk and capital risk (the risk of changes in the capital value of an investment) operate in opposite directions in their effects on the slope of the yield curve.

According to the market segmentation approach, interest rates for different maturities are determined independently of one another. That is, investors (and borrowers) do not consider successions of short-term investments (or borrowings) as substitutes for long-term ones. So the interest rate for short maturities is determined by the supply of and demand for short-term funds. Likewise, long-term interest rates are those that equate the sums that investors wish to lend long-term with the amounts that borrowers are seeking.

3

—————— ∾ ——————

Equity investment

Stock valuation

Investment analysts need to produce estimates of what stock prices should be. Market makers need such estimates for the purpose of generating appropriate quotes and investors need them for ascertaining which stocks are over- or underpriced in the market. There are two major approaches. One proceeds by obtaining estimates of the price—earnings ratio and of prospective earnings. The other discounts prospective future dividends in order to arrive at their present value.

DISCOUNTING CASH FLOWS

A sum of money received (or paid) in the present is worth more than the same sum received in the future. One explanation for this runs in terms of the fact that money can earn interest. A unit of money received now is worth more than the same unit received one year from now because it can earn interest over the year. If the interest rate is 10 per cent p.a., then receipts in the present are worth 10 per cent more than identical receipts one year hence.

To render a future cash flow comparable with a current one the future sum is discounted. This involves dividing the future sum by one plus the (decimalised) rate of interest. In the case of a receipt of S one year hence when the interest rate is 10 per cent the present value, PV, is given by:

$$PV = S/(1.1).$$

More generally:

$$PV = S/(1 + i)$$

where i is the decimalised rate of interest.

If the cash flow is to occur two years from now, then (assuming a rate of interest of 10 per cent p.a.) because of compound interest an identical sum in the present is worth 21 per cent more. The present value would be:

$$PV = S/(1.1)^2 = S/(1.21).$$

More generally:

$$PV = S/(1 + i)^2$$

Correspondingly the present value of a sum three years hence is $S/(1 + i)^3$, four years hence $S/(1 + i)^4$, and so on. It follows that the present value of a future stream of cash flows is:

$$PV = S/(1 + i) + S/(1 + i)^2 + S/(1 + i)^3 + \ldots + S/(1 + i)^n$$

where the final receipt (or payment) occurs n years from the present. This can be more formally expressed as:

$$PV = \sum_{k=1}^{n} S/(1 + i)^k$$

which states that the present value equals the sum of the discounted cash flows (the cash flow amounting to S at the end of each year) relating to the next n years.

The time period may not necessarily be a year. If it is not, then an adjustment is required to the interest rate. For example for six-monthly cash flows an interest rate of 10 per cent p.a. would need to be expressed as a rate of 5 per cent.

The cash flow may not be the same at the end of each time period, in which case the equation becomes

$$PV = S_1/(1+i) + S_2/(1+i)^2 + S_3/(1+i)^3 + \ldots + S_n/(1+i)^n$$

or

$$PV = \sum_{k=1}^{n} S_k/(1+i)^k$$

where $S_1, S_2, S_3, \ldots, S_n$ are the cash flows at the end of periods 1, 2, 3, $\ldots$, n respectively. There may also be a different interest rate (rate of discount) for each time period.

DISCOUNTING FUTURE DIVIDENDS

This approach to stock price valuation uses variations on the discounted cash flow model:

$$P = D_1/(1+r_1) + D_2/(1+r_2)^2 + D_3/(1+r_3)^3 + \ldots + D_N/(1+r_N)^N$$

where $D_1, D_2, D_3, \ldots, D_N$ are the dividends per share of stock expected at points of time in the future. The final point of time, indicated by N, would usually be treated as being infinitely distant. The rates of discount are indicated by $r_1, r_2, r_3, \ldots, r_N$. These discount rates might be based on returns on alternative investments, such as government bonds, with some upward adjustment to reflect the fact that riskier investments (i.e. corporate stock) would be required to yield a higher rate of return.

In ascertaining the required rate of return for a stock, and hence the rate at

---

Required rate of return
= Risk-free real interest rate
+ Expected rate of inflation
+ Risk premium

Figure 3.1 Required rate of return on corporate stock

which its expected future dividends are to be discounted, one approach might be to start with the yield curve for government bonds. The yields on distant maturity (long duration) government bonds could be taken as the basis. Then a risk premium (additional required rate of return) would be added and the result used as the rate of discount.

Rates of return on conventional government bonds can be seen as incorporating a real interest rate and compensation for expected inflation. Rates of yield on index-linked government bonds (which automatically compensate for inflation) indicate the real rate of interest. The excess yield of conventional government bonds over index-linked ones reflects the market's expectation of inflation.

The required rate of return on a corporate stock can be subdivided into three (see Figure 3.1). First, the real rate of return; secondly, compensation for expected inflation; and finally, a risk premium reflecting the fact that corporate stocks are riskier than government bonds.

Exercise 3.1

Data
The redemption yield on conventional long gilts is 9 per cent p.a.
The redemption yield on index-linked gilts is 4 per cent p.a.
The average rate of dividend yield on equities is $4\frac{1}{2}$ per cent p.a.
The risk premium on equities, relative to conventional gilts, is 3 per cent p.a.

Question
What does the market expect the real rate of return on equities to be? How much of this will come from capital gains?

Answer
The nominal rate of return on equities should equal the return on conventional gilts plus the risk premium:

9% p.a. + 3% p.a. = 12% p.a.

The expected long-term average rate of inflation equals the redemption yield on conventional gilts minus the redemption yield on index-linked gilts:

9% p.a. $-$ 4% p.a. $=$ 5% p.a.

The expected real rate of return on equities is the expected nominal rate of return minus the expected rate of inflation:

12% p.a. $-$ 5% p.a. $=$ 7% p.a.

If $4\frac{1}{2}$ per cent of the real rate of return comes from dividends then $2\frac{1}{2}$ per cent would be expected to arise from an increase in the real value of share prices, that is, capital gains.

The investment analyst using this approach would need to generate estimates of future dividend payments and also ascertain appropriate discount rates. For the discount rates there would be a source of information, from which to work, in the form of the yield curve. No convenient source of information exists for the formation of expectations of dividends and so the analyst needs to develop a model of future dividend flows.

The simplest approach is to assume that dividends will remain constant at their current levels. It is more usual to assume that dividends will grow. There are several types of growth path that might be assumed. One takes the form of a constant rate of growth. If the rate of growth is denoted by g the model may be described by:

$$P = D/(1+r_1) + D(1+g)/(1+r_2)^2 + D(1+g)^2/(1+r_3)^3 + \ldots + D(1+g)^{N-1}/(1+r_N)^N$$

where D is the dividend at the end of the first period (which may be six months or a year) and g is the assumed growth rate per period. By assuming a discount rate that is the same for all future points in time the above model can be rewritten as:

$$P = D/(1+r) + D(1+g)/(1+r)^2 + D(1+g)^2/(1+r)^3 + \ldots + D(1+g)^{N-1}/(1+r)^N$$

If N is treated as being infinitely distant (as it normally is in stock valuation since corporates typically do not have foreseeable termination dates), this latter form of the model can be expressed as:

$$P = D/(r-g)$$

This is often referred to as the Gordon growth model. (It is to be noted that the model requires r to exceed g and that a constant dividend would generate a stock price of D/r.) (See Figure 3.2.)

Other models involve dividend growth that is forecast to occur at rates that differ according to the time period. The two-period model assumes growth at an untypical rate for a period after which growth proceeds at a normal or typical rate. If the untypical growth rate is denoted by capital G, the typical rate by small g, and the untypical growth is expected to occur for N periods at the end of which the stock price is small p (with the current stock price denoted by capital P), then the current stock price can be expressed as:

The Gordon growth model

$$V = \frac{D}{(1+i)} + \frac{D(1+g)}{(1+i)^2} + \frac{D(1+g)^2}{(1+i)^3} + \cdots$$

$$V = \frac{D}{(i-g)}$$

$$i = \frac{D}{V} + g$$

V is the present value of the expected future flow of dividends (and is the fair price of the stock). The third equation indicates that the rate of discount (which equals the required rate of return) equals the expected rate of dividend yield, D/V, plus the expected rate of capital growth of stock g (which equals the expected growth rate of dividends).

Figure 3.2 The Gordon growth model

$$P = D/(1+r) + D(1+G)/(1+r)^2 + D(1+G)^2/(1+r)^3 + \cdots$$
$$+ D(1+G)^{N-1}/(1+r)^N + p/(1+r)^N$$

The stock price at the end of N periods, small p, can be expressed in terms of the Gordon growth model:

$$p = D_{N+1}/(r-g)$$

where D_{N+1} is the dividend at the end of period $N + 1$ (which is the first period of normal growth) and is equal to:

$$D(1+G)^{N-1}(1+g)$$

Some investment analysts use the three-period models in which the period of untypical growth is followed by a period during which growth changes from the untypical to the typical rate. At the end of the transition period the third period, during which growth proceeds at a normal rate, begins.

Forecasting dividends can be particularly difficult. Even if projections of sales can be produced with a reasonable degree of reliability there remain problems in deducing prospective future dividends. Dividends are more prone to fluctuation than sales because of business risk and financial risk. Business risk arises from fixed costs that have to be met with the effect that a particular level of sales is necessary merely to meet these fixed costs. So profits will fall to zero even when sales are still substantial. It also follows that profits will be more volatile than sales.

Financial risk stems from the presence of debt obligations that must be met before any dividends can be distributed to shareholders. A level of operating profit is required merely to meet the servicing costs of debts such as bank loans and bonds. So a positive level of operating profits may be absorbed completely by debt servicing costs, leaving nothing for distribution to shareholders. Profits available for distribution as dividends to the shareholders are more variable than operating profits. Between them, business risk and financial risk render dividend

1. *Business risk*   The risk of variation in company profits. If there are fixed costs the percentage variations in profit exceed the percentage variation in sales. A level of sales is required merely to meet fixed costs.

2. *Financial risk*   The risk of variation in the level of dividends on ordinary shares (common stock). If there are debt obligations (e.g. bonds or bank loans), the percentage variations in dividends exceed the percentage variations in profit. An amount of profit is needed merely to meet debt servicing.

3. *Business risk* and *financial risk*   Together imply that fluctuations in a firm's sales often cause much greater fluctuations in funds available for the payment of dividends on shares.

Figure 3.3 Sales and dividends

forecasting very hazardous. Sales forecasts are very difficult and unreliable themselves. Translating sales forecasts into expectations of dividends encounters further sources of uncertainty (see Figure 3.3).

Exercise 3.2

Question
Lotek plc has just paid its annual dividend of 10p per share. The required rate of return is 12.5 per cent p.a.

1. If that level of dividend payment is expected to be constant into the future what is the fair price of the shares?
2. If the next dividend payment is expected to be 7.5 per cent higher than the last and if that rate of dividend growth is expected to be maintained throughout the future, what then is the fair price of the shares?
3. How would the answer change if the 7.5 per cent p.a. dividend growth rate were expected for three years after which the dividend growth rate was expected to slow to 2.5 per cent p.a.?

Answer
1. $V = D/r$ where V is the fair price of the shares, D is the expected constant dividend yield and r is the required rate of return. So

   $$V = 10/0.125 = 80p$$
2. $V = D/(r-g)$ where g is the expected dividend growth rate. So

   $$V = 10.75/(0.125 - 0.075) = 215p$$
3. First ascertain the fair price of the shares three years hence:

   $$D = 10(1.075)^3(1.025) = 12.734$$
   $$V = D/(r-g) = 12.734/(0.125 - 0.025)$$

   so

   $$V = 127.34p$$

The current fair price is thus

$$V = 10.75/1.125 + 11.56/(1.125)^2 + 12.42/(1.125)^3 + 127.34/(1.125)^3$$
$$= 9.56 + 9.13 + 8.72 + 89.43$$
$$= 116.84p \ (117p \text{ to nearest whole pence})$$

Exercise 3.3

Question
The risk-free interest rate is 3 per cent p.a. The risk premium on the market portfolio is 4 per cent p.a. The stock of XYZ has a beta of 0.5 and an expected rate of dividend yield of 10p per year.

1. What is the expected rate of return on XYZ stock?
2. What is the fair price of XYZ shares?
3. What would be the fair price of XYZ shares if dividends were expected to grow by 3 per cent p.a. from the current level of 10p?

Answer
1. The equation for the securities market line is:

   $$E(R_i) = r_f + B[E(R_m) - r_f]$$
   $$E(R_i) = 0.03 + 0.5 [0.04]$$
   $$= 0.05$$

   So the expected rate of return on XYZ stock is 5 per cent p.a.
2. According to the dividend discount model, share price = dividend/expected rate of return

   Price = 10p/0.05 = 200p
3. According to the Gordon growth model, share price = dividend/(expected rate of return minus expected rate of growth)

   Price = 10p/(0.05 − 0.03)
   = 10p/0.02 = 500p

Ratio analysis

When analysing a company for the purpose of ascertaining an appropriate price for its shares various ratios may be employed. There is a substantial number of ratios in use and the following are merely some of the more important ones. Just as the analysis of stocks involves consideration of expected return and risk, so too the ratios used for company analysis can be divided between those concerned with return and those indicating levels of risk.

Two ratios concerned with return are the *return on equity* and the *return on investment*. The return on equity (alternatively known as return to ordinary shareholders) is calculated as profit net of tax and interest as a proportion of equity (where equity is the total value of the ordinary shares or common stock). The return on investment is the same net profit divided by total capital, where total capital is defined as equity plus debt (debt including bonds and preference shares).

Ratios that help to measure risk include the current ratio, which is the ratio of current assets to current liabilities. The liquid assets ratio subtracts the value of inventories from current assets before dividing by current liabilities. The interest coverage (or debt coverage) ratio divides profit before interest and taxes by total interest payments. High values of these ratios suggest low risk.

Debt/equity ratios are indicative of gearing (leverage), and hence of risk. Such ratios include those that divide long-term debt (e.g. bonds issued) by either equity or equity plus long-term debt. If such ratios are high, return on equity will tend to experience extreme swings, performing very well in upturns and very poorly in downturns. (If shares are looked upon as call options with the value of debt constituting the option strike price, a high ratio indicates a high strike price.)

The dividend payout ratio is calculated as dividends divided by earnings (profits). Although the dividend payout ratio is not directly a measure of risk, historically safer companies have tended to pay out larger proportions. So the payout ratio indicates how management evaluates corporate risk.

Also a high dividend yield — that is, dividends per share divided by the market price of the share — tends to be associated with a high overall rate of return (relative to the shares of other firms). The same can be said of earnings per share divided by the market price of the shares. This latter ratio is probably better known as the reciprocal of the price–earnings ratio.

PRICE–EARNINGS RATIOS

The price–earnings ratio, P/E, is the ratio of the price of shares in a particular stock to the earnings (pre-tax profits) per share. There are numerous ways of ascertaining the price–earnings ratio. One is to use the average of past price–earnings ratios for the stock. Another is to discover what factors affect the ratio, and how they affect it. The ratio can then be calculated on the basis of the current values of such factors. A variant of this approach uses regression analysis to produce equations for the determination of the price–earnings ratio. Such an equation might take the form of:

$P/E = 3 + 2$ (growth rate in earnings) $+ 0.5$ (dividend payment rate).

This hypothetical equation states that the price–earnings ratio for a particular stock is equal to three plus twice the rate of growth of earnings plus half the proportion of those earnings that is paid out in dividends. The price–earnings ratio is then multiplied by current or prospective earnings in order to arrive at an estimate of what price shares in the stock should be.

Another way to ascertain the price-earnings ratio is to make use of the Gordon growth model. The Gordon growth model is used to estimate the fair price of the stock. This estimate is then divided by earnings in order to ascertain a price–earnings ratio.

$$P_1/E_2 = (D_2/E_2)/(r-g)$$

P_1 is the current fair price of the stock, D_2 is the dividend expected one year hence and E_2 is the expected level of earnings over the coming year. From this formulation it appears that the price–earnings ratio is positively related to the dividend payout rate (D/E) and the expected growth rate of dividends g but inversely related to the required rate of return r (and hence to interest rates). Instead of using the Gordon growth model to directly estimate the stock price the price–earnings ratio can be calculated from the expected values of the dividend payout rate, required rate of return, and growth rate of dividends. The resulting estimate of the price–earnings ratio is then multiplied by a forecast of earnings in order to ascertain a stock price.

In obtaining a forecast of earnings per share one approach might be to estimate sales per share and multiply the result by a prediction of the operating profit margin (earnings or profit as a proportion of sales revenue). One way of forecasting dividends per share in the coming year would be to multiply the earnings per share by the anticipated dividend payout rate (dividends as a proportion of earnings).

THE VALUE OF THE FIRM

If the firm is entirely financed by ordinary shares (common stock), then its value is the price of a share multiplied by the number of shares in existence. If the firm is financed by both equity and debt (stocks and bonds) then the value of the firm is the sum of the values of the shares and the bonds. If there are other forms of finance, such as bank borrowing, then they too should be included in the valuation of the firm. In other words, the value of the firm is the sum of the values of the various claims on the firm's earnings, which amounts to the value put on the firm by its owners.

It is possible that the composition of a firm's liabilities can affect its value. Such would be the case if the returns on different types of liability had different tax implications. For example, if interest on bonds and bank borrowing could be treated as costs from the tax viewpoint, then the use of such financing could reduce the tax liability and result in a lower tax payment by a firm leveraged in this way. The lower tax payment leaves more to be distributed to those with a claim on the firm's earnings and this greater income distribution leads to a higher valuation of those claims, and hence of the firm.

RIGHTS ISSUES

When a company seeks to raise further capital by an additional issue of shares it may do so via a rights issue; in fact, in many countries companies are obliged to make the initial offering of new shares via a rights issue. A rights issue involves offering the new shares to existing shareholders in proportion to the number of shares that they already hold. For example, a one-for-two rights issue involves offering one new share for every two shares already held.

Usually the new shares are offered at a discount to the current stock price. If the current stock price is 100p the new shares might be offered at 70p each. It would be irrational for an investor to ignore a rights issue since the offer price would be less than the new stock price, which would fall somewhere between the previous stock price and the offer price of the new shares. For example, an initial stock price of 100p and an offer price of 70p in a one-for-two rights issue might be expected to result in a new stock price of 90p, which is based on (100p + 100p + 70p)/3. As an alternative to accepting the offer of new shares a shareholder might sell the rights to another investor (who might be prepared to pay up to nearly 20p for the right to pay 70p for shares that will be worth 90p). A shareholder who completely ignores a rights issue will experience a loss as the stock price falls.

It is likely that a rights issue will be underwritten. This involves a bank agreeing, for a fee, to buy the shares not taken up by existing shareholders. As an alternative to having a rights issue underwritten, and paying the underwriter's fee, the firm raising the capital could take the deep discount route. The main risk that is insured against by underwriting is the possibility that the stock price will fall below the rights issue offer price. In the event of such a fall it would not be rational for shareholders to take up the new issue since they would be paying more than the subsequent market value of the shares. If the deep discount route is taken the offer price of the new issue of shares would be so low that it would be virtually impossible for the stock price to fall below it. So, instead of a one-for-two rights issue at 70p per share the company might arrange for a one-for-one (one new share for each share already held) at 35p per share. This will raise the same amount of money (twice the number of shares at half the price) but since the share price is highly unlikely to fall below 35p it is unnecessary to incur the expense of having the share issue underwritten.

PREFERENCE AND PREFERRED SHARES

Although they are called shares, preference and preferred shares are in many ways more similar to bonds that to common stock (ordinary shares). Preference and preferred shares are basically the same except that preferred shares receive the lower priority in terms of dividend payments, so the following discussion will be in terms solely of preference shares.

Preference shares typically pay a fixed dividend to their holders each year, similar to the coupon payments from bonds. Like bonds, preference shares do not constitute part ownership of the firm and do not provide voting rights to their holders. However, unlike bonds the firm is not obliged to make the dividend payments on preference shares if profits are not sufficient.

Preference shares come in various types, as follows:

- cumulative;
- non-cumulative;
- participating;
- redeemable; and
- convertible preference shares.

With the exception of the first two characteristics these are not mutually exclusive. So, for example, it may be possible to buy non-cumulative participating redeemable convertible preference shares.

Cumulative preference shares require the corporation to make good any missed dividend payments when profits become adequate. Back payments of missed dividends must be made before any dividends on common stock (ordinary shares) can be paid. In the case of a non-cumulative preference share there is no obligation on the issuer to pay any previously missed dividends. So a missed dividend may be lost forever.

Participating preference shares provide participation in particularly good profit levels. If the corporation's profits are very substantial the payments to the holders of participating preference shares will exceed the normal dividend level. Redeemable preference shares may be redeemed by the issuing company: that is, the original sum invested may be paid to the holder of the preference share in return for which the preference share ceases to exist. There could be a specific redemption date or the issuing company may be able to redeem at any time (in which case, the company has a call option on the shares). Convertible preference shares are similar to convertible bonds in that the holder has rights to convert the holding of preference shares into a holding of ordinary shares (common stock) on predetermined terms.

Forecasting

Forecasting is based on either technical analysis or fundamental analysis (sometimes they are combined). Technical analysts look for patterns in the behaviour of prices sometimes with reference to data on volumes traded. This is alternatively known as chartism. The belief is that prices follow patterns that are frequently repeated, such that if the early stages of a standard pattern can be identified, prices can be forecast to behave in the way suggested by the later stages of that standard pattern.

Different chartists tend to identify different patterns from the same data set and hence frequently arrive at differing conclusions as to future price movements. Of course those who happen to get the price forecast correct tend to ensure that investors learn about their success, whereas those who are wrong are prone to keep quiet about it. So one hears about successful technical analysis more often than about failures. Together with the natural human tendency to try to see an order in events this helps to explain why some people believe in this form of analysis.

An enormous amount of research effort has been put into testing whether price patterns can be used for forecasting. Overwhelmingly the evidence indicates that they cannot. There are two possible exceptions. The first is the self-fulfilling prophecy. If the number of chartists forecasting a price fall exceeds the number forecasting a rise, chartists would be net sellers. That in itself could cause the predicted price fall. This tendency of prices to follow the predicted path does not mean that the chartists make profits. Many of the sellers would be selling at artificially low prices. This is a recipe for losses. The converse behaviour would be a forecast-induced price rise and resulting purchases at artificially high prices. In these ways technical analysts might induce instability in markets (causing unwarranted price movements) but would tend to incur losses (and go out of business). Such behaviour is sometimes referred to as destabilising speculation.

The other exception to the rule that technical analysis is of no predictive value occurs in situations in which governments intervene in financial markets in order to prevent (or induce) particular price movements. The currency markets are particularly prone to this. One chartist technique is to look for resistance or support levels of prices. These are seen as maximum or minimum prices. If governments are trying to maintain maximum or minimum prices, then the chartists' belief in resistance or support levels is well founded. The technical analysis in such circumstances might discover the maximum or minimum price aimed at by the government. A one-way (no lose) speculation opportunity might thereby be identified. For example, buying at a minimum price gives a profit opportunity without a loss potential.

Fundamental analysis is concerned with evaluating all relevant information. In the case of ascertaining the appropriate price for ordinary shares (common stock), fundamental analysis is likely to focus on factors such as the management of the company, its market environment, the general economic outlook and so on. Fundamental analysts may use price—earnings ratio analysis and models that involve the discounting of expected future dividends.

The efficient markets hypothesis

According to the *efficient markets hypothesis* securities prices behave as if they follow a random walk. A random walk is a pattern of price movements in which one day's price movement is totally unrelated to price movements on previous days. An implication of this is that recent price patterns (as used by chartists) provide no clues as to future price movements. Also, adjustments to relevant information must occur almost immediately, otherwise one day's price movement might be part of a lagged adjustment that could be inferred from the previous day's partial adjustment. According to the efficient markets hypothesis, only new information can cause a price movement. This price movement would take place very quickly (too quickly for profits to be made from the new information) and is equally likely to cause price increases as price falls. The best forecast of tomorrow's price is today's price; however, tomorrow's price will differ from today's in a way that reflects the news occurring between today and tomorrow. That news could be either good or bad.

This leads on to the postulation of three forms of the efficient markets hypothesis. These are the weak, semi-strong, and strong forms. The weak form states that present prices reflect all the information contained in previous prices such that there is no profit potential from using historical price data. In other words, chartism is futile. A large number of empirical studies have supported the weak form of the efficient markets hypothesis.

The semi-strong form states that current prices reflect all publicly available information. Publicly available information encompasses not only past prices but also published data on individual companies and the economy as a whole. An implication of the semi-strong form is that there is no scope for making profits from publicly available information since the effect of such information on prices will occur too quickly. A large body of empirical evidence is supportive of the semi-strong form.

The strong form suggests that privately held information is already embodied in prices and hence cannot be used to generate profits from forecasting price movements. Private information can be subdivided into the results of investment analysis which are known only to the analyst (or the fund manager for whom he or she works) and information arising from having access to privileged information. Use of the latter is illegal in many countries and, not surprisingly, there is evidence to suggest that it can be used to make profits from forecasting prices. As for the private information that is based on investment analysis it would appear from the empirical evidence (which is based on institutional investors like mutual funds, unit trusts, and so forth) that such information is not already embodied in prices and that as a result it can be used to make profits. Unfortunately it appears that on average such profits are merely sufficient to cover the cost of the investment analysis.

Stock exchanges

THE PURPOSE OF A STOCK EXCHANGE

The main purpose of a stock exchange could be seen as the facilitation of the transfer of money from investors to those wishing to borrow. The investors buy stocks or bonds from borrowers and thereby transfer money to the borrowers in exchange for potential future cash flows.

The direct transfer of money from lender to borrower, without a financial intermediary such as a stock exchange, would be problematical for a number

---

The need for a stock exchange

1. Companies want:
   - To raise large amounts of money.
   - Long-term or permanent capital.

2. Investors on the other hand want:
   - To invest small amounts to spread risk.
   - Liquidity (money back when they want it).

A stock exchange overcomes this basic mismatch.

Figure 3.4 The primary role of a stock exchange

of reasons. First, there would be the difficulty of how lenders and borrowers are to find each other. Secondly, corporates want to borrow large sums of money whereas individual investors normally wish to invest relatively small amounts in any particular firm (partly because individual investors have limited amounts to invest, and partly because they usually prefer to spread their investments amongst a number of companies so as to avoid the risk of suffering heavily from the poor performance of one firm). A stock exchange is said to provide a size transformation, relatively small sums from each of a large number of investors are aggregated so as to provide a large sum for a borrower.

Thirdly, a stock exchange provides a maturity transformation. Corporates have a need to borrow on a long-term basis, whereas investors often prefer to lend short-term. A stock exchange provides a means of reconciling these two objectives (see Figure 3.4). A firm may sell securities with distant maturities (or, as in the case of ordinary shares and common stock, with no maturity date) whilst the buyers of such securitites can obtain quick access to their money by selling the securities.

Another function of a stock exchange, which is performed as a byproduct of the financial intermediation, is to communicate information about the companies whose securities are being traded. The prices of stocks and bonds reflect the evaluation of investors and dealers (some of whom carry out very detailed analyses of the firms) of the performance of the firms. Stock prices, and their changes, can communicate information of value to those both outside and inside the corporates whose securities are being traded.

PRIMARY AND SECONDARY MARKETS

Trading in securities can be subdivided between the primary and secondary markets (see Figure 3.5). When stocks and bonds are initially issued they are said to be sold in the primary market. Subsequent to their initial sale they are

---

Stock markets

1. *Primary markets* For new issues whereby firms or governments can obtain money.
2. *Secondary markets* For trading existing stocks and shares. The ability to sell stock on a secondary market makes investors more willing to buy in the primary market.

The vast majority of trades are on the secondary markets.

Figure 3.5 Trading in securities

---

traded in the secondary markets. So primary trading involves buying and selling newly created securities, whereas secondary trading involves stocks and bonds that are already in existence. The fact that financial investments can be sold in a secondary market renders them more liquid, and hence more attractive. This enhanced liquidity renders investors more willing to buy in the primary market, and causes them to be less demanding in terms of required rates of return. An active secondary market improves the operation of the primary market and allows corporates to borrow money easily and on favourable terms. Normally, secondary market trading volume far exceeds the level of primary market dealing.

TYPES OF STOCK EXCHANGE

Most economically developed countries have stock exchanges (see Figure 3.6). In many cases there are both national and regional exchanges. National exchanges tend to trade high-capitalisation stocks: that is, the stocks of large corporations. National exchanges tend to impose demanding listing conditions. If shares in a company are to trade on a national stock exchange they must be listed. The exchange may lay down criteria for listing in terms of history of the company, its profits, its capital, the integrity of its management and possibly other factors. Shares in a firm can be traded on a stock exchange if the stock exchange authority gives its approval: that is, lists the stock.

Stock exchanges

1. *National* For example, New York stock exchange, American stock exchange, London stock exchange, Tokyo stock exchange, Paris Bourse, Frankfurt stock exchange.
2. *Regional* For example, Pacific and Midwest in US, Osaka and Nagoya in Japan, Munich and Hamburg in Germany. Regional exchanges list stocks in small companies (they have less stringent listing conditions than national exchanges) and cater for small stockbroking firms (by offering cheaper membership than the national exchanges).
3. *Over the counter* No restrictions on what stocks are traded, who trades them or where they are traded. Can operate by direct contact between buyers and sellers.

Figure 3.6 Types of stock exchange

Global market

The national stock exchanges together provide a global market since national exchanges list foreign stocks so that stocks in major companies may be traded on two or more exchanges (e.g. London trades in more than 600 foreign stocks). As a result, national stock markets tend to integrate into a global market.

Figure 3.7 Global trading of stocks

Regional exchanges tend to cater for the stocks of smaller companies. Their listing requirements are often less stringent than those of the national exchanges. The financial costs involved in obtaining a listing also tend to be lower. So it is easier for a corporate to get its stocks traded on a regional exchange, but probably at the cost of a less liquid marketplace.

There may also be trading that is not formally regulated by an authorised exchange and does not require the stocks to be listed. In such markets any financial investment may be traded and anyone may be involved. It is likely that deals in such markets are less open than on formal exchanges, often being on a private one-to-one basis.

Stocks of very large multinational companies may be simultaneously traded on more than one national stock exchange. So trading in such stocks is effectively global (see Figure 3.7) and may operate on a 24-hour basis (as one exchange closes, trading may continue on others). This is one dimension of the globalisation of financial markets: that is, the tendency for financial markets in different countries to become integrated into a single market. A major factor leading to such globalisation has been the development of telecommunications; other factors have been the tendencies towards international diversification of portfolios, and deregulation of national financial markets.

At the other extreme, regional exchanges frequently specialise in firms that are located in the same geographical area. Such regional exchanges tend to trade the shares of relatively small local companies whose stocks are analysed by, and traded through, small local stockbroking firms.

Stock market trading systems

THE QUOTE-DRIVEN SYSTEM

The dominant system in the United Kingdom is a quote-driven system in which market makers quote selling (offer) and buying (bid) prices. These prices are displayed on Stock Exchange Automated Quotation (SEAQ) screens, and stockbrokers or institutional investors then transact with the market makers on the basis of the quotes shown. So the market maker is proactive and the investor reactive in terms of the prices.

Market makers, or dealers as they are alternatively known, trade as principals.

That is, they buy and sell for their own account and will normally hold positions in the stocks for which they make a market. In terms of transactions they are reactive rather than proactive and hence must move their price quotes if they wish to change their stock positions.

If investors are net buyers, then market makers would find that their stockholdings tend to decline. They might seek to prevent or offset such a decline by raising their offer prices, so as to deter buyers, and raising their bid prices, so as to encourage sellers. Conversely, net sales by stock brokers on behalf of clients or by institutions would tend to raise the stockholdings of market makers to undesirable levels. In response, market makers would lower offer prices in order to encourage buyers and lower bid prices so as to deter sellers. In this way the price quotes of market makers respond to the pressures of demand and supply.

The excess of the offer price over the bid price is known as the bid–offer spread. It provides a source of profit for the market maker as well as compensating for the risks inherent in the process of market making. The market bid–offer spread is the excess of the lowest offer price over the highest bid price and is normally lower than the spreads of individual market makers.

THE ORDER-DRIVEN SYSTEM

The order-driven system operates on the basis of matching buy and sell orders. Investors are proactive in terms of both price and quantity. Orders to buy and sell determine stock prices at which orders to buy are matched by orders to sell. This can be depicted by demand and supply curves as illustrated in Figure 3.8.

In Figure 3.8, P_A is the offer (or ask) price, which is the price at which investors buy. P_B is the bid price, at which investors sell. Investors offering P_A or more will buy at P_A. Sellers requiring P_B or less will sell at P_B. The quantity that buyers demand at P_A matches the quantity that sellers wish to supply at P_B. The excess of P_A over P_B (the bid–offer or bid–ask spread) constitutes a payment to the stock exchange, or other agent, for carrying out the matching process.

So in an order-driven system stock prices are determined directly by demand and supply. The agent or body facilitating the trading process holds no position in shares and is entirely reactive to those seeking to buy or sell.

THE MARKETS IN WHICH THESE SYSTEMS OPERATE

As mentioned earlier, the quote-driven, or dealer, system is the predominant one in the United Kingdom. It is also the dominant one in the United States. On the New York Stock Exchange market makers, normally referred to as *specialists*, have the additional function of ensuring orderly and continuous markets. This function requires them to ensure that price changes between one

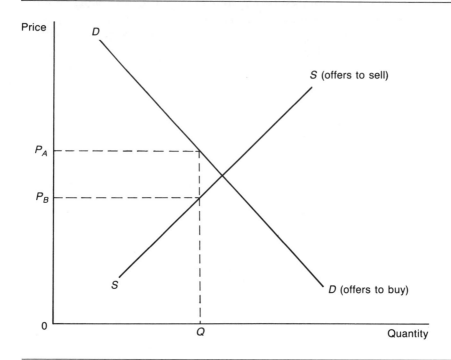

Figure 3.8 The auction/matching system

deal and the next are small and they must accept any resulting changes in their stock positions. This in effect means that they must sell in rising markets and buy in falling markets thereby trading in such a way as to foster smooth transitions between price levels. The computer-based National Association of Securities Dealers Automated Quotation (NASDAQ) market, which is very similar to the London screen-based system, also involves market makers but without the additional functions required by the New York Stock Exchange of its specialists.

In both the United Kingdom and the United States the market-maker system has difficulty with illiquid stocks, which tend to be those of smaller companies. If trades are infrequent (perhaps as little as one or two per month), the income from market making is small and the market makers may be left with undesirable stock positions for long periods of time. In the cases of such stocks, alternative, order-driven, systems may be used such as the bulletin board in the United Kingdom. The bulletin board involves investors, or their brokers, putting offers to buy or sell at particular prices on the board and leaving the offers thus displayed for other investors to respond to should they wish. This, like other order-driven systems, entails the risk that the desired purchase or sale will not take place.

Equity investment

Order-driven systems predominate for stocks in Japan and many European exchanges. On the Tokyo Stock Exchange the *saitori* members constantly adjust prices so that offers to buy from them match offers to sell to them. Unlike market makers in New York and London they do not operate as principals trading on their own account. Saitori members avoid taking stock positions themselves and seek to operate purely as intermediaries between buyers and sellers. Consequently they simply provide the mechanism for equating demand and supply in an order-driven system. However, their inability to take positions on their own accounts prevents them from trading in such a way as to stabilise market prices.

POSSIBLE FUTURE DIRECTIONS

Trading systems appropriate for some stocks are inappropriate for others. Major blue-chip stocks traded on several national exchanges enjoy high trading volumes, particularly since they tend to be favoured by institutional investors (since only by holding stocks in large corporations can the large institutional investors reconcile the objective of holding a manageable range of stocks with the objective of not holding a high proportion of any one company's stock). For such stocks, market making is a profitable activity that can serve to stabilise markets by means of the market makers taking positions to offset temporary imbalances between demand and supply caused by timing differences between buy and sell orders.

At the other extreme there are shares in small companies whose trading is limited both geographically and in terms of frequency. The limited trading volumes render market making unprofitable. So alternative trading systems — order-driven systems — must be employed for such stocks. Of course, the relative uncertainties concerning the ability to sell and the selling prices would render such smaller company stocks less attractive. However, these disadvantages would tend to cause their prices to be relatively low and hence their rates of dividend yield relatively high.

4

~

Options, warrants and convertibles

Call options

A call option gives the buyer of that option the right, but not the obligation, to buy shares at a particular price. That price is known as the exercise, or strike price. At the time of buying the option there would be at least two exercise prices available to choose from. For example, when the price of BP shares was 302p on 19 August 1993 the option exercise prices available were 300p and 330p. If the holder of a call option decides to exercise it he or she will buy a specific number of shares at the strike price chosen when buying the option. The number of shares covered by one option contract varies from country to country; examples are USA 100, UK 1,000, Germany 50.

It would be profitable to exercise a call option if the market price of the stock turns out to be higher than the strike price. In the event of the market price being lower than the strike price the option holder is not obliged to exercise, and presumably would not, since exercising would realise a loss. The buyer of an option thus has potential for profit without the risk of a loss. For this favourable situation the buyer of an option pays a premium. Continuing the previous example, the premiums for BP call options, at the close of trading on 19 August 1993, were as shown in Table 4.1. October, January and April were expiry months. The expiry month of an option is the month in which it ceases to be exercisable. Option premiums (i.e. prices) are expressed in the same currency units as the shares; for example, pence in the UK, dollars in the USA. Premiums are payable at the time the option is bought.

Table 4.1 Premiums for BP call option

Exercise (strike) price (p)	Premium (p)		
	October	January	April
300	15	$21\frac{1}{2}$	$26\frac{1}{2}$
330	4	$9\frac{1}{2}$	14

Source: *Financial Times*, 20 August 1993.

63

THE PROFIT/LOSS PROFILE AT EXPIRY

Since an option buyer is not obliged to exercise an option he has the right to simply disregard it. In such an event the premium paid is lost, but there would be no further loss. The premium paid is the maximum loss that can be incurred. On the other hand, the profit potential is subject to no limits. In principle there is no upper limit to the stock price and hence no upper limit to the potential profit. Figure 4.1 shows the profit/loss profile of a call option at expiry.

The option used for the illustration is the October 300p BP call whose premium is 15p. If the buyer holds the option to the expiry date and the share price turns out to be 300p or less there would be no point in exercising the option. There is no benefit from exercising an option to buy shares at 300p when those shares can be bought at the same, or a lower, price in the market. In such a situation the option buyer makes a net loss because of the payment of the 15p premium, which is non-returnable. This is shown in Figure 4.1 which depicts a loss of 15p at all prices up to 300p.

If the price of the share turns out to be greater than 300p it would be worthwhile to exercise the option. The option holder could choose to exercise the option to buy at 300p and then immediately sell the shares at the higher price, thereby realising a profit. At a share price of 315p this profit would exactly offset the premium paid. Hence 315p is the breakeven price at which net profit is zero. At prices above 315p the gross profit exceeds the premium, so that there is a net profit. (These figures would need some adjustment if bid−ask spreads and commission costs are to be taken account of.)

The gross profit referred to is alternatively known as the intrinsic value of

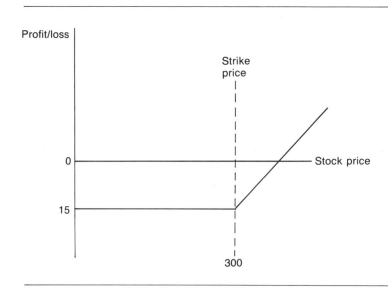

Figure 4.1 Profit/loss profile of a call option at expiry

the option. Intrinsic value can be defined as the profit to be obtained by immediately exercising the option (disregarding the premium) and is equal to the difference between the exercise price and the market price of the stock when the option is in-the-money.

An in-the-money call option is one whose exercise price is less than the market price of the stock, and which therefore offers an immediate gross profit. An at-the-money option is one whose exercise price is equal to the market price. An out-of-the-money call option is one whose exercise price is greater than the market price. Only in-the-money options have intrinsic value.

THE PROFIT/LOSS PROFILE PRIOR TO EXPIRY

At the time that a traded option expires its price (premium) will be equal to its intrinsic value. Prior to expiry the premium would normally exceed the intrinsic value. This excess of the price of the option over the intrinsic value is known as the time value. When an option is exercised only the intrinsic value is realised. The seller of an option would obtain a price that incorporates some time value as well as the intrinsic value.

When account is taken of the time value the profit/loss profile of an option differs from the at-expiry profile depicted in Figure 4.1. A prior-to-expiry profile is shown by the broken line in Figure 4.2. Time value is at its highest when the option is at-the-money. Time value declines as the option moves either into- or out-of-the-money and will approach zero as the market price of the stock diverges substantially from the exercise (strike) price.

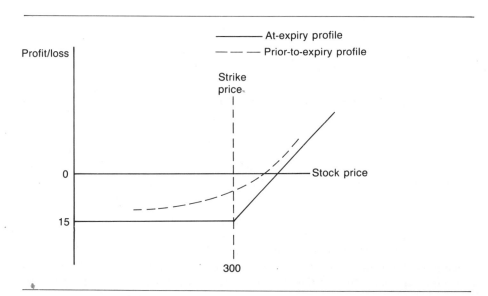

Figure 4.2 Profit/loss profile of a call option prior to expiry, showing its time value

The broken line indicates the market price of the option minus the initial premium paid (15p in this case). When an option is purchased the premium paid will be the market price and the profit/loss profile (broken line) will intersect the horizontal axis indicating zero net profit at the ruling stock price. (This is equivalent to saying that at the moment of purchase the value of the option is equal to the price paid for it.) As time passes and the stock price changes the net profit will cease to be zero. The net profit shown by the prior-to-expiry profile is the price that the trader could sell the option for minus the price (premium) that was paid for it.

Below the exercise price the price of the option consists of time value only but above the exercise price the price consists of both time and intrinsic value. This ensures that the gradient of the prior-to-expiry profile increases as the share price rises. This gradient is known as the option delta and can alternatively be expressed as the change in the price of the option as a proportion of the change in the price of the stock. The delta approaches zero as the option becomes deeply out-of-the-money and approaches one when it is deep in-the-money. The delta is approximately 0.5 when the option is at-the-money.

DETERMINANTS OF THE PREMIUM

The explanation of an option premium subdivides into ascertaining intrinsic value and assessing the influences on time value. The intrinsic value of a call option is equal to the stock price minus the exercise price of the option, with zero being the minimum intrinsic value. In principle the option premium cannot fall below the intrinsic value. If the option premium were below the intrinsic value there would be a guaranteed profit from buying the option and immediately exercising it (and selling the shares acquired). It would be irrational for anyone to sell an option for a price that is less than its intrinsic value, since more could be obtained from exercising it.

The determination of time value is more complex. Major influences on time value are the expected volatility of the stock price, the length of the period remaining to the expiry date, and the extent to which the option is in- or out-of-the-money.

The higher the expected volatility, the greater will be the premiums. An option on a volatile stock has a strong chance of acquiring intrinsic value at some stage prior to expiry. Similarly the probability of an option acquiring intrinsic value prior to expiry rises with the length of time remaining to its expiry date. It can be seen from Table 4.1 that the options with the more distant expiry dates have the higher premiums.

Time value is at its peak when the option is at-the-money and declines as the option moves either into- or out-of-the-money. Out-of-the-money options have less time value than at-the-money options because the stock price has further to move before intrinsic value is acquired. In-the-money options have less time value than at-the-money options since their prices contain intrinsic value which is vulnerable to a fall in the stock price, whereas at-the-money option premiums contain no intrinsic value. The risk that existing intrinsic value might be lost reduces the attractiveness of the option and lowers its price.

Put options

A put option gives its holder the right, but not the obligation, to sell shares at a specified price at any time prior to the expiry date of the option.

The holder of an option can exercise it, sell it, or allow it to expire. It is worthwhile exercising an option — that is, exercising the right to sell shares at the strike price — only if the market price of the stock turns out to be lower than the strike price. If the strike price is greater than the stock price the option is said to have intrinsic value. The intrinsic value would be equal to the excess of the strike price over the stock price. An option without intrinsic value might simply be allowed to expire since its holder is not obliged to exercise it, and presumably would not if the strike price were below the market price of the stock.

The buyer of an option pays a premium, which is the price of the option. The premium consists of the intrinsic value, if there is any, plus time value. It is likely that the holder of an option would choose to sell it in preference to exercising it or allowing it to expire. By selling the option he would receive the time value as well as any intrinsic value (whereas exercising the option realises the intrinsic value only).

Table 4.2 shows the premiums of BP put options at the close of trading on 19 August 1993. The price of BP shares was 302p. The months referred to in Table 4.2 are expiry months. All the option contracts in the table belong to one class, namely BP puts. Within that class there are six series. Each series is characterised by a strike price and an expiry date (e.g. 300 October, 330 April). So at any one time the buyer of a BP put option would have three to choose from at each strike price. When the October expiry date is reached options with a July expiry date would be introduced.

All prices in Table 4.2 are in pence. So, for example, it would cost $30\frac{1}{2}$p (per share) to buy an option that provides the holder with the right to sell shares at 330p each at any time up to the October expiry date. (Since each option in the UK relates to 1,000 shares the actual price of the option would be £305.) Substantial movements of the stock price would invoke the introduction of new strike prices, so that there are strike prices either side of the stock price.

Table 4.2 Premiums for BP put option

Exercise (strike) price (p)	Premium (p)		
	October	January	April
300	$10\frac{1}{2}$	$15\frac{1}{2}$	$18\frac{1}{2}$
330	$30\frac{1}{2}$	$33\frac{1}{2}$	36

Source: *Financial Times*, 20 August 1993.

THE PROFIT/LOSS PROFILE AT EXPIRY

In the case of traded stock options the premium is usually payable in full on the day following the purchase of the option. However, since the buyer is not obliged to exercise the option, and presumably would not do so if it involves selling at a loss relative to the market price of the share, the premium paid is the maximum loss that the buyer of the option can incur. So, for example, a buyer of BP October 330p puts faces a maximum loss of $30\frac{1}{2}$p per share, which amounts to £305 per contract since each put option contract is for the sale of 1,000 shares.

The maximum profit is limited only by the fact that stock prices cannot fall below zero. Since it is conceivable that a stock price can fall to zero the net gain from a put option can, in principle, be as much as the strike price minus the premium paid. The buyer of October 330p BP puts stands to gain as much as 330p $-$ $30\frac{1}{2}$p per share. This amounts to £2,995 per option contract. The option holder could buy shares at 0p and, by exercising the option, sell them at 330p.

Figure 4.3 shows the profit/loss profile of BP October 330p puts at expiry (that is, on the day in October upon which the option ceases to be capable of being exercised).

If the stock price is 330p or higher when the option expires, the holder of the option records a net loss of $30\frac{1}{2}$p per share (£305 per option contract). If the stock price turns out to be less than 330p there is a gross profit to be made

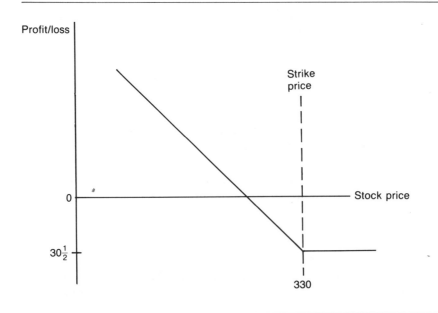

Figure 4.3 Profit/loss profile of a put option at expiry

by exercising the option. Exercising the option would allow the option holder to sell shares at 330p whilst buying them at a lower price. This gross profit from exercising the option minus the premium paid is the net profit. If the stock price lies between $299\frac{1}{2}$p and 330p there is a net loss, whereas below the breakeven stock price of $299\frac{1}{2}$p there is a net profit.

THE PROFIT/LOSS PROFILE PRIOR TO EXPIRY

At expiry an option would have only intrinsic value, which could be equal to zero. Prior to expiry the option would have time value as well as intrinsic value. The profit/loss profile of Figure 4.3 is based on intrinsic value only. Since intrinsic value is the gross profit to be made from exercising the option it will be zero at or above the strike price of 330p, whereas below 330p it will be equal to the difference between the stock price and the strike price. The net profit or loss at expiry is equal to the intrinsic value minus the premium paid.

Prior to expiry the price of an option will exceed the intrinsic value. This excess is the time value and is shown by the vertical distance between the prior-to-expiry profile and the at-expiry profile in Figure 4.4. The prior-to-expiry profile indicates the current market price of the option minus the price that the present holder paid for it. As time passes the prior-to-expiry profile will tend

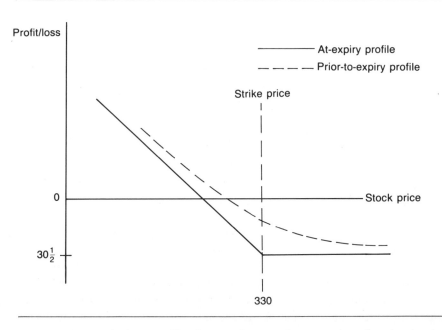

Figure 4.4 Profit/loss profile of a put option prior to expiry, showing its time value

to converge on to the at-expiry profile, with the convergence becoming complete as expiry is reached.

This convergence reflects the tendency for the time value of an option to decline with the passage of time. This erosion of time value can be explained in terms of the likelihood of a substantial increase in intrinsic value falling as the time available for the requisite stock price movement declines. A second factor affecting time value is the expected volatility of the stock price. With high volatility there is a relatively high chance of subtantial gains in intrinsic value at some stage prior to expiry. So, the greater is the expected volatility of a stock price, the greater will the time value of an option on that stock tend to be.

A third factor affecting time value is the relationship between the stock price and the strike price of the option. Time value is at its highest when the stock price is equal to the strike price. When the stock price is equal to the strike price the option is said to be at-the-money. As the stock price and strike price diverge, in either direction, time value declines.

When the stock price exceeds the strike price the put option is said to be out-of-the-money. A better price can be obtained by selling the shares in the market than by exercising the option. Time value declines as the option moves further out-of-the-money (in other words as the stock price rises), reflecting the decreasing likelihood of the stock price declining sufficiently to cause exercise of the option to become profitable.

When the stock price is lower than the strike price the put option is said to be in-the-money. A better price can be obtained by exercising the option than by selling the shares in the market. It is possible to make a profit by buying shares at the market price and selling them at the price guaranteed by the option contract. Time value declines as the option becomes deeper in-the-money (that is, as the stock price falls). This can be understood in terms of there being an increasing amount of intrinsic value that is at risk of being lost. The price of an in-the-money option contains the intrinsic value of that option. The buyer of an in-the-money option bears this risk, whereas the buyer of an at-the-money option does not. The risk borne rises as the option becomes deeper in-the-money. This risk is reflected in the time value. The buyer of an at-the-money option pays a higher price for time value than the buyer of an in-the-money option, with the price paid for time value declining as the option becomes deeper in-the-money.

The gradient of the prior-to-expiry profile is known as the delta and represents the ratio between the change in the price of the option and the change in the stock price. In the case of put options deltas are negative. The delta increases in absolute value as the option moves deeper in-the-money (as the stock price falls). As the option becomes increasingly deep in-the-money the prior-to-expiry profile approaches the 45° line of the at-expiry profile because of the decline in time value. This means that the delta approaches -1 when a put option becomes very deep in-the-money.

The delta decreases in absolute value as the option moves further out-of-the-money. The prior-to-expiry profile approaches the horizontal line of the at-expiry profile since time value diminishes as the stock price moves away from the stroke price of the option. The delta tends towards zero as the option becomes very deep out-of-the-money.

Exercise 4.1

Question
Dixons shares are trading at 140p. The option prices are as follows:

Strike price	Calls			Puts		
	December	March	June	December	March	June
140	8	7	18	8	12	16
160	2	$6\frac{1}{2}$	10	19	25	27

Do any of the options appear to be mispriced? If so what pricing principles are violated?

Answer
The March 140p call is underpriced because time value should rise with increasing time to expiry. The December 160p put is underpriced because the option price should not be below the intrinsic value.

Using call options

Options may be used to either reduce or increase risk. Reducing risk could be regarded as hedging and increasing risk as speculating.

HEDGING ANTICIPATED PURCHASES

Options can be used to hedge intended purchases of stock. Suppose it is 19 August 1993 and that a portfolio manager intends to buy BP shares with funds expected to become available in November. The current price of BP stock is 302p and the portfolio manager wishes to avoid the risk of having to pay a much higher price in November. The prices of BP call options are found to be as shown in Table 4.1 (p. 63). The portfolio manager could buy January 330p call options at $9\frac{1}{2}$p per share. Each option contract provides the right, but not the obligation, to buy 1,000 BP shares at a price of 330p per share. The price of the option is $9\frac{1}{2}$p per share which amounts to £95 ($9\frac{1}{2}$p × 1000) per option contract.

If, when the stock was purchased in November, the price were 360p the portfolio manager could exercise the option and thereby buy shares at 330p, a saving of 30p per share at a premium cost of $9\frac{1}{2}$p per share and a net profit of $20\frac{1}{2}$p per share.

By exercising the option the hedger obtains its intrinsic value. If, instead, he or she sold the option they would receive the time value as well as the intrinsic value. The time value might, plausibly, be 6p and hence the sale price of the option would be 36p. The portfolio manager would have bought options for $9\frac{1}{2}$p and sold them for 36p. There would have been a net profit of $26\frac{1}{2}$p per share rather than the $20\frac{1}{2}$p obtained from exercising the option. The $26\frac{1}{2}$p per share profit from the option partially offsets the increased price of the share whose effective price becomes $333\frac{1}{2}$p ($360 - 26\frac{1}{2}$).

If the share price were 330p or less at the time the shares were purchased the options held would have no intrinsic value and therefore could not be profitably exercised. However, they would still have time value. For example, if the share price were still 302p, the January 330p call options might, plausibly, be selling at 6p. The options would have been bought for $9\frac{1}{2}$p and sold for 6p (a bid– offer spread would increase this difference). The net cost of $3\frac{1}{2}$p (that is, £35 per contract covering 1,000 shares) compares favourably with the net cost of $9\frac{1}{2}$p (£95) incurred if the option is allowed to expire unexercised.

HIGHLY GEARED POSITION TAKING

Call options can be used for obtaining much higher percentage returns than those available from holding the stocks to which the options relate. However, this is at the risk of much higher percentage losses. Options allow exposure to the movements of the stock price with an outlay equal to the option premium rather than the stock price.

Consider the example used hitherto. A trader expecting a rise in the price of BP shares and wishing to profit from that rise could either buy the shares or buy call options. If the shares were purchased at 302p and subsequently sold for 360p the percentage profit would have been 19.2 per cent. Alternatively the trader could have bought January 330p calls at $9\frac{1}{2}$p and subsequently sold them for 36p, thereby making a 278.9 per cent profit.

Although taking advantage of the high gearing offered by options can produce high percentage profits it can also lead to heavy percentage losses. Suppose that instead of rising by 58p the stock price fell by 58p, to 244p. In such a circumstance the option price might, plausibly, have fallen to 1p. There would have been a 89.5 per cent loss compared to the 19.2 per cent loss from buying and selling the shares themselves.

Options, unlike shares, have expiry dates. When that date has passed, the option has no value (it ceases to exist). So if the share price remains at 302p until the expiry date there would be a 100 per cent loss on an option held to that date, whereas there would have been neither profit nor loss from holding the shares (disregarding any dividends). Since the passage of time erodes time value there would be a tendency for profits to decline, and losses to increase, as time passes. An option that expires unexercised would provide its holder with a 100 per cent loss.

A trader who fears a sharp fall in stock prices, or who wishes to take profits following a market rise, but wishes to profit from any further upward movement can use the 90/10 strategy. This involves the investor selling his or her shares and holding most of the proceeds on deposit while using a small proportion to buy call options. For example, 1,000 BP shares might be sold for £3,020 of which £215 is used to buy a January 300p call.

Should there be a sharp fall in the price of the stock the investor still retains at least £2,805 (£3,020 − £215). The investor's capital cannot fall below £2,805. At the same time the investor would benefit in the event of a rise in the stock price because of the call option held. However, the ability to profit from a rise in the stock price is only temporary. After the January expiry date there is no exposure to the market, unless part of the £2,805 is used to buy another call option with a more distant expiry date.

Using put options

Options can be used to fine-tune the amount of risk that an investor faces. A holder of shares may use options either to reduce or to increase the exposure of the value of the shareholding to movements of the stock price.

A put option guarantees a minimum selling price for a block of shares. Table 4.2 (p. 67) shows the premiums of BP put options at the close of trading on 19 August 1993, at which time the price of BP shares was 302p.

A holder of 5,000 BP shares would be able to ensure that the value of the shareholding could not fall below £15,000 (5,000 × 300p) by buying five 300p put options. These options would provide the right to sell 5,000 BP shares at 300p. The option prices are expressed in pence per share, so the cost of providing such protection until the January expiry date would be £775 (5,000 × $15\frac{1}{2}$p). Of course, should the stock price remain in excess of 300p the shareholder would not exercise the right to sell at 300p.

Although the shareholder has the right to exercise the option and thereby sell shares at 300p he is more likely to sell, rather than exercise, the option. This can be understood by considering the elements that make up an option premium. The premium (that is, price) of an option can be subdivided into its intrinsic value and its time value. The intrinsic value represents the gross profit that could be obtained by immediately exercising the option. For example, an October 330p put option has an intrinsic value of 28p when the stock price is 302p since, by exercising the option, shares can be sold at 28p more than they are bought at (ignoring bid−offer spreads). The difference between the option premium and the intrinsic value is termed time value, which is $2\frac{1}{2}$p in the case of the October 330p put options. Time value can be regarded as a payment for the possibility that intrinsic value will increase prior to the date on which the option expires (that is, the date beyond which it cannot be exercised).

If a shareholder exercises an option, only the intrinsic value is received, whereas if the option is sold both the intrinsic and time values are obtained. It thus makes sense to sell an option in preference to exercising it.

In Table 4.2 the 300p puts have an exercise price below the stock price. Therefore they cannot be immediately exercised at a gross profit and have zero intrinsic value. Their price consists entirely of time value. Put options with exercise prices below the market price of the stock are said to be out-of-the-money. When the stock price is equal to the exercise price the option is said to be at-the-money. Put options with exercise prices above the stock price (the only ones with intrinsic value) are termed in-the-money.

Time value is at its highest when the option is at-the-money and declines as the stock price moves away from the exercise price (in either direction). If the shareholder bought January 300p put options at $15\frac{1}{2}$p per share on 19 August and saw the stock price fall by 20p the following day he would simultaneously have seen the price of his options rise. A new option price of 26p would seem plausible (an intrinsic value of 18p plus a time value of 8p).

Faced with the choice between exercising the options and thereby selling shares at the exercise price of 300p and following the alternative route of selling shares at the new market price of 282p and simultaneously selling the options at 26p, the investor will clearly favour the latter procedure. The 26p premium would include time value of 8p, whose receipt via selling the options gives an effective share price of 308p ($292\frac{1}{2}$p after taking account of the original cost of the options) instead of the 300p from exercising the option ($284\frac{1}{2}$p after deducting the $15\frac{1}{2}$p original cost).

TAKING A SHORT POSITION

Put options provide a means of making profits from a fall in stock prices. If a trader in options believes that the price of a particular stock will fall, that trader can seek to profit from such a fall by buying put options.

In the example used above the trader, expecting a fall in the price of BP stock, could buy January 300p put options at $15\frac{1}{2}$p per share. The following day the stock price falls to 282p and the price of the options rises to 26p. Put options provide a right to sell at a particular price and that right becomes more valuable as the stock price falls.

In this context it is worth noting that whereas in-the-money and at-the-money options will give the highest absolute profits (because of the enhancement of intrinsic value), out-of-the-money options could provide the higher percentage returns because of the lower initial premiums.

Options, warrants and convertibles

Writing options

For every buyer of an option there must be a seller. The seller of an option is usually referred to as the writer. The buyer of an option is said to have a long option position whereas the writer of the option is said to have a short position. The profit/loss profile of a short (written) option is the mirror image of that of the long (bought) option. Profits of the buyer must equal losses of the seller, and vice versa. Figures 4.5 and 4.6 compare long and short positions for call and put options respectively.

The premium paid by the buyer obviously equals the premium received by the writer. The profit (loss) of the buyer will always equal the loss (profit) of

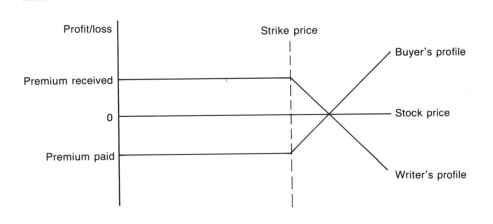

Figure 4.5 Call option (at expiry) profiles

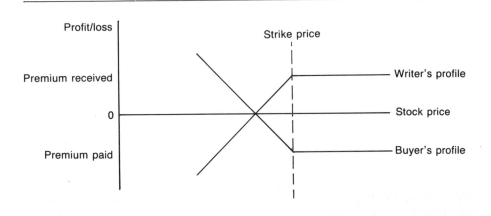

Figure 4.6 Put option (at expiry) profiles

the writer. It should be noted that the buyer of a call option has loss potential limited to the premium paid but unlimited profit potential. Conversely the writer of a call has a maximum profit equal to the premium received but unlimited loss potential. In the case of put options the buyer has a maximum loss equal to the premium, which constitutes the maximum profit of the writer. With put options the maximum profit of the buyer (maximum loss of the writer) occurs at a stock price of zero.

Exercise 4.2

The GEC option prices are as follows whilst the share price is 236p:

Strike price	Calls			Puts		
	October	January	April	October	January	April
220	19	30	39	$1\frac{1}{2}$	7	12
240	5	17	27	9	14	22
260	1	11	18	25	28	32

Questions
1. Draw the profit/loss profile for the buyer of a January 220p call option. (a) What is the breakeven price at expiry? Indicate (b) the maximum profit and (c) the maximum loss.
2. Draw the profit/loss profile for the writer of an April 260p call option. (a) What is the breakeven price at expiry? Indicate (b) the maximum profit and (c) the maximum loss.
3. Draw the profit/loss profile for the buyer of an April 240p put option. (a) What is the breakeven price at expiry? Indicate (b) the maximum profit and (c) the maximum loss.
4. Buy 1,000 shares and buy one January 240p put option. Draw the profit/loss profile of the combined position. Identify (a) the breakeven share price at expiry; (b) the maximum profit; and (c) the maximum loss.
5. Buy 1,000 shares and write one January 240p call option. Draw the profit/loss profile of the combined position. Identify (a) the breakeven share price at expiry; (b) the maximum profit; and (c) the maximum loss.

Answers
1. (a) 250p; (b) no maximum profit; (c) 30p.
2. (a) 278p; (b) 18p; (c) no maximum loss.
3. (a) 218p; (b) 218p; (c) 22p.
4. (a) 250p; (b) unlimited profit potential; (c) 10p.
5. (a) 219p; (b) 21p; (c) 219p.

Anticipatory hedges

Anticipatory hedges are used in cases in which there is a wish to delay the purchase of an asset (or delay the sale). A purchase may, for example, be delayed because the requisite finance is not yet available. If the intention is to buy stock, then call options on that stock could be purchased; for stock portfolios stock index options could be used.

A fund manager intending to purchase a particular stock might buy call options on that stock. Alternatively he or she could write deep in-the-money puts. A deep in-the-money put entails a high chance of the writer being assigned (exercised against); indeed, absence of assignment would occur only if the stock price had become unattractively high. The effective purchase price of the stock is the strike price minus the option premium received.

Covered writing

Covered writing refers to selling call options corresponding to assets held or selling put options when the liquidity for the purchase of the underlying is held. So covered writing involves the portfolio manager being prepared for the eventuality of being exercised against.

It may be the case that a portfolio manager has in mind a share price at which he would be prepared to buy and another at which he would be prepared to sell (see Figure 4.7). For example, he might be prepared to buy more shares in XYZ plc if the stock price falls to 180p and sell some of his existing holding if the price reaches 220p. In such a situation it might make sense for the fund manager to write 180p puts and write 220p calls. Writing these options would provide premium receipts whilst bringing about the desired transactions in the event of the stock price passing 180p or 220p.

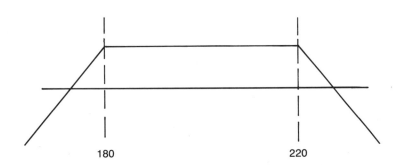

- The fund manager wishes to buy at 180 or sell at 220.
- If the put is exercised the fund manager buys at 180.
- If the call is exercised the fund manager sells at 220.
- Whatever happens to the stock price the fund manager receives the premiums from the two options.

Figure 4.7 Illustration of covered writing

Covered writing would also be a strategy that arises from a view that the market will be stable for a period of time.

Using call options in a stable market

If a fund manager expects the market to be stable, writing (that is, selling) call options that are covered by his or her portfolio is a rational strategy. The premiums received from such covered writing (selling) augment the returns on the portfolio.

The analysis can be expressed in terms of options on individual stocks covered by holdings of those stocks (for delivery if the option seller (writer) is assigned), or in terms of stock index options covered by a portfolio of shares.

Suppose it is 19 August and a fund manager has a balanced portfolio of UK equities with a value of £1,000,000 and a beta of approximately 1. Suppose further that the FTSE 100 index stands at 3067 and the FTSE 100 call options for September expiry with a strike price of 3100 are priced at 32. Since each contract relates to stock worth £10 per index point (3067 × £10) the fund manager can write up to 32 option contracts whilst being fully covered, £1,000,000/£30,670 = 32.6. (Note that the denominator is £10 multiplied by the current index and not £10 multiplied by the strike price.)

Selling 32 contracts would yield 32 × £320 = £10,240 (ignoring the bid−offer spread and other transactions costs). This yield is in addition to the dividend yield from the shares held. The drawback is that if the market rises by more than 33 points over the remaining life of the option the fund manager will forego any market rise beyond those 33 points; so this strategy would be attractive only if no strong market rise in the short term is expected.

RATES OF RETURN

The yield can be expressed as a rate of return on the net investment. The net investment is the expenditure on shares minus the receipts from selling options. For example:

Initial value of portfolio	£1,000,000
Less option premiums received	−£10,240
Net cash investment	£989,760

The potential rate of return can be expressed as 'return if unchanged' or as 'return if exercised'. The 'return if unchanged' is the rate of return in the event of the FTSE 100 index remaining at 3067, in which event the 3,100 calls would not be exercised.

Unchanged value of portfolio	£1,000,000
Less net cash investment	−£989,760
Profit	£10,240

Rate of return = £10,240/£989,760 or 1.03 per cent. It is to be emphasised that the appropriate denominator is the net cash investment and not the value of the portfolio.

When ascertaining the 'return if exercised' (which is the maximum return) it is necessary to take into account the profit on the portfolio arising from the market movement. (For clarity of exposition, dividends and transactions costs will continue to be ignored.)

Portfolio value upon exercise	£1,010,760	(£1,000,000 × 3100/3067)
Less net cash investment	—£989,760	
Profit	£21,000	

Rate of return = £21,000/£989,760 or 2.12 per cent. It is to be noted that in the case of stock index options, 'portfolio value upon exercise' refers to the new value of the original portfolio minus the cash settlement made upon assignment. (Stock index options are cash settled — that is, there is no delivery of stock if the option is exercised; instead, there is a cash settlement equal to the intrinsic value of the option.)

Exercise 4.3

Question
It is 15 March. FTSE option prices on LIFFE are:

Strike price	Calls			Puts		
	March	April	May	March	April	May
1800	64	88	110	23	47	65
1850	35	60	83	45	73	88
1900	16	38	60	77	103	115

The FTSE 100 Index is 1839.

A portfolio manager has a balanced fund worth £1,000,000, with a beta equal to the beta of the FTSE 100 index. Describe a strategy that could be pursued in order to increase returns in a stable market environment. Ignoring transactions costs and dividend receipts, calculate the rate of return achieved if on the option expiry date the FTSE 100 Index is (i) 1750, (ii) 1839 and (iii) 1950.

Answer
Write April 1850 call options. The number of contracts required for near complete cover is 54 (£1,000,000/£18,390 = 54.38).

Value of stock	£1,000,000
Less option premiums received	—£32,400
Net cash investment	£967,600

In cases (i) and (ii) the option would be unexercised:

(i)
Value of stock	£951,604	$\left(\dfrac{1750}{1839} \times £1m\right)$
Less net cash investment	−£967,600	
Net profit/loss	−£15,996	
Rate of return	$\dfrac{-£15,996}{£967,600} \times 100 = -1.65\%$	

(ii)
Value of stock	£1,000,000
Less net cash investment	−£967,600
Net profit/loss	£32,400
Rate of return	$\dfrac{£32,400}{£967,600} \times 100 = 3.35\%$

In case (iii) the option would be exercised:

(iii)
Value of stock	£1,005,982	$\left(\dfrac{1850}{1839} \times £1m\right)$
Less net cash investment	−£967,600	
Net profit/loss	£38,382	
Rate of return	$\dfrac{£38,382}{£967,600} \times 100 = 3.97\%$	

(In case (iii) the rate of return would be a little higher than indicated since 0.38/54.38 = 0.7 per cent of the portfolio would not be matched by options and would therefore benefit from the full rise in the index to 1950.)

DOWNSIDE PROTECTION

The option premiums received can be looked upon as providing some protection against a fall in the value of the portfolio. In the previous case a decline in the value of the original portfolio to £989,760 after selling the options would leave the fund manager in his or her original position of holding assets to the value of £1,000,000 (£989,760 plus the option premiums received of £10,240). The written options might thus be regarded as providing 1.024 per cent downside protection.

Thus covered call writes provide additional yield, which can be interpreted as downside protection, at the cost of foregoing some (or all) of the upside potential (see Figure 4.8).

VALUATION TRADING

The fund manager could be indulging in a form of valuation trading. He or she may sell the call options because they consider them to be overpriced. It would seem to be irrational for him or her to sell underpriced options. Individual estimates of fair prices depend upon individual estimates of market volatility.

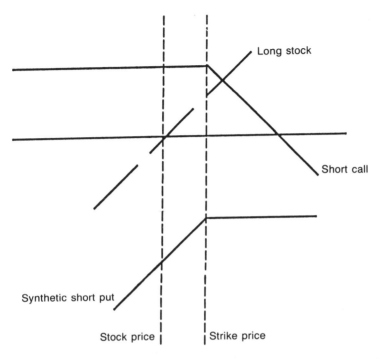

Figure 4.8 Covered call writing (buy—write)

- The premium from the short call could be viewed as an enhancement to yield or as downside protection.
- Combining a stockholding with a written call is equivalent to writing a put.

The current price of an option reflects the market's expectation of volatility. An individual investor will consider the option to be overpriced if he or she considers that the market has overestimated volatility.

PACKAGED BUY—WRITE FUNDS

The covered writing, or buy—write, strategy of buying stock and writing (selling) call options against that stock is sometimes marketed by institutions to small investors as funds that produce exceptionally high rates of income yield. The receipts from the sale of options is added to the dividends from the stock providing a relatively high cash flow to the investor. The investor should be aware, however, that this high rate of income yield is at the expense of a fund that has exposure to downward movements in stock prices without a corresponding upside exposure. In consequence, the investor is likely to experience a fall in the capital value of the investment over time.

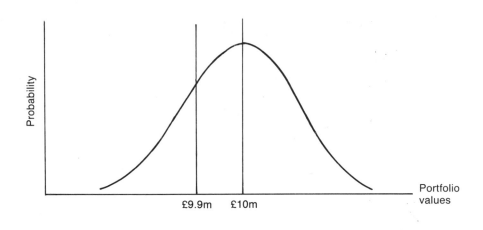

Figure 4.9 Probability distribution of possible values of a portfolio of equities

Using cylinders to reduce portfolio risk

The risk of a portfolio is frequently expressed in terms of the variance of the distribution of possible outcomes. This is illustrated by Figure 4.9 which shows a fund manager's subjective evaluation of the probability of various possible values of a portfolio of equities three months from the present. The average of the possible values (weighted by their probabilities) — in other words, the statistical expectation — is £10,000,000. This value of £10,000,000 reflects a rate of return over the current value of the portfolio (which might, for example, be £9,900,000). An apparent cost of this expected profit is, however, considerable uncertainty as to the outcome, with the range of possibilities including values less than £9,900,000.

The portfolio manager could reduce the extent of possible variation at negligible (if any) cost in terms of option premiums by means of an options cylinder (see Figure 4.10). This involves buying FTSE 100 put options in order to impose a minimum prospective value on the portfolio, and financing this purchase by writing (that is, selling) call options at a higher strike price.

Suppose it is mid-October and the portfolio manager is considering the prospective value of the fund in mid-January. Suppose further that the current FTSE 100 index stands at 1980 and that January 1950 put options can be bought for 80 whilst January 2050 call options can be sold for 77. This implies a premium cost of £30 [(80−77) × £10] per pair of options.

A 1950 put option gives the fund manager the right to sell a notional quantity of stock for £19,500. That notional quantity would sell for £19,800 at the current FTSE 100 index value of 1980. A 2050 call option that has been written obliges the fund manager to sell that same quantity of stock at £20,500 to the

82

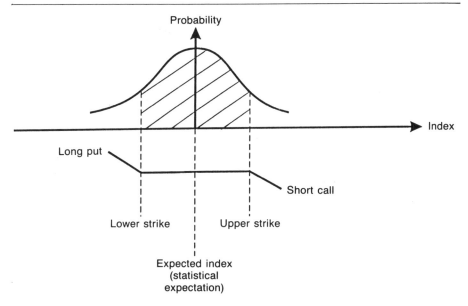

• If the options are to be held to expiry then an index portfolio will have a probability distribution that corresponds to the shaded part of the normal distribution

Figure 4.10 Using an options cylinder to reduce portfolio risk

buyer of the option, should that buyer choose to exercise the option. The fund manager would choose to exercise a 1950 put option if the index fell below 1950 and would be exercised against by the holder of the 2050 call option if the index rose above 2050. So the cylinder constrains the fund manager to an index range of 1950 to 2050. In so doing it reduces the variance of the value of the portfolio and hence reduces the risk faced by the fund manager.

Exercising stock index options does not involve stock being delivered. Effectively the fund manager would be locked into a range of values (£9,750,000 to £10,250,000 if the beta of the portfolio is the same as the beta of the FTSE 100 index), by being compensated with a positive cash flow in the event of a decline beyond the bottom of the range and suffering by way of a monetary loss in the event of the value rising above the top of the range.

A WORD OF WARNING

Finally, a word of warning about using the financial options market. The prices of options are determined by the forces of demand and supply in the market. Market participants should be alert to the liquidity of the markets (in the sense of the volumes traded). In an illiquid market the user's purchases or sales could move prices to his or her disadvantage. So a user may need to spread purchases or sales across a number of strike prices and expiry dates so as to avoid an excessive impact on the market for contracts of a particular series. The user may even feel that it is necessary to buy or sell less than the desired number of contracts and hence tolerate a risk reduction that is less than the hoped for reduction.

90/10 funds

90/10 funds provide exposure to stock market movements whilst ensuring a degree of capital certainty. They involve most of the portfolio being invested in capital-certain assets — for example, three-month deposits — whilst the remainder is used to buy stock or stock index call options in order to allow upside capture from market rises.

Despite their generic name these funds do not necessarily comprise 90 per cent capital-certain assets and 10 per cent equity-related options. The percentages are discretionary and would be determined by factors such as attitude to risk and the confidence with which a bullish view is held.

A fund manager might, for example, invest in twelve-month money-market securities the proportion of the fund that would yield the original value of the fund from such securities over one year. Having thus secured the capital value of the fund the remainder could be used to buy call options so as to obtain upside exposure to the stock market.

These funds provide security together with upside exposure. As with other funds, increased profit potential is obtained at the cost of increased risk. The greater the proportion of the fund in options, the lower is the capital certainty. Raising the proportion of the fund that is used to buy options will raise the delta of the fund (the delta being the relationship between changes in the value of the fund and changes in the prices of the stocks that underlie the options). The proportion of the fund in options can be raised by buying a greater number of options or by buying deeper in-the-money (or fewer out-of-the-money) options; either way, the delta of the fund would be increased.

If the wish is to obtain exposure to the stock market in general rather than specific stocks, then stock index options would be better than options on individual stocks. Such an approach spreads the risk so that adverse developments which are specific to particular stocks can be diluted (and offset by favourable developments in other stocks). The avoidance of stock-specific risk reduces option premiums. Volatility is an important determinant of option premiums. Since a stock index avoids the risks that are specific to individual stocks (and bears only the general market risk that is common to all stocks) it tends to be less volatile than individual stock prices. Consequently, option premiums for stock index options tend to be lower than those for individual stocks. This is a good reason for using stock index options rather than individual stock options.

Finally, it might be noted that 90/10 funds provide a means of reducing the currency risk that normally accompanies investment in overseas stock markets.

A fund that is 90 per cent invested in sterling deposits and 10 per cent invested in US options has considerably less exposure to the risk of a fall in the value of the US dollar than a fund that is 100 per cent invested in US stocks, although they might have identical exposures to the US stock market.

Exercise 4.4

Question
An institution offers a one-year investment yielding either 12 per cent or half of the FTSE 100 appreciation, whichever is the greater. The current FTSE 100 is 2000 and one-year interest rates are 15 per cent.

1. Beyond what value of the FTSE 100 does the stock-appreciation-based return exceed the guaranteed minimum return?
2. How could the fund be constructed?
3. What is the price of the implicit option?

Answer
1. A rise in the FTSE 100 to 2480 would provide a 240 index point return for the investor. The 240 amounts to 12 per cent. Beyond an index level of 2480 the index-based return would exceed 12 per cent.
2. The institution providing the investment needs to provide 12 per cent plus half of any index increase beyond 2480. Depositing 80 per cent of the fund at 15 per cent p.a. would yield a return equal to 12 per cent of the whole fund. A call option with a strike price of 2480, and relating to half the size of the fund, would provide a return equal to half the index rise above 2480.
3. Eighty per cent of the fund needed to be deposited in order to generate the guaranteed 12 per cent return on the whole fund. The interest return on the remaining 20 per cent can be used to purchase the option. This interest return amounts to 3 per cent of the total fund. The present value of this sum can be used for the option premium, and amounts to about 6 per cent of the sum to which the option initially relates (strictly speaking, the present value of that 6 per cent).
   So the implicit option premium is £3/(1.15) for every £100 of the original investment.

Exercise 4.5

Question
1. The current FTSE 100 stands at 2500 and the two-year interest rate is 10 per cent p.a. A 90/10 fund offers full upside exposure to the FTSE 100 with a guaranteed minimum payment of the original investment after two years. Suggest two ways of constructing such a fund on the assumption that two-year options are available. How much is available for the purchase of the options? What is the cost of downside protection to the investor?
2. How would the answers change if the fund promised a minimum 10 per cent return at the end of the two years?
3. Comment on the relative likelihood of calls and puts being used.

Answer

1. For every £100 of the initial investment £100/(1.1)^2 = £82.65 should be deposited so that £100 is available after two years. A two-year call option with a strike price of 2500 should be purchased. £100 − £82.65 = £17.35 is available for the purchase of the option. When compared with the alternative of buying stock the cost of downside protection to the investor amounts to the dividends foregone.

   An alternative means of constructing the fund would be to invest fully in stocks and buy a two-year put option with a strike price of 2500. The money available for the purchase of the option is the present value of the future dividends. Again, the cost of downside protection to the investor amounts to the dividends foregone.

2. For every £100 of the initial investment £110/(1.1)^2 = £90.91 should be deposited so that £110 is available after two years. A two-year call option with a strike price of 2750 should be purchased. (A strike price of 2750 rather than 2500 is appropriate otherwise the rise from £100 to £110 would be provided by both interest receipts and stock appreciation.) £100 − £90.91 = £9.09 is available for the purchase of the option. Alternatively stock could be purchased and a two-year put option with a strike price of 2750 could be purchased. The cost of the downside protection to the investor (when compared to buying stock) consists of the dividends foregone.

3. In the case of item 1, £17.35 is available for an at-the-money call and the present value of the dividends is available for an at-the-money put. In the case of item 2, £9.09 is available for an out-of-the-money call and the present value of the future dividends would pay for an in-the-money put. In item 2, expected dividends must be high for this to provide sufficient finance for the purchase of the put.

Warrants

Warrants are long-term options. They may have expiry dates that lie five years or more in the future (in contrast to stock options, which often have a maximum life of nine months).

Most warrants are issued by the company upon whose shares they are based. If they are exercised the company will issue new shares. So unlike options, warrants are usually used as a means of raising corporate finance. The issuing company receives the money from the sale of the warrants and subsequently receives the money paid upon exercise. In contrast to options, warrants tend to entail the expansion of the number of shares in issue.

Warrants are often attached to company debt, such as loan stock, when they are issued. The presence of such warrants renders the debt more attractive to the investor and hence the issuing company can raise money on more advantageous terms in that they pay a lower rate of interest than would otherwise be the case. In most instances the warrant is detachable from the host debt instrument and can be traded in its own right. Some warrants are issued naked — in other words, without the presence of corporate debt instruments. Since warrants normally pay no dividend or coupon, they provide an issuing company with a source of finance that involves no initial servicing costs.

Some warrants are not connected with the raising of corporate finance. Third-party warrants (sometimes misleadingly named 'covered' warrants) might be written by a bank without any involvement of the company on whose stock the warrants are based. One type of third-party warrant is, however, used for the raising of corporate finance. This involves the company raising the finance issuing warrants on the stock of another company.

Another form of third-party warrant is the stock index warrant. An important way in which these differ from most of the warrants described hitherto is in the existence of puts as well as calls (gilt warrants also include puts as well as calls).

In many respects warrant pricing is similar to option pricing. There is an intrinsic value based on the difference between the warrant exercise price (normally referred to as the subscription price) and the price of the shares. Call warrants are normally deep out-of-the-money when issued. There is also a time value influenced by the relationship between the subscription and spot prices, expected stock price volatility, time to expiry, expected dividends and interest rates. The greater longevity of warrants renders them more difficult than options to price accurately.

Convertibles

A convertible might be looked upon as a corporate bond with an attached call option. Convertibles are often referred to as convertible loan stock (or convertible unsecured loan stock since most are unsecured), and involve the right to convert the loan stock into shares at specified rates and points of time. Convertible preference shares are preference shares with the right to convert to ordinary shares. Some convertibles provide the right to convert to other loan stock rather than shares.

The number of shares for which the bond can be exchanged is referred to as the conversion rate. So, for example, the convertible may allow the conversion of £100 par value of loan stock into 20 shares. Multiplication of the conversion rate by the share price provides the conversion value. A share price of £6 would imply a conversion value of £120. Convertible loan stock would also exhibit an investment, or straight bond, value. This is the value of the bond (or preference share) in the absence of the right to convert. The investment value is the price of a corresponding straight bond or preference share.

The market value of the convertible would normally be higher than the greater of the conversion and investment values. The excess of the market value over the greater of the conversion or investment value is often referred to as the premium. Figure 4.11 illustrates the relationship between the conversion, investment, and market values of a convertible. It is assumed that the conversion rate is 20 and that the investment value is £90 per £100 par value.

Figure 4.11 illustrates the convertible as a loan stock with an attached option.

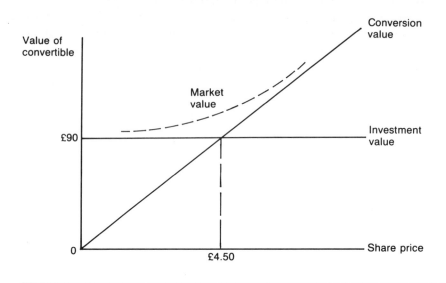

Figure 4.11 Relationship between the conversion, investment and market values of a convertible

The investment value is that of the naked loan stock whilst the excess of the market value over the investment value corresponds to the option premium. In this example the option has a strike price of £4.50. The excess of the conversion value over the investment value corresponds to the intrinsic value of the option.

It must be realised that the investment value, and hence the strike price of the implicit option, is not immutable. A rise in interest rates would lower the investment value and strike price. Similar effects would arise from a decline in the credit standing of the company, such a decline requiring a higher rate of return, which, given a constant coupon or dividend, implies a fall in the price of the loan stock (or preference share).

Convertibles are hybrids in that they constitute a compromise between bonds and shares. They provide more upside exposure to share price movements than bonds but less than ordinary shares. They provide less downside protection than bonds, but more than shares. The percentage rate of dividend or coupon yield would be less than that of a straight bond (because the market value exceeds the investment value), but probably more than that of the ordinary share (a rate of dividend yield on the share that exceeds the rate of coupon yield on the convertible would probably induce conversion of the convertible into the share).

The fact that the convertible involves a lower rate of coupon yield than a straight bond renders it attractive to the issuer. The attached option causes the investor to require a lower coupon yield. Convertibles thus provide a cheaper source of finance than loan stock or preference shares. Their advantage over ordinary shares, from the point of view of the issuer, is that they constitute a form of deferred equity. In particular the voting rights do not accrue to the holder until conversion takes place.

Holders of a convertible have the right to convert during a conversion period. If conversion does not take place during that period the convertible might simply become a loan stock or preference share. So, for example, a convertible might offer the right to convert on 1 June of the sixth, seventh, eighth, ninth or tenth year of its life, and if conversion does not take place on any of those dates it then becomes unsecured loan stock maturing at the end of a life of a further ten years, at which point it would be redeemed at par. The conversion rate would normally imply a high purchase price of the share (if acquired through conversion) on the issue date of the convertible so that a significant share price advance would be necessary for conversion to become worthwhile. It is to be noted that this conversion price per share, based on the issue price of the convertible, is not the same as the strike price of the implicit option as illustrated in Figure 4.11 (which is based on the investment value). The conversion price is the market value of the convertible divided by the number of shares obtained upon conversion. At the time of issue the conversion price will be greater than the share price.

The price of the option component of the convertible is determined in the same way as the price of any other option. Its value is influenced by time to expiry, volatility, interest rates, and the share price, in the same way as other options. However, the strike price will be variable since it is dependent upon the investment (straight bond) value of the convertible. The investment value of the convertible is influenced by interest rates and the credit standing of the issuing corporation.

The question arises as to why the holder of a convertible would exercise the right to convert, since it might be expected that the market value would exceed the conversion value so that the sale of the convertible would appear to be preferable to conversion. The circumstances in which conversion would take place are (i) call by the issuing corporation, (ii) the existence of a final conversion date, or (iii) the dividend yield of the share rising above the coupon yield of the convertible.

Sometimes the issuer of the convertible has the right to call it. This means that the holder must either accept redemption of the convertible (probably at the par value of the loan stock) or convert it into shares. If the latter provides the greater value, conversion will take place. When the final conversion date passes, the implicit option disappears, leaving only the investment value of the convertible. If the conversion value exceeds the investment value on the final conversion date it would be rational to exercise the right to convert.

The excess of the conversion price over the share price, when expressed as a percentage of the share price, is known as the conversion premium:

$$\text{conversion price} \quad = \quad \frac{\text{market value of convertible}}{\text{number of shares on conversion}}$$

$$\text{conversion premium } (\%) \; = \; \frac{\text{conversion price} \; - \; \text{share price}}{\text{share price}} \; \times \; 100.$$

In most circumstances the conversion premium would be positive. However a time may come when the dividend on the share exceeds the coupon on the convertible (the coupon is fixed whereas the dividend is likely to rise over time). If conversion dates are at distant intervals (such as a year apart) the prospect of a lower rate of yield on the convertible than on the share could render it less valuable than the shares into which it might be converted. So a share dividend above the coupon of the convertible, together with a long time before the next conversion date, could entail a negative conversion premium. The prospect of a negative conversion premium subsequent to a conversion date could lead to conversion on that date.

Appendix: Determining the appropriate strike price when using stock index options

A fund manager may wish to guarantee a minimum portfolio value by hedging with put options. That minimum value could be a percentage of the present portfolio value and relate to a future point in time.

It is tempting to take the view that there is a proportionality between the value being guaranteed and the strike price used. For example it might be supposed that protection against a fall in the value of the portfolio of more than 10 per cent would be obtained from a put option with a strike price 10 per cent below the current stock index. However, such an approach is appropriate only when the hedged portfolio and the index portfolio have identical betas and expected dividend yields.

One approach to the determination of the strike price would be to apply the *capital asset pricing model*, and, in particular, the securities market line. The securities market line determines the required, or expected, return on a portfolio. It can be expressed as

$$E(R_p) \; = \; R_f \; + \; B \, [E(R_m) \; - \; R_f]$$

where $E(R_p)$ is the expected rate of return on the portfolio being held, R_f is the risk-free rate of return (for example, the Treasury bill rate or LIBOR), B is the beta of the portfolio being held, and $E(R_m)$ is the expected rate of return on the market portfolio (which might be treated as synonymous with the portfolio on which the stock index is based). The term $B[E(R_m) - R_f]$ can be seen as the reward for accepting risk. Risk and the reward for risk bearing (specifically, it is the general market risk, known as systematic risk, that is being referred to) are both directly related to the beta of the portfolio.

Options, warrants and convertibles

When ascertaining the appropriate strike price (where the strike price is a stock index value) it is necessary to see the maximum portfolio decline in terms of an excess rate of return. The excess rate of return is the difference between the portfolio rate of return and the risk-free rate (specifically, the portfolio rate minus the risk-free rate, $R_p - R_f$). The portfolio return embodies dividends as well as capital gain or loss. In the event of a fall in the stock index the rate of dividend yield has to be subtracted from the portfolio value decline when calculating the negative excess return.

The beta of the portfolio being held gives the relationship between the excess return of that portfolio and the excess return of the stock index portfolio (whose beta is usually assumed to equal one). The stock index portfolio has an expected excess rate of return of $E(R_m) - R_f$ whereas other portfolios have expected excess rates of return of $B[E(R_m) - R_f]$. So when the excess rate of return corresponding to the maximum fall in the protected portfolio is found, the corresponding excess rate of return on the stock index portfolio can be found by dividing by beta.

Since the excess return on the stock index portfolio is one that corresponds to a price fall in the hedged portfolio, it too can be expected to be negative. The actual return on the stock index portfolio will equal the risk-free interest rate minus the calculated excess return. This actual return includes the expected dividend yield. Subtraction of the dividend yield provides the capital gain or loss component of the rate of return. When this rate of capital gain or loss is added to, or subtracted from, the current stock index value, the result is the stock index value that corresponds to the minimum portfolio value. In other words it is the stock index to be used as the put option strike price when designing the portfolio hedge.

Exercise 4.6

Question
The FTSE is at 2000, its yield is 4 per cent p.a. and the rate of interest is 10 per cent p.a. You hold a portfolio with a value of £10m, a beta of 2 and a yield of 2 per cent p.a. and wish to insure against the value of this falling below £9m after a year (with dividends distributed). At what exercise price should the puts be bought?

Answer
It is necessary to ascertain the FTSE index that would correspond to a portfolio of £9m after a year.

A 10 per cent fall in the portfolio value to £9m implies a total return on the portfolio of −8 per cent (10 per cent capital loss with a 2 per cent yield). This in turn implies an excess return over the risk-free rate of −18 per cent (treating the interest rate as the risk-free rate). Since the portfolio has a beta of 2 the corresponding excess return on the FTSE portfolio would be −18/2 per cent = −9 per cent. With an interest rate of 10 per cent an excess return of −9 per cent implies an actual return of 1 per cent. Since the FTSE has a yield of 4 per cent a return of 1 per cent implies a decline in the FTSE by 3 per cent to 2000 × 0.97 = 1940.

So the FTSE 100 index that would correspond to a portfolio value of £9m is 1940. A minimum portfolio value of £9m thus corresponds to a minimum index value of 1940. The puts therefore should have a strike price of 1940. In equation form:

$$-0.08 = 0.1 + 2\,[E(R_m) - 0.1]$$

$$-0.18/2 = E(R_m) - 0.1$$

$$0.01 = E(R_m)$$

$$0.01 - 0.04 = -0.03$$

$$(1 - 0.03) \times 2000 = 1940$$

5

~

Foreign investments: the currency dimension

Why invest abroad?

Two reasons for buying foreign securities are the diversification effects on stock risk and the reduction of currency risk. In Chapter 1 it was shown that holding a diversified portfolio of investments reduces risk since unexpected negative returns on some assets would tend to be offset by unexpected positive returns on others (that is, deviations from expected returns in one direction would tend to be cancelled by deviations in the other direction). It was seen that a well-diversified portfolio could reduce risk to the systematic risk, which is the risk of movements in the market as a whole.

Stock markets in different countries do not correlate perfectly. The correlation between national markets is not zero, as was demonstrated by the global nature of the stock market crash of October 1987 and as would be expected from the fact that many stocks are traded on more than one national stock exchange. However, since the correlation is not perfect there is scope for further reducing risk by diversifying into foreign investments. The systematic risk of a global portfolio would be less than that of a portfolio of stocks from a single national market.

The second reason, cited above, for investment abroad is the reduction of currrency risk. This might seem strange since holding foreign securities provides exposure to the currencies of the respective countries. What is often overlooked is that most people already have a currency exposure to the extent that they buy imported goods (or goods with imported components). For example, oil is priced in US dollars and, for non-US residents, a rise in the US dollar against the domestic currency tends to raise the prices of oil-based products in terms of the domestic currency. To the extent that expenditures are on goods ultimately priced in foreign currencies, it is risk reducing to have income sources in foreign currencies. So an appreciation of a currency against the home currency, while raising the home currency price of imported goods, would simultaneously raise the domestic currency value of the income receipts from investments in that foreign currency.

A FALSE REASON FOR INVESTING IN OTHER COUNTRIES

Sometimes higher expected rates of return from foreign stock markets, or higher interest on foreign currency deposits, are proposed as reasons for investing in foreign countries or currencies. It is necessary to be wary of such reasoning. First, high interest rates on a currency probably reflect high expected inflation in the country concerned and the likelihood of exchange rate depreciation. In other words, high foreign currency interest rates tend to be offset by a fall in the value of the foreign currency in terms of the domestic currency (this is sometimes referred to as the *international Fisher effect*). Although the difference between domestic and foreign interest rates is unlikely to be exactly matched by currency movements (unless forwards or futures are used to hedge currency risk), deviations in one direction are as likely as deviations in the other. It is as likely that the net interest receipts (when account is taken of currency movements) would be below those on the domestic currency as above, and of course the uncertainty of net returns is much higher.

A reason for expected higher returns from foreign stock markets might be the higher expected risk. A Third World emerging stock market may offer the potential for high returns but at the cost of a correspondingly high level of risk.

Currency risk

Currency risk is present when an investor stands to lose from exchange rate changes. One way to eliminate currency risk is to ensure that foreign currency income receipts (for example, interest and dividends from foreign investments) match foreign currency expenditures (for example, on imports). To the extent that these foreign currency receipts and expenditures do not match precisely, there is currency risk.

Income from foreign investments will fall if the relevant foreign currency depreciates. Dividends from a portfolio of US stocks will be worth less in terms of the home currency if the US dollar falls in value against the home currency. If it is felt desirable to reduce or eliminate such currency risk the risk management might be carried out by the individual investor, but the nature of risk management instruments renders this impractical unless the value of the portfolio is very substantial. It is more likely that institutional investors such as pension funds or mutual funds (unit trusts) would undertake such risk management, since the size of their portfolios would render such risk management practical.

Before moving on to examine techniques for currency risk management it should be mentioned that the direct effect of exchange rate movements on the value of foreign currency receipts is just one type of currency risk (one that corresponds to the transactions risk faced by corporate treasurers). There is also the effect of exchange rate changes on the domestic currency valuation of foreign investments (corresponding to the translation risk of the corporate treasurer). A third type of currency risk facing the investor corresponds to the economic risk faced by a company treasurer. This is more indirect and hence difficult to measure. An investor with no foreign securities in his or her portfolio would still have a currency risk if the companies invested in were exposed to currency price movements. For example, exchange rate movements might affect the stock prices of companies involved in exporting or importing. Also, changes in exchange rates can affect domestic stock prices by affecting the domestic currency valuation of foreign subsidiaries in the company's balance sheet.

REMOVING UNWANTED EXPOSURES IN INTERNATIONAL INVESTMENT

A portfolio of foreign stocks provides the fund manager with several exposures, some of which may be unwanted. There is exposure to the non-systematic risk of the individual stocks — that is, the risk that is unique to a stock or its sector rather than being related to the market as a whole. There is exposure to the foreign stock market or markets. Currency exposure is also present.

So an investor simultaneously takes positions in individual stocks, stock markets, and currencies when acquiring a portfolio of foreign stocks. This requires the fund manager to have expertise in stock selection, market timing, and currency forecasting. It also requires that the investor is simultaneously bullish on individual stocks relative to the market, the market as a whole, and the relevant currency. These co-requisites of foreign investment are unlikely to exist simultaneously in one person and at one time. Derivatives may be used to neutralise, or reverse, the unwanted dimension or dimensions of foreign investment.

ELIMINATING THE CURRENCY DIMENSION

Suppose that a UK fund manager is bullish on some specific US stocks and on the US stock market but is uncertain or bearish on the US dollar. Currency futures may be used to remove the exposure to the US dollar. The chosen portfolio consists of 10,000 shares of Aetna Life, 20,000 shares of American Express, 20,000 shares of Bethlehem Steel, and 10,000 shares of Boeing. The stock prices, and values of the stock holdings, are shown in Table 5.1.

The US dollar exposure of $2,015,000 can be removed by buying sterling currency futures. The adverse effects of a fall in the dollar (rise in the pound) would be offset by profits on the sterling currency futures. Suppose that the futures price of sterling is $1.60 = £1. The number of sterling currency futures to be bought on the Chicago Mercantile Exchange (where each contract relates

Table 5.1 The portfolio stock prices and values of stock holdings

Stock	Price ($)	Number of shares	Value of shares ($)
Aetna Life	53⅛	10,000	531,250
American Express	30	20,000	600,000
Bethlehem Steel	21⅝	20,000	432,500
Boeing	45⅛	10,000	451,250
			2,015,000

to £62,500) is $2,015,000/($1.60 × 62,500) = 20.15, which rounds down to 20 contracts (it is not possible to trade in fractions of futures contracts).

Currency futures are not the only instrument available for the management of exchange rate risk. Other instruments include forwards, options, swaps, and currency accounts.

THE FORWARD FOREIGN EXCHANGE MARKET

A forward purchase is an agreement to buy foreign currency on a specified future date at a rate of exchange determined in the present; likewise a forward sale. This technique removes uncertainty as to how much future payables or receivables are worth in terms of domestic currency.

If the forward rate for a currency exceeds the spot rate, that currency is said to be at a premium. For example, if the spot rate of sterling in terms of US dollars is £1.40, whilst the six-month forward rate is £1 = $1.45, then sterling is said to be at a premium against the dollar. Conversely, if the forward rate is less than the spot rate, the currency is said to be at a discount. With a spot exchange rate of £1 = $1.40, a forward rate of £1 = $1.35 means that sterling is at a discount against the US dollar (correspondingly the dollar is at a premium against sterling).

Table 5.2 shows how forward rates against sterling are reported in the *Financial Times*. The letters 'pm' indicate that the currency is at a premium against sterling and 'dis' indicates a discount. The forward rates are obtained by subtracting the premium from, or adding the discount to, the quoted price of sterling. For example, the spot price for sterling at the close of business is quoted as US$1.9510−1.9520 (sterling can be sold for $1.9510 per £1 and bought for $1.9520), and the dollar is at a three-month premium of 2.53−2.50 cents. This implies a forward rate of $1.9257−1.9270.

Table 5.3 shows how forward rates against the US dollar are quoted in the *Financial Times*. On the date concerned (7 December 1990) every currency stood at a discount to the US dollar. In most cases the discount of the currency against the US dollar is signified by 'dis'. In the cases of the British pound, Irish punt and the ecu it is signified by 'pm' because these three currencies use the direct form of quotation against the US dollar (dollars per unit of foreign currency), whereas the other currency quotes are based on the indirect form (number of units of foreign currency to the US dollar). The rule of thumb is that the adjustment for the premium or discount produces a forward bid−offer spread that is greater than the spot bid−offer spread. Take, for example, the yen against the dollar (see Table 5.4). The discount or premium should be added or subtracted with the result that the forward spread is greater than the spot spread. As another example, consider a direct form of quote, that of the ecu against the dollar (see Table 5.5). In both cases adjustment for the premium or discount widens the bid−offer spread. In the first case, the dollar is worth more yen forward than spot, so the yen is at a discount against the US dollar. In the second

Table 5.2 Pound spot — forward against the pound

December 7	Day's spread	Close	One month	% p.a.	Three months	% p.a.
US	1.9430–1.9520	1.9510–1.9520	0.95–0.93 cpm	5.78	2.53–2.50 µm	5.16
Canada	2.2570–2.2665	2.2620–2.2630	0.38–0.32 cpm	1.86	0.68–0.59 pm	1.12
Netherlands	3.2500–3.2625	3.2500–3.2600	1⅜–1¼ cpm	4.84	3½–3¼ pm	4.15
Belgium	59.50–59.95	59.85–59.95	24–18 cpm	4.21	58–48 pm	3.54
Denmark	11.0950–11.1400	11.1050–11.1150	3¾–3⅜ orepm	3.85	8⅝–7 3/7 pm	2.95
Ireland	1.0780–1.0920	1.0815–1.0825	0.30–0.25 cpm	3.05	0.75–0.63 pm	2.55
Germany	2.8790–2.8900	2.8850–2.8900	1¼–1 pfpm	4.68	3–2¾ pm	3.98
Portugal	253.25–255.15	254.00–255.10	1–22 cdis	−0.54	97–158 dis	−2.00
Spain	183.80–184.95	183.85–184.15	2–10 cais	−0.39	36–49 dis	−0.92
Italy	2171.75–2177.50	2174.50–2175.50	4–3 lirepm	1.93	8–6 pm	1.29
Norway	11.2950–11.3375	11.3125–11.3225	3⅝–2¼ orepm	3.11	5⅝–5⅛ pm	1.90
France	9.7750–9.8050	9.7925–9.8025	3⅜–3⅛ cpm	3.98	7⅞–7½ pm	3.14
Sweden	10.8475–10.8925	10.8700–10.8800	par–¼ oredis	−0.14	2⅜–3¼ dis	−1.03
Japan	255.25–256.75	255.70–255.80	1¼–1⅛ ypm	5.57	3⅜–3¼ pm	5.18
Austria	20.25–20.30	20.26–20.29	8⅛–7⅜ gropm	4.59	22⅝–20¼ pm	4.23
Switzerland	2.4575–2.4675	2.4575–2.4675	1⅛–1 cpm	5.18	2⅞–2¾ pm	4.57
Ecu	1.4025–1.4120	1.4100–1.4110	0.46–0.42 cpm	3.74	1.04–0.99 pm	2.88

Source: Commercial rates taken towards the end of London trading; six-month forward dollar 4.45–4.49 cpm; 12-month 7.86–7.76 cpm

Table 5.3 Dollar spot — forward against the dollar

December 7	Day's spread	Close	One month	% p.a.	Three months	% p.a.
UK[1]	1.9430–1.9520	1.9510–1.9520	0.95–0.93 cpm	5.78	2.53–2.50 pm	5.16
Ireland[1]	1.7935–1.8055	1.8045–1.8055	0.30–0.25 cpm	1.83	1.20–1.10 pm	2.55
Canada	1.1575–1.1630	1.1585–1.1595	0.38–0.40 cdis	−4.04	1.09–1.13 dis	−3.83
Netherlands	1.6650–1.6775	1.6680–1.6690	0.16–0.19 cdis	−1.26	0.54–0.58 dis	−1.34
Belgium	30.60–30.75	30.65–30.75	2–4 cdis	−1.17	9–15 dis	−1.56
Denmark	5.6900–5.7250	5.6900–5.6950	0.90–1.10 oredis	−2.11	3.20–3.80 dis	−2.46
Germany	1.4755–1.4880	1.4790–1.4800	0.12–0.14 pfdis	−1.05	0.47–0.50 dis	−1.31
Portugal	130.55–131.51	130.60–130.70	62–72 cdis	−6.15	230–260 dis	−7.50
Spain	94.40–95.05	94.50–94.60	47–52 cdis	−6.28	145–155 dis	−6.35
Italy	1112.50–1121.50	1114.25–1114.75	3.50–4.00 liredis	−4.04	11.20–12.20 dis	−4.20
Norway	5.7900–5.8300	5.7975–5.8025	1.35–1.70 oredis	−3.16	4.80–5.40 dis	−3.52
France	5.0100–5.0450	5.0175–5.0225	0.68–0.73 cdis	−1.69	2.66–2.76 dis	−2.16
Sweden	5.5665–5.5940	5.5700–5.5750	2.60–2.90 oredis	−5.92	8.60–9.20 dis	−6.39
Japan	130.40–132.15	131.05–131.15	0.01–0.03 ydis	−0.18	0.06–0.09 dis	−0.23
Austria	10.4175–10.4480	10.4175–10.4225	0.50–1.10 gdis	−0.92	2.30–3.60 dis	−1.13
Switzerland	1.2585–1.2710	1.2620–1.2630	0.07–0.10 cdis	−0.81	0.24–0.29 dis	−0.84
Ecu	1.3800–1.3900	1.3900–1.3815	0.25–0.23 cpm	2.09	0.85–0.79 pm	2.38

Note: [1] UK, Ireland and ecu are quoted in US currency. Forward premiums and discounts apply to the US dollar and not to the individual currency.
Source: Commercial rates taken towards the end of London trading.

Table 5.4 The spot and forward bid—offer spreads

	Yen/$		Yen/$
Spot	131.05—131.15	Spot spread	0.10
One-month forward discount	0.01—0.03	Spread on discount	0.02
One-month forward rate	131.06—131.18	One-month forward spread	0.12

Table 5.5 The spot and forward bid—offer spreads

	$/ecu		$/ecu
Spot	1.3805—1.3815	Spot spread	0.0010
One-month forward premium	0.0025—0.0023	Spread on premium	0.0002
One-month forward rate	1.3780—1.3792	One-month forward spread	0.0012

case, the ecu is worth fewer dollars forward than spot, so the US dollar is at a premium against the ecu.

The premiums and discounts are also reported in terms of per cent per annum. In Table 5.2 the dollar premium is quoted as 5.16% p.a. This percentage is ascertained from the following formula:

$$\frac{\text{premium} \times 365 \times 100}{\text{spot rate} \times \text{number of days to maturity}}$$

This formula can be more readily understood by rewriting it as:

$$\text{percentage} = \frac{\text{premium}}{\text{spot rate}} \times \frac{365}{\text{number of days to maturity}} \times 100$$

The first component, premium/spot rate, expresses the premium as a proportion of the spot rate. The second component, 365/number of days to maturity, annualises the figure. It alters the first ratio to produce the number that would be found for the twelve-month premium if the twelve-month forward premium was proportional to the three-month (or whatever) premium. So in the case of three-month forwards this adjustment would multiply the first ratio by four, whilst in the case of one-month forwards the multiplication would be by about twelve. Finally, the resulting figure is multiplied by 100 in order to convert the decimal into a percentage (see Example 5.1).

Example 5.1

Spot £1 = $1.9510 − 1.9520
3-month forward premium = 2.53 − 2.50 cents
3-month forward rate is £1 = $1.9257 − 1.9270

Rate of premium (% p.a.)
For seller of sterling:

$$\frac{0.0253}{1.9510} \times 4 = 0.0519 \ (5.19\% \ \text{p.a.})$$

For buyer of sterling:

$$\frac{0.0250}{1.9520} \times 4 = 0.0512 \ (5.12\% \ \text{p.a.})$$

Mid-price quote:

$$\frac{0.02515}{1.9515} \times 4 = 0.0516 \ (5.16\% \ \text{p.a.})$$

The bid—offer spread (the difference between the buying and selling prices) is always larger for forward foreign exchange than for spot. From Table 5.2 it can be seen that, in the case of the US dollar, the spot spread is 0.1 cent ($1.9510—$1.9520) whilst the three-month forward spread is 0.13 cent (see Example 5.2). It is thus possible to see whether there is a premium or a discount even in the absence of a direct indication. The quoted numbers should be added to, or subtracted from, the spot numbers according to whichever increases the bid—offer spread. So in the case of the three-month forward rate against the US dollar the spread is increased by subtracting 2.53—2.50 from the spot prices. It follows that the US dollar is at a premium against the pound (the pound is at a discount against the dollar). In the case of the Spanish peseta the numbers for the three-month forward rate are 36—49. The bid—offer spread is increased by adding these to the spot rates to yield 184.21—184.64. The peseta is thus at a discount against sterling.

Example 5.2

Spot £1 = $1.9495—1.9505
Three-month forward premium = 2.50—2.47 cents
Three-month forward rate is £1 = $1.9245—1.9258
Spot bid—offer spread = $0.0010
Forward bid—offer spread = $0.0013
Forward spread > spot spread
Forward spread = spot spread + premium spread

Determination of forward rates

To build up the picture of how forward exchange rates are determined it is useful to begin with considering how a bank might deal with a customer's request to buy or sell foreign currency forward. For example, a customer wishes to sell

Foreign investments: the currency dimension

US$1 million for sterling six months forward. To avoid exchange risk the bank could sell dollars at the time that the forward deal is agreed. The dollars might be obtained by borrowing them at the current eurodollar rate and the sterling obtained would be invested. Suppose that eurodollar six-month interest rates are 15 per cent p.a. and eurosterling six-month rates are 10 per cent p.a. The position of the bank immediately after the forward deal is agreed is:

10 March
Borrows $930,232 ($1,000,000/1.075) at 15% p.a.
Buys   £620,155 (930,232/1.5) at the spot exchange rate of
                £1 = $1.50
Deposits   £620,155 at 10%

10 September
Receives $1,000,000 from customer
Repays $930,232 capital plus $69,768 interest (totalling
                $1,000,000)
Receives   £620,155 capital plus £31,008 interest (totalling
                £651,163)
Pays customer   £651,163

On 10 March the bank agrees to pay the customer £651,163 in exchange for $1,000,000 on 10 September. The forward exchange rate is thus:

$$\$1,000,000/£651,163 = \$1.5357/£1$$

(Note that for this example, figures have been rounded to the nearest whole pound or nearest whole dollar.) Although it is possible, rather than probable, that a bank would follow this procedure, its possibility means that should the forward rate differ from £1 = $1.5357, the bank could profitably use this technique. Competition between profit-maximising banks in the pursuit of customers would then move the forward rate towards the one calculated above.

The forward exchange rate calculated above can alternatively be calculated by means of the following equation:

$$\frac{R_F - R_D}{1 + R_D} = \frac{F - S}{S}$$

where R_F is the eurocurrency interest rate on the foreign currency, R_D is the eurocurrency interest rate on the domestic currency, F is the forward (or futures) exchange rate, and S is the spot exchange rate. The condition depicted by this equation is known as interest rate parity. Using the figures from the example above (and treating sterling as the domestic currency), gives:

$$\frac{0.075 - 0.05}{1.05} = \frac{F - 1.5}{1.5}$$

$$F = 1.5357$$

A point to be noted is that since six-month forwards are being dealt with, the annual interest rates need to be converted to six-month rates by dividing by 2 (e.g. 15 per cent p.a. equals 7.5 per cent over six months, which in decimal form is 0.075). Secondly, the exchange rate needs to be quoted using the indirect method (units of foreign currency per unit of domestic currency) if the equation above is to be used. If the direct quotation method (number of units of domestic currency per unit of the foreign currency) is used the equation becomes:

$$\frac{R_D - R_F}{1 + R_F} = \frac{F - S}{S}$$

The interest rate parity relationship can alternatively be looked upon in terms of arbitrage possibilities, and in particular, covered interest arbitrage. Interest returns should be the same on all currencies (specifically eurocurrencies) when account is taken of forward premiums and discounts. Thus there is no significant difference in terms of return between investing in a dollar deposit (in the case above, at 15 per cent p.a.) on one hand and buying sterling spot, whilst selling it forward and investing that sterling between purchase and sale on the other hand. The forward premium on sterling offsets the interest differential between dollar and sterling deposits. This is the interest rate parity relationship.

The 'rule of thumb' is that if interest rates on foreign currency deposits are higher than those on domestic currency deposits, then the domestic currency will be at a premium against foreign currency; if, however, the domestic currency interest rates are the higher, then the domestic currency will be at a discount. The premium or discount compensates for the interest rate differential between deposits in the two currencies (note that the relevant rates are those on eurocurrency deposits).

The interest rate parity relationship may be maintained by covered interest arbitrage. Taking the example of the Deutschmark against the US dollar, the arbitrage may take one of the following forms:

1. Borrow dollars, buy spot Deutschmarks with the borrowed dollars; deposit the Deutschmarks purchased, sell those Deutschmarks plus interest forward; use the dollar receipts to repay the dollar borrowing. This is illustrated by Figure 5.1.
2. Borrow Deutschmarks, sell those Deutschmarks in the spot market for US dollars; deposit the dollars, buy forward Deutschmarks against the original dollars plus anticipated interest; use the Deutschmark receipts to repay the Deutschmark borrowing. This is illustrated by Figure 5.2.

It is to be emphasised that all values are known at the outset: dollar interest rates, Deutschmark interest rates, spot exchange rates, forward exchange rates. Since all relevant values are known no risk attaches to the arbitrage transactions. So, if interest rate parity fails to hold, one of the two arbitrage processes illustrated will yield a riskless profit.

The arbitrage process will tend to restore interest rate parity if it is deviated

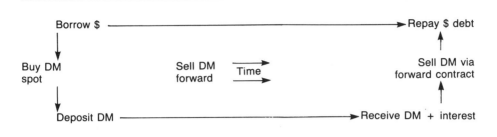

Figure 5.1 Covered interest arbitrage process (1). Borrow $, buy DM, deposit DM, sell DM forward

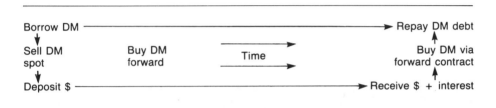

Figure 5.2 Covered interest arbitrage process (2). Borrow DM, sell DM, deposit $, buy DM forward

from, and hence the interest rate parity relationship is maintained by the mechanism of covered interest arbitrage. This arbitrage involves making profits from divergences between the interest rate differential, on the one hand, and the premium/discount expressed as a percentage change from the spot exchange rate on the other.

Suppose that the sterling short-term interest rate is 10 per cent p.a., whilst the corresponding dollar rate is 8 per cent p.a. The dollar stands at a premium against sterling and this premium implies an appreciation of the dollar at a rate of 2 per cent p.a. Suppose further that this interest rate parity relationship is disturbed by an increase in the dollar interest rate to 9 per cent p.a. An opportunity for arbitrage profits emerges. A bank in the UK could borrow sterling at 10 per cent p.a., exchange it for dollars, deposit those dollars at 9 per cent p.a. and simultaneously sell the principal plus interest forward. Inclusive of the 2 per cent p.a. guaranteed appreciation of the dollar, the dollar deposit yields 11 per cent p.a. in terms of sterling. There is a net gain of 1 per cent p.a., and there is no risk involved. This arbitrage is illustrated by Figure 5.3. (Note that for the purposes of exposition there has been some rounding to the nearest whole number.)

The process of taking advantage of the arbitrage opportunities tends to restore interest rate parity. In particular, the spot purchase of dollars tends to raise

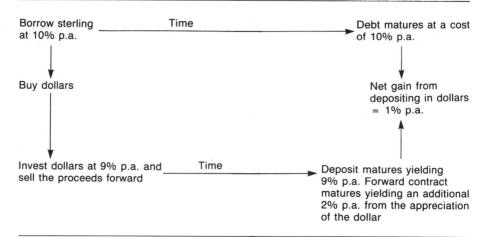

Figure 5.3 Covered interest arbitrage process (3). Borrow £, sell £, deposit $, buy £ forward

the spot price of dollars, and the forward sale of dollars tends to depress the forward price. The rising spot price and falling forward price reduces the dollar's premium. The premium will decline so long as the arbitrage is pursued and the arbitrage will be pursued so long as the premium exceeds the interest rate differential. In Figure 5.3 there is scope for arbitrage profits so long as the dollar's premium against sterling exceeds 1 per cent p.a. (In addition, borrowing sterling and lending dollars tends to raise sterling interest rates relative to dollar rates, so that a widening interest rate differential may contribute to the restoration of interest rate parity.)

Exercise 5.1

Question
The interest rate parity relationship can be expressed as:

$$\frac{R_\$ - R_£}{1 + R_£} = \frac{F - S}{S}$$

where $R_\$$ = US dollar interest rate, $R_£$ = sterling interest rate, F = forward price of sterling and S = spot price of sterling. If twelve-month rates are:

£ $13\frac{11}{16} - 13\frac{9}{16}$

$ $8\frac{5}{16} - 8\frac{3}{16}$

and spot £1 = $1.9260−1.9270:

1. Between what forward prices (for twelve-month forwards) would there be no opportunity for arbitrage profits?
2. If the interest rates above were three-month rates, what would be the theoretical prices of forward contracts maturing in three months?

Answer

1. Borrow \$, buy spot £, deposit £, sell £ forward:

$$\frac{0.083125 \; - \; 0.135625}{1.135625} = \frac{F \; - \; 1.9270}{1.9270}$$

$$F = \$1.8379/£1$$

Borrow £, sell spot £, deposit \$, buy £ forward:

$$\frac{0.081875 \; - \; 0.136875}{1.136875} = \frac{F \; - \; 1.9260}{1.9260}$$

$$F = \$1.8328/£1$$

There would be no scope for arbitrage profits between:

$$£1 = \$1.8328 \text{ and } £1 = \$1.8379$$

It must be remembered that money is borrowed at the offer rate (which is the higher rate) and deposited at the bid rate (which is the lower rate). Currency is bought at the offer (higher) price and sold at the bid (lower) price.

2. For the range of theoretical prices of forward contracts:

$$\frac{0.020781 \; - \; 0.033906}{1.033906} = \frac{F \; - \; 1.9270}{1.9270}$$

$$F = \$1.9025/£1$$

$$\frac{0.020469 \; - \; 0.034219}{1.034219} = \frac{F \; - \; 1.9260}{1.9260}$$

$$F = \$1.9004/£1$$

So the range of theoretical forward prices would be:

$$\$1.9004/£1 \text{ to } \$1.9025/£1$$

CAUSE AND EFFECT

Interest rate parity establishes a close relationship between the spot exchange rate and the forward exchange rate. The question arises, however, as to whether the spot rate is determined by market forces and the forward rate follows it, or whether the forward rate takes the lead and the spot rate follows. There are advocates of both views. There are two good reasons for supposing that the foward rate determines the spot rate. First, changes in the underlying economic and political circumstances seem likely to lead to a greater volume of forward deals than spot deals. Bodies deciding to hedge previously unhedged positions because of the changes would do so in the forward market. Speculators seeking to profit from their anticipations of exchange rate movements are likely to do so using forward rather than spot exchange because of the higher leverage involved in forward positions. (Futures could be used as alternatives to forwards and would behave in a similar way.)

Secondly, there is reason to believe that the forward rate corresponds to the expected rate and is therefore not determined by the spot rate. Speculators have expectations about the level of future exchange rates and if forward rates differ from these expectations there is a perceived scope for speculative gains. Furthermore the pursuit of these speculative gains would tend to move the forward rate towards the expected rate. Suppose, for example, that the three-month forward rate was above the rate that was generally expected. It would be worthwhile to sell forward with a view to honouring the contract by means of buying spot when the contract matures. If the expectation is correct the currency is bought at a lower price than that at which it is sold. Conversely, a forward rate lower than the expected rate would lead speculators to buy forward in anticipation of selling at a higher price when the contract matures. In the former case the forward sales by speculators would depress the forward rate towards the expected rate whereas in the latter case their forward purchases would raise the forward rate towards the expected rate. So there is reason to believe that the forward rate would tend to represent the expected rate. Since the expected rate is unlikely to be mechanistically determined by the spot rate it seems plausible that the line of causation goes from the forward rate to the spot rate.

For example, if sterling looks as though it might weaken because oil prices have fallen, previously unhedged positions might become hedged. Potential hedgers may be prepared to leave positions exposed until the fear of a sterling depreciation emerges. The emergence of such a fear leads to forward sales in order to avert the risk of loss from a considerable depreciation. Traders may also enter the forward market in the anticipation of making profits. If a trader expects the future spot rate to be below the forward rate he or she sells forward with a view to meeting the forward contract when it matures by buying spot at a lower price. The total effect is to drive down the forward price of sterling.

An increasing forward discount (or decreasing premium) for sterling would render sterling deposits less attractive relative to deposits in other currencies. The rate of depreciation of sterling would exceed the interest differential in favour of sterling. Arbitrageurs would sell sterling spot in order to switch their investments from sterling to other currencies. This puts downward pressure on spot sterling which declines in value, thereby maintaining interest rate parity. Thus the forward sales of sterling bring about matching depreciations of forward and spot sterling, leaving the premium/discount unaffected (unless there has been some impact on the interest rate differential).

Finally, in this context, it is interesting to note that futures rates are frequently used as a source of information by operators in the spot market. This use of futures rates suggests that they are seen as being determined independently of spot rates. Since forward rates are unlikely to diverge significantly from futures rates it follows that forward rates are also seen as being determined independently of spot exchange rates.

Foreign investments: the currency dimension

FORWARD RATES AS FORECASTS

There is reason to believe that the forward rate corresponds to the expected rate. Speculators have expectations about the levels of future exchange rates and if forward rates differ from these expectations there is a perceived scope for speculative gains. Furthermore the pursuit of these speculative gains would tend to move the forward rate towards the expected rate.

The forward rate may not precisely reflect expectations of the future rate because no forecast is held with certainty. The speculator's forecast may turn out to be wrong and, as a result, a loss might be incurred. The expected profit must be sufficient at least to compensate for this risk. If the forward rate does not differ from the expected rate by enough to offer an expected profit more than sufficient to offset the risk, the forward purchase or sale would not be undertaken. In addition to compensating for the risk the profit must also cover the transactions costs (commissions and bid—offer spreads). So there will be a range of forward prices, around the expected price, that do not offer sufficient profit to entice speculators. The greater the perceived risk, and the higher the transactions costs, the wider this range will be. In highly volatile, and hence very risky, market conditions the extent of the range may be considerable. Under such circumstances the value of forward, or futures, prices as market forecasts is much reduced.

There is therefore reason to believe that the forward rate would tend to approximate to the expected rate. Forward and futures prices are frequently used as sources of price information by operators in the spot market. This use of forward and futures prices suggests that the expected rate is reflected in forward and futures rates.

It appears that the forward rates are generally as likely to overestimate as to underestimate future currency prices. The absence of any significant tendency towards overestimation or underestimation suggests that forward rates are unbiased predictors of future rates. An unbiased predictor has no net tendency towards either underestimation or overestimation, but may none the less be typically inaccurate. Perfect accuracy of any forecast is impossible since not all circumstances that will affect an exchange rate can be foreseen. The most that can be hoped for is that the market for forward foreign exchange is efficient. An efficient market is one that utilises all available information in the determination of prices and in which the price adjustments are made quickly. If the markets for forward currency are not efficient there may be scope for obtaining better forecasts from other sources, for example, when other sources utilise all the available information.

FORECASTING SERVICES

If forward exchange rates do not fully reflect all the available information then there is scope for professional exchange rate forecasters to provide more accurate forecasts by making more effective use of the available information. Also, if a forward exchange rate differed from the expected spot rate because of a risk premium or transaction costs, there would be scope for professional forecasters to provide a better prediction than that obtained by observing the forward exchange rate. In the view of many, including the present author, any suggestion that professional forecasts tend to be more accurate than forward rates must be regarded as not proven. Indeed, if it were the case that professional forecasts were better predictors of rates because they made better use of the available information, it is to be expected that the process of obtaining speculative profit would pull forward rates into line with the forecasts, thereby eliminating the superiority of the forecasts.

Currency funds

Currency funds involve short-term bank deposits (or other short maturity money market investments such as Treasury bills) in foreign currencies. An investor may choose currency funds that invest in single currencies or might invest in a managed currency fund that moves money between currencies in an attempt to profit from exchange rate movements (taking money out of currencies likely to fall and putting it into currencies that the fund manager expects to rise).

A portfolio of single currency funds would be suitable for an investor seeking a reduction in currency risk through the holding of a diversified portfolio of currencies. Such an investor may believe that the home currency is going to decline relative to other currencies as a whole without having a view as to which particular foreign currencies this decline will be against (or strongest against). Investors in these funds should always bear in mind the tendency for currency movements to be offset by interest rate differentials. A currency prone to appreciate against other currencies can be expected to yield a relatively low rate of interest.

Managed multicurrency funds might be chosen by investors who believe that the fund managers have the expertise to forecast successfully relative currency movements. Such expertise could provide profits from selling currencies that are due to fall and buying currencies that will rise. Such managers need to be able to utilise information more effectively or more quickly than other currency traders. Currency traders are largely involved in forecasting the behaviour of other currency traders. It might be a zero-sum game in which the profits of some are matched by the losses of others.

Circumstances in which currency traders, as a whole, might earn profits include attempts by central banks to hold currency values against market pressure. For example, in September 1992 the Bank of England bought billions of pounds in an attempt to prevent its decline. The attempt was unsuccessful and as a result the Bank of England (on behalf of UK taxpayers) had bought billions of pounds that subsequently fell in value. Correspondingly, currency traders, in aggregate, made profits measured in billions of pounds.

Another circumstance that allows currency speculators, as a whole, to profit is the willingness of hedgers to accept small losses, on average, in order to avoid currency risk. It amounts to hedgers paying speculators to take on their currency risk. This can be seen most clearly in relation to futures markets (and currency funds may utilise currency futures). If hedgers in aggregate wish to sell futures on a particular currency the futures price will tend to fall below the expected future currency price. So speculators can expect to profit by buying the underpriced futures. They thereby guarantee a buying price that lies below the expected price of the currency.

A currency trader, whether operating as a private investor or as a manager of a currency fund, needs to be aware of the factors that influence exchange rates.

Influences on exchange rates

The foreign exchange markets trade currencies for both spot and forward delivery. They do not have a specific location and take place primarily by means of telecommunications both within and between countries. There are a number of major financial centres in which the markets are particularly active — New York, London, Tokyo, Frankfurt, Singapore, Hong Kong, and Bahrain among others. Much of the market involves trades between banks, whether acting as agents for customers or on their own behalf. Central banks (such as the US Federal Reserve, Bank of Japan, Bundesbank, Bank of England, etc.) tend to be particularly active participants in the foreign exchange markets, often acting in concert with each other. This intervention by central banks can cause situations in which currency dealers can make trading profits.

Exchange rates are determined by demand and supply (see Example 5.3). The purchases and sales of currencies stem partly from the need to finance trade in goods and services, although this accounts for only a small percentage of the total (typically much less than 5 per cent). A very substantial proportion is for the finance of investment, and in particular, the temporary investment in short-term money market instruments such as bank deposits, that might be regarded as speculation on currency movements (buying and investing the currencies that are expected to appreciate in value). A third source of demand or supply arises from the participation of central banks, a participation that would emanate from a desire to influence the direction, extent or speed of exchange rate movements.

Although short-term speculative movements account for the bulk of currency deals, the more fundamental factors of trade in goods and services (see Example 5.4), long-term investment and government policy are crucial to currency price movements. Not only do these more fundamental factors have a direct impact but they are in large part the basis for the speculative flows.

Example 5.3

Determination of exchange rates

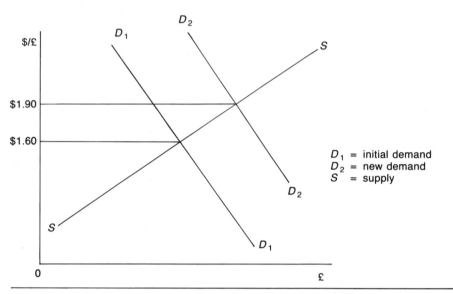

Figure 5.4 Demand and supply determine the international price of the pound

Factors that influence demand and supply
1. The balance of payments on current account (that is, exports and imports of goods and services).
2. The balance of payments on capital account (that is, investment flows into and out of the United Kingdom).
3. Central bank (e.g. Bank of England) intervention.

Figure 5.4 shows the determination of the price of sterling, in terms of the US dollar, by the interaction of demand and supply. The demand for sterling can come from foreign residents paying for UK exports, from foreign residents wishing to invest in the UK, or from the Bank of England (or other central banks) buying sterling in order to support its value. Figure 5.4 illustrates a case in which, as a result of an increase in demand from one or more of these sources, the demand curve for sterling shifts to the right and raises the US dollar value of the pound.

The supply of sterling can arise from UK importers selling pounds in order to obtain the currency required to pay for the imports. It can stem from UK investors wishing to acquire foreign currency in order to invest abroad.

Alternatively, one or more central banks may be selling sterling in order to depress its value. Rightward or leftward shifts (reflecting increased or decreased supply) of the supply curve would generate declines or rises respectively in the price of sterling.

Example 5.4

The influence of trade in goods and services on the exchange rate

- Exports generate a demand by residents of other countries for the sterling required to pay for the UK exports.
- Imports generate a demand by UK residents for the foreign currencies needed to pay for imports. Sterling is supplied in payment for the foreign currencies.
- An excess of exports over imports implies that the demand for sterling exceeds its supply and vice versa for a deficit.
- A current account surplus causes excess demand for sterling and hence an appreciation.
- A current account deficit causes an excess supply of sterling and hence a depreciation.
- A major cause of surpluses and deficits in the balance of payments on current account is the differences between the UK inflation rate and inflation rates abroad.

PURCHASING POWER PARITY

Purchasing power parity is a theory of exchange rate behaviour that is useful for explaining long-term currency movements. However, the long term may be as much as five years and purchasing power parity is of little help in explaining short-term changes, particularly day-to-day currency price movements. Despite its shortcomings, purchasing power parity is an important concept. There are two forms of the purchasing power parity theory, the absolute and the relative. The absolute form states that tradable goods should sell at the same price in all countries when adjustments are made for exchange rates and transport costs. If there are differences, then arbitrage should take place involving purchasing in the low-price countries and selling in the high-price countries. Such arbitrage would affect both the prices of the goods concerned and also the prices of the currencies, since the arbitrage trade would involve currency transactions. General misalignments resulting from disequilibrium exchange rates would generate so much arbitrage-based currency trading (that is, buying the currency in which goods are cheap and selling the currency in which they are expensive) that currency prices would be moved towards the values consistent with the absolute form of purchasing power parity. The evidence is not supportive of the absolute form of purchasing power parity but is consistent with the relative form (in the long run).

111

The relative form of the purchasing power parity hypothesis states that exchange rates will move so as to offset differences between domestic inflation rates. A country experiencing a relatively high inflation rate will tend to experience balance of payments deficits as its goods and services become uncompetitive in international markets. The deficit would put downward pressure on the international value of its currency. Conversely, a country whose inflation rate is low in comparison with that of other countries would find that its exports gain in price competitiveness whilst its imports rise in price relative to domestic production. Its exports would rise and its imports fall. The resulting balance of payments surplus would tend to cause an upward movement in the foreign exchange value of its currency. So the relative form of purchasing power parity predicts that exchange rates will move so as to offset differences between national inflation rates (see Figure 5.5).

Thus observations of relative rates of inflation, or of the underlying causes such as differences in rates of money supply growth, can be used to ascertain the direction of movement of exchange rates. However, this approach is not suitable for short-run forecasts of exchange rates. Rates can differ from those implied by purchasing power parity for several years and at any one time the actual rates are strongly influenced by short-run factors. Not surprisingly, the proportion of exchange rate variability explained by purchasing power parity is greater when there are large differences between countries in the extent to which prices change between two points in time. So the usefulness of the theory is greater when inflation rates differ substantially and when longer time periods are considered, since longer time periods would be associated with larger price-level movements.

Numerous studies, the earliest being soon after the First World War, have tested the relative version of purchasing power parity. On the whole, the studies have shown that over long periods exchange rate variations are well explained by price-level changes.

Exchange rates fluctuate around the rates suggested by purchasing power parity. At any time a currency is likely to be overvalued (relative to the rate

---

If the UK inflation rate is 4% p.a. higher than the German inflation rate, then purchasing power parity predicts a 4% p.a. fall in sterling against the Deutschmark.

UK has higher inflation

↓

Loss in international competitiveness

↓

Balance of payments deficits

↓

Depreciation

Figure 5.5 Purchasing power parity: exchange rate movements reflect differences in inflation rates

implied by purchasing power parity) against some currencies and undervalued against others.

The movement towards purchasing power parity may occur through exchange rate adjustments, price-level changes, or both, and can take a long time. Studies have suggested that the full adjustment to purchasing power parity can take more than five years, although most of the adjustment is typically achieved within two years.

So currency prices should change so as to offset inflation rate differentials. A high inflation rate leads to devaluation of the domestic currency. Devaluation should, in principle, restore the loss in competitiveness from high inflation. Devaluation renders exports cheaper, and hence more competitive. It also causes imports to be more expensive (since the currencies in which they are priced become more expensive). So exports should increase and imports fall. However, devaluation of the domestic currency causes a rise in import prices. Such a rise in import prices can fuel domestic inflation further, especially if it stimulates increases in the level of wage settlements. This vicious circle is shown in Figure 5.6.

In the short-to-medium term (perhaps for as much as a year following the initial devaluation), there is a strong possibility that a devaluation would weaken the balance of payments and thereby cause an excessive exchange rate adjustment. This can arise from the J-curve effect (see Example 5.5). Trade volumes take time to respond to price changes. Existing orders and contracts will determine trade flows for the first few months. Quantities traded will change only when new orders and contracts are made. However, the price changes are immediate. A country whose currency devalues will face higher import prices from the time of the devaluation. So initially the prices of imported goods rise in domestic currency terms, whilst export and import volumes are unchanged. In the period immediately following the devaluation, expenditure on imports rises with no offsetting increase in export revenues. The initial effect of the devaluation on the balance of payments is to increase the deficit. This worsening

Figure 5.6 The vicious circle of inflation

of the balance of payments would put further downward pressure on the international value of the domestic currency. So in the short term the depreciation of the currency may be greater than is required for the restoration of balance of payments equilibrium. There is exchange rate overshooting.

Example 5.5

The J-curve effect
- The rise in import prices directly worsens the balance of payments on current account.
- The changes in the volumes of imports and exports need to be sufficient to offset this direct effect. Trade volumes take time to respond to changes in export and import prices.
- Initially volumes show insufficient change, but over time the response increases.
- The balance of payments on current account gets worse before it gets better.
- This is known as the *J*-curve effect.

Appendix: Calculating numbers of futures contracts required for hedging

Basis is the difference between a spot (cash market) price and the corresponding futures price. Changes in basis reduce the efficiency of hedging with futures. One source of basis change arises directly from price movements. Futures prices tend to stand at premiums (or discounts) to cash market prices. This relationship between futures and cash prices, which is based on cost of carry, extends to the relationship between changes in futures prices and changes in cash prices. In the absence of a change in cost of carry a futures premium would entail the extent of movement in the futures price exceeding that of the cash price. This means that basis changes as a result of price changes. The analysis that follows demonstrates that this source of basis change can be eliminated by an appropriate calculation of the number of futures contracts, a calculation that may seem to be counter-intuitive.

The requisite number of contracts depends on the currency of the sum to be hedged (for example, sterling or US dollars, against which the derivatives are quoted) and upon the expected point in time at which closing out will occur. This analysis uses the Chicago Mercantile Exchange sterling currency contracts and assumes an awareness that the locked-in rate depends on the closing-out date — the spot rate if contracts are closed out immediately; the initial futures rate if contracts are held to maturity; or an average of the two, weighted according to the period of time for which the contracts are held.

Suppose that there is a need to hedge £10,000,000 against $US and that the pound is trading at a 2 per cent premium against the dollar. Spot £1 = $1.50 and six-month futures £1 = $1.53. Further suppose that the £10,000,000 is covered by 160 sterling currency contracts (160 × £62,500 = £10,000,000).

Now consider two scenarios:

1. An immediate rise in the pound to £1 = $2.00, followed immediately by closing out (with no change in relative £/$ interest rates).
2. A rise in the pound to £1 = $2.00 by the futures maturity date, with closing out on the futures maturity date.

In the first case, the futures price would rise to $2.04. The cash market loss would be $0.50/£, whereas the futures profit would be $0.51/£ (because the futures profit includes the premium). So the initial number of contracts should ideally be margined down to an extent that offsets the premium. This could be achieved by dividing the initial US dollar value of the hedged sterling by the futures price:

$$\$15,000,000/\$1.53 = £9,803,922$$

In principle, futures contracts corresponding to £9,803,922 (in practice probably 157 contracts) should be entered into.

In the second scenario the futures price reaches $2, providing a futures profit of $0.47/£. The effective price of sterling is thus $1.53 — the number of contracts does not need to be margined. In other words, a number of contracts equivalent to the initial dollar value of the hedged sterling divided by the initial spot exchange rate would be appropriate:

$$\$15,000,000/\$1.50 = £10,000,000.$$

One hundred and sixty futures contracts (£10,000,000/£62,500) are required. If contracts are to be closed out or exercised before maturity, the requisite number of contracts would lie between 157 and 160 and be a direct function of time to closing out (approaching 160 as the closing-out date approaches the maturity date of the contract).

In order to ascertain the number of contracts needed to hedge a dollar sum, a sterling equivalent must be found. Consider two possibilities:

1. Hedging $15,000,000 with a view to closing out almost immediately (that is, hedging an imminent sum of $15,000,000).
2. Hedging $15,300,000 with a view to holding the futures contracts to maturity (that is, hedging a sum of $15,300,000 anticipated for six months hence).

In both cases, suppose that the initial spot rate is £1 = $1.50 and the initial (six-month) futures price is £1 = $1.53. Suppose, further, that the spot price moves immediately to £1 = $2 in the first case, and to £1 = $2 by the futures maturity date in the second.

In the first case the sterling value of the dollars falls from £10,000,000 to

£7,500,000. At £1 = $2 the requisite dollar profit from futures would be $5,000,000. This would be obtained from contracts relating to £9,803,922 ($15,000,000/$1.53) since the futures profit per £1 would be $0.51, bearing in mind the 2 per cent premium. So the appropriate number of contracts would be based on dividing the dollar sum to be hedged by the initial futures exchange rate.

In the second case, the dollar profit from the futures required to ensure that the $15,300,000 is worth £10,000,000 (that is, to ensure that the $15,300,000 is converted at the original futures price) is $4,700,000. This would be obtained from futures based on £10,000,000, since the futures profit would be $0.47 per £1. Again, the appropriate number of contracts is based on dividing the dollar sum to be hedged by the initial futures exchange rate.

So whether the futures are to be closed out almost immediately, or are to be held to maturity, the dollar sum should be divided by the initial futures price of sterling in ascertaining the sterling value to be covered by futures. It follows that whenever the contracts are to be closed out the dollar sum should be divided by the initial futures rate. So the number of contracts is independent of the point in time at which the exposure is due to appear (the date on which the currency flow is expected).

This conclusion conflicts with the intuitive idea that the exchange rate at which conversion takes place should be the forward rate relating to the close out date, which would be a weighted average of the initial spot and futures exchange rates.

THE ROLE OF BASIS

The reason for ascertaining the appropriate number of sterling contracts to cover a dollar-denominated exposure by dividing the dollar sum by the futures exchange rate (relating to the futures maturity date), rather than by the implied forward rate (relating to the date of the exposure), can be seen in terms of avoiding part of the basis risk. If the interest rate structure between the two currencies remains unchanged, movements in the general level of exchange rates would cause changes in basis. With futures prices at a discount (or premium) against the spot, futures price movements would be smaller (or larger) than the spot price changes. As a result basis changes, and hedges would tend to be imperfect.

To compensate for such changes in basis, numbers of futures contracts need to be factored up or down. In the case of a futures discount, the number of contracts needs to be factored up by the same percentage as the discount. In the presence of a premium, factoring down by the same percentage as the premium would be appropriate. Dividing the dollar sum to be hedged by the futures price, rather than by an implied forward price for the exposure date, would provide the factoring required. A futures discount leads to an increase in the number of contracts by the required percentage; vice versa for a premium.

Foreign investments: the currency dimension

AN ILLUSTRATION

The points raised can be illustrated by means of a hypothetical example. It is 28 October and prices for sterling currency futures are as outlined below:

> December futures $1.7595 (18 December maturity)
> March futures $1.7475 (18 March maturity).

A treasurer anticipates that $20 million will be received on 18 January and decides to hedge the exposure using the March futures.

The implied forward rate for 18 January can be obtained by interpolating, between the December and March futures prices; it is $1.7555. The number of contracts suggested by the implied forward rate for 18 January is:

$(20,000,000/1.7555)/62,500 = 182$ (to the nearest whole number)

whereas the number of contracts suggested by using the March futures price as the divisor is:

$(20,000,000/1.7475)/62,500 = 183$ (to the nearest whole number).

On 18 January the new spot (offer) rate is $1.90. There has been no change in the interest-rate structure between the currencies, so that the futures discount remains at the same percentage. The January—March discount was $0.008/$1.7555 = 0.004557. The new money value of the futures discount will be $1.90 × 0.004557 = $0.0087, which implies a new March futures price of $1.90 − $0.0087 = $1.8913.

The profit from each March futures contract is therefore ($1.8913 − $1.7475) × 62,500 = $8,987.5. The two hedging strategies generate futures profits of:

$$\$8,987.5 \times 182 = \$1,635,725 \; (\pounds860,907.9)$$

and

$$\$8,987.5 \times 183 = \$1,644,712.5 \; (\pounds865,638.2)$$

Meanwhile, the loss on the underlying exposure was ($20,000,000/$1.7555) − ($20,000,000/$1.90) = £866,449.8.

The hedging strategy using the March futures price for determining the number of contracts produces the more efficient hedge. The factoring up of the number of contracts largely compensates for the 0.07 cent ($0.0087 − $0.008) change in basis, though the compensation was less than complete since some rounding down was required in order to ascertain the nearest whole number of futures contracts.

6

$\approx$

Collective investments and performance evaluation

Collective investments are provided by institutional investors and include pension funds, insurance funds, and mutual funds (unit trusts and investment trusts). Investing through the medium of such funds can provide a number of advantages:

1. Collective investments provide a degree of diversification that might not otherwise be possible for a small investor. A fund might have holdings spread across one hundred or more stocks. Most individual investors would not find it practical to have such a large number of stock holdings. A fund might also have other types of investment such as commercial property. A diversified spread of property holdings would be even more difficult for the small investor.

2. Collective investments provide professional portfolio management. Most individual investors lack the time, resources, and expertise to manage a portfolio. Institutional investors are in a position to carry out the requisite monitoring, analysis and transactions on a continual basis.

3. Collective investments often have a particular focus. This focus may be geographical: for example, a fund might invest solely in the stocks of a single country such as Japan or the United States or in the stocks of a region such as Europe or South East Asia. A fund might concentrate on particular types of stock: for example, growth stocks, smaller company stocks, or high income stocks. A service that a fund manager may provide for the investor is the maintenance of a particular focus: for example, a stock may cease to provide a higher than average rate of dividend yield and so would need to be replaced in a high income fund.

4. There may be other advantages to the investor. These other advantages might vary from country to country: for example, investing through pension funds often attracts tax advantages. Other advantages depend upon the individual: for example, some investors welcome the savings discipline that arises from a commitment to regular monthly investments. Some advantages would be more universal, such as the convenience of having the day-to-day administration of a portfolio in the hands of professionals so that the individual need pay no attention to the investment after it has been made.

Mutual funds (unit trusts and investment trusts)

Mutual funds are available in open-end (unit trust) and closed-end (investment trust) forms. Open-ended mutual funds expand and contract as investments are received or repaid. Investors buy units in the fund with each unit representing an equal fraction of the value of the fund. When investors are buying more units than they redeem the fund managers can buy more shares. Net redemptions by investors may force the fund managers into selling stock. Fund managers must pay attention to liquidity. A heavy commitment to illiquid stocks could produce a situation in which redemptions by investors cannot be honoured. Such a possibility may inhibit the investment strategy of the fund.

Closed-end mutual funds tend to operate as companies that invest in the stocks of other companies. After the initial offer for sale there may be no further equity investment into the fund. Subsequent investors would need to buy shares in the fund from existing investors. Also, investors cannot take money out of the fund. To realise their investment in the fund they would need to sell their shares to other investors. As a result the fund managers do not need to be concerned about the liquidity of their investments and may be able to take a longer view than the managers of open-end funds.

A potential disadvantage of the closed-end fund to the investor is the fact that the aggregate value of the shares in the fund may not match the total value of the investments held by the fund. In the case of the open-ended funds the sum of the values of the units equals the value of the assets held in the fund. Such is not the case for closed-end funds and it is not unusual for the share price to be less than (at a discount to) the value of assets per share. The tendency for the price of shares in the fund to deviate from the value of the assets in the fund, per share, provides an additional source of uncertainty and risk. It is possible for investment trust share prices to fall while the value of the fund is rising.

Another feature that distinguishes closed-end funds from open-ended ones is the ability (in most countries) of closed-end funds to borrow money, for instance through the sale of bonds. This produces a source of leverage. If investment returns exceed interest rates the rate of return to the holders of shares in an investment trust will be enhanced.

VARIATIONS ON CLOSED END FUNDS

Closed-end funds have become the source of various financially engineered investments. One approach has been to divide such funds into income shares and capital shares. Buyers of income shares receive all of the income from the fund but are entitled only to a pre-set amount of capital when the fund is wound up. (Another feature that distinguishes closed-end funds from open-end funds is the facility to have a date on which the fund is liquidated and the proceeds paid to the shareholders; all funds that are divided between income and capital

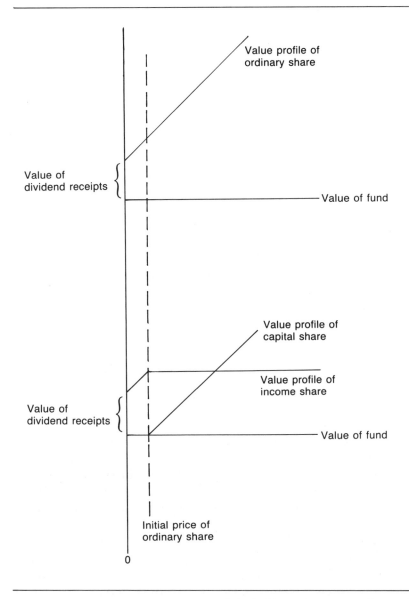

Figure 6.1 The combined position of the holders of income and capital shares

shares have such a winding up date.)

The holders of the capital shares of a split-capital trust receive all or most of the capital growth from the fund. In effect they hold call options on the fund, with the capital returnable to the holders of income shares providing the strike price of the call options. The holders of the income shares of a split-capital trust are effectively the sellers (writers) of put options. The combined position of the holders of the income and capital shares is illustrated by Figure 6.1. Adding the values of the income and capital shares produces the value of an ordinary share (an ordinary share constitutes an income share plus a capital share). Figure 6.1 illustrates the case in which the capital returnable to the holders of income shares equals the initial (issue) price of the ordinary shares.

Another way in which a closed-end fund (investment trust) might take a split-capital form is through division into highly geared ordinary shares and zero-dividend preference shares. Highly geared ordinary shares get all of the income and some of the capital growth. The zero dividend preference shares would have redemption values above the initial issue price of the ordinary share. The ordinary share price would need to rise above the redemption value of the zero dividend preference shares before the holders of highly geared ordinary shares become eligible for any capital gain. A highly geared ordinary share might be looked upon as an ordinary share partly financed through borrowing by means of the issue of zero-dividend preference shares.

It might even be the case that zero-dividend preference shares are used to add leverage to capital shares when a split-capital investment trust divides into income and capital shares. In such a case the holders of capital shares receive nothing until the zero-dividend preference share holders and the income share holders have been paid their redemption values. The capital share holder receives what is left. Capital share holders have the lowest priority for redemption payments when a fund is wound up.

With-profits funds

A type of fund that is particularly suitable for the very risk-averse investor is the with-profits fund. Such a fund might be the basis of a pension plan or an endowment policy. If an investor puts a lump sum into a with-profits pension plan, for example, the value of that investment cannot fall irrespective of what happens in stock or bond markets. Furthermore the pension scheme provider (typically an insurance company) will add a sum of money to the investor's personal fund each year (this sum is known as an annual, regular, or reversionary bonus). Once added, such bonuses cannot be taken away, whatever happens to the value of the investments in the underlying fund. So the money value of the investor's personal fund can only grow, it cannot fall. The pension provider will normally add a further bonus, known as the terminal bonus, on the date that the investor's pension scheme matures.

So the with-profits investment provides a high degree of security. It further reduces risk through the smoothing of investment returns over time. The insurance company (or other provider) will have a fund that will typically consist of stocks, bonds, property and bank deposits (and other money-market investments). Investments into a with-profits scheme will go into this underlying fund and the profits on the fund will pay for the bonuses. The provider of the with-profits scheme will put some of these profits into a reserve in years in which the underlying fund performs particularly well and will take money out of the reserves in order to pay bonuses in years that show poor investment performance. So good and bad years are averaged out and the private investor in the with-profits scheme is protected against the extremes of stock market fluctuations.

From the perspective of the pension scheme provider the value of the private investors' pension funds constitutes a liability, whereas the underlying portfolio is an asset. The surplus (or excess) is the amount by which the value of the assets of the underlying fund exceed the aggregate value of the liabilities (the total value of the individual with-profits policies). Companies providing the pension schemes are required to maintain a minimum surplus known as the solvency margin.

The surplus remaining above the required minimum solvency margin will be divided between the reserves (available for bonus payments in future years), dividends for shareholders (this is not applicable if the company is mutual and hence owned by its policyholders — a mutual has no shareholders), and the current payments of bonuses to the pension scheme members (or other policy holders).

It is sometimes argued that the annual bonuses reflect the current income on investments (dividends, interest, etc.) whilst the terminal bonuses arise from capital gains on the investments. This cannot be precisely true since in many years annual bonus rates deviate substantially from rates of return available on investments. Nevertheless there may be a kernel of truth in the idea. Another way of looking at the terminal bonus is to see it as the return of the investor's share of the solvency margin and reserves. The reserves available for the terminal bonus may be related to the capital appreciation of the underlying portfolio of assets.

An interesting question concerns the cost of the risk reduction. At one level the risk reduction might be seen as more apparent than real, in that instead of fluctuations in the current value of the policy there is uncertainty as to the size of the terminal bonus. The terminal bonus could be seen as the difference between the value of the policy (prior to the terminal bonus) and the value of the fund that could have been bought instead of the with-profits policy (which might be alternatively regarded as the policyholder's share of the underlying portfolio). From this perspective the risk reduction is more apparent than real. However, with-profits policies do provide a form of disaster insurance; in the event of an extreme collapse of asset prices the policyholder is protected.

It is possible that this disaster insurance is more apparent than real. It is conceivable that an insurance company (or other provider) could be rendered unable to meet its obligations to policyholders in the event of a heavy crash in asset prices. This risk may be reduced by accumulating some reserves that are not paid to policyholders. In such a case the cost of risk reduction is in the form of reduced terminal bonuses. An alternative means of providing the disaster insurance is for the portfolio manager to purchase put options. These put options would be at progressively higher strike prices as annual bonuses are added to policies (a succession of put options at progressively higher strike prices, each option replacing the previous one, is known as a cliquet option). If this approach were to be taken the cost of the disaster insurance would be in the form of the option premiums paid.

Annuities

An annuity provides the right to a future flow of income receipts. The usual time for the purchase of an annuity is retirement; the income receipts are then seen as pension payments. An individual would typically buy an annuity from an insurance company, possibly but not necessarily the same insurance company as that with which the pension fund has been built up (the pension fund is used to buy the annuity).

If the income flows are annual, then the annual receipt, d, is given by the formula:

$$d = P / \left[\frac{1 - (1 + r)^{-T}}{r} \right]$$

where P is the price of the annuity, r is the interest rate, and T is the number of years for which the payments will be made.

Three further points need to be made. First, r is the redemption yield of bonds with a maturity equal to T. Second, for income payments that are more frequent than a year, d and r should be divided by the number of payments per year and T multiplied by that number (so in the case of monthly payments the number would be 12). Third, when an annuity is purchased for the purpose of providing a pension, T would be based on average life expectancy.

It can be deduced from the equation that higher redemption yields on bonds lead to higher income payments. So people who retire when bond yields are high receive higher pensions. This can alternatively be seen from the insurance company's point of view. The insurance company will finance the payments by investing in bonds (frequently government bonds such as gilts or treasuries). If the insurance company receives high returns on its investments it is able to make large payments to its annuity holders.

It can also be seen from the equation that a higher T produces a lower d. The longer the period for which the insurance company expects to pay out, the smaller will be the periodic payments. Since women tend to live longer than men they have lower annuity rates.

Evaluating fund management performance

The performance of fund managers is often measured in terms of just one characteristic, the average compound rate of growth (either inclusive or exclusive of reinvested dividends). Furthermore fund managers tend to choose beginning and end dates that put the fund performance in the most favourable light.

Collective investments and performance evaluation

The performance of a fund cannot be measured in isolation. The rate of return achieved can be compared with (a) interest rates, (b) inflation rates, (c) stock indices, and (d) the performance of other funds. When comparing the performance of different funds identical beginning and end dates should be used. The performance of a fund can be made to look artificially good if the performance relates to a period which starts with a depressed stock market and ends with a buoyant one.

If a fund consists of equities, then the appropriate yardstick against which to measure its performance might be a stock index, such as the S & P 500, FTSE 100, Nikkei 225, CAC 40, or DAX. It is necessary to ensure that either both or neither the fund and the index are inclusive of dividends.

There is often consternation when it is observed that most managed funds fail to outperform a relevant stock index. Such failure to outperform should not be surprising. At best, average fund performance should match the index since fund managers are involved in a zero-sum game. Outperformance by some will correspond to underperformance by others; after all, the index measures the average (or aggregate) performance of investors. There are reasons to expect the average fund manager to underperform the index. First, funds incur charges that are not incurred by the index portfolio. Secondly, some investors will benefit from the use of inside information. Inside information is unlikely to be available to the managers of institutional funds (and in most countries such managers would avoid using inside information because its use is illegal).

The realisation of average underperformance has led to the emergence of index funds which merely attempt to track a stock index. Such funds may consist of the stock index portfolio itself (all the stocks in the index with relative quantities based on their weightings within the index), a portfolio whose beta matches that of the index portfolio, or may be constructed using futures on the stock index (the futures prices tend to rise and fall in line with the price of the stock index portfolio). The retail investor must ensure that charges are not such that the dividend yield on the fund is substantially below that on the stock index portfolio; a large difference in dividend yields means that the fund is not truly replicating the index.

Since equity funds can, on average, be expected to underperform stock indices an alternative benchmark is often employed. That benchmark is an average of similar funds. This has the advantage of allowing a degree of risk adjustment. Simply focusing on rates of return ignores other dimensions of performance such as risk. A fund may have a relatively high return simply because it has a greater risk. Comparing a fund with other funds with a similar risk level provides a more meaningful comparison of performance. It should also be borne in mind that funds should meet their objectives and that failure to do so constitutes poor performance. For example, a fund that claims to yield a high income should be seen as performing badly if its rate of income yield is lower than that of stock index portfolios (or the average rate of yield available in the market).

There are three other approaches to risk adjustment, although they are probably not frequently used. All three look at returns in excess of the riskless rate (the rate on Treasury bills or deposits in banks with high credit ratings). The difference between the rate of return on the fund and the riskless rate is referred to as the 'excess return'.

The reward-to-variability ratio, also known as the Sharpe measure, is the ratio of excess return to the standard deviation of returns on the portfolio. The reward-to-volatility ratio, also known as the Treynor measure, is the ratio of excess return to the portfolio beta. The Treynor measure accepts the tenet of the Capital Asset Pricing Model that only non-diversifiable risk (measured by beta) should be compensated for with enhanced returns, a portfolio manager can be expected to enhance returns by increasing systematic (non-diversifiable) risk but not by accepting additional non-systematic (diversifiable) risk.

The third approach is also based on the Capital Asset Pricing Model and is known as alpha (or Jensen's alpha). It compares the excess return on the portfolio with the excess return that would be expected on the basis of the portfolio beta. A positive alpha indicates a greater than expected excess rate of return, and vice versa for a negative alpha. In equation form:

$$a = (r_p - r_f) - B (r_m - r_f)$$

where a is alpha, r_p is the portfolio return, r_f is the risk-free interest rate, B is the portfolio beta, and r_m is the return on the market portfolio (normally approximated by the return on a stock index portfolio).

It is increasingly common to see a measure of risk, normally a standard deviation of returns or prices, quoted alongside figures on rates of return. Although this does not provide a risk adjusted measure of return it does provide information which the individual investor may use to find a risk adjusted rate of return. Such information also allows individual investors to tailor the risk—reward characteristics of their investments to their own risk—reward preferences: for example, an investor willing to accept high risk in order to obtain high returns can determine which funds, or types of fund, provide increased returns to reflect greater risk.

Finally, it is worth pointing out a deficiency with the use of standard deviation (or variance) of returns to measure risk. Typically, annual standard deviation is used. This assumes that one year is an appropriate investment horizon for all investors. That may not be the case. Consider the extreme example of a fund manager with a single future liability of £100,000 payable in ten years. That fund manager could buy a zero-coupon bond with a ten-year maturity (that is, a bond that pays no interest or coupons but merely provides a redemption value at maturity). The fund manager can be certain that the value of the asset will match the value of the liability ten years from the present. Fluctuations in the bond price during the ten-year period are of no concern. Annual standard deviation is not a relevant measure of risk.

Also consider a 25-year-old investing for retirement at 65. It is likely that during the intervening 40 years periods of relatively poor performance will be largely offset by periods of good returns. There is time diversification. The investor has a portfolio of time periods as well as a portfolio of investments. The annual standard deviation of returns is not important; what matters is the 40-year standard deviation. Annual standard deviations are not necessarily good guides to 40-year standard deviations.

ATTRIBUTION OF FUND PERFORMANCE

The performance of a fund manager depends partly on the allocation of the portfolio between asset classes (for example, between equities, bonds, and deposits) and partly upon selection within classes (which stocks to buy). If a portfolio contains foreign currency investments there is a currency dimension to the returns, profits or losses arising from currency price movements. It is possible to measure the contribution of each of these different decisions (asset allocation, stock picking, and currency choice) to the overall performance of the portfolio.

To separate the effects of asset allocation from those of stock picking it is necessary to compute an average return for all investments (weighted by the total market value of each asset class). Then an average rate of return within each asset class is calculated. The results may be those illustrated by Table 6.1. It can be seen that equities overperform by 1.8 per cent p.a., bonds underperform by 2.2 per cent p.a., and deposits underperform by 4.2 per cent p.a.

The next step is to compare the portfolio that is being evaluated with the average portfolio. The average portfolio reflects the total values of the different asset classes available to be held. Table 6.2 compares hypothetical figures for a portfolio being evaluated and an average portfolio.

Table 6.1 Rates of return on asset classes

Asset class	Rate of return (% p.a.)
Equities	10
Bonds	6
Deposits	4
All investments	8.2

Table 6.2 Comparison of evaluated portfolio with average portfolio

Asset class	Average portfolio (%)	Evaluated portfolio (%)
Equities	60	75
Bonds	30	20
Deposits	10	5

Table 6.3 Asset allocation contribution to portfolio performance

Asset class	Overweighting (1)	Overperformance (2)	Contribution to performance (1)×(2)
Equities	0.15	1.8%	0.27%
Bonds	−0.10	−2.2%	0.22%
Deposits	−0.05	−4.2%	0.21%

It can be seen that the portfolio being evaluated is 15 per cent overweight in equities, 10 per cent underweight in bonds, and 5 per cent underweight in deposits. The portfolio return arising from the asset allocation decision is based on the extent to which it is overweight in the overperforming asset class and underweight in the underperforming asset classes. The asset allocation contribution to portfolio performance is thus calculated as shown in Table 6.3. It can be seen that the total contribution of the asset allocation decision to portfolio performance is:

$$0.27\% + 0.22\% + 0.21\% = 0.7\% \text{ p.a.}$$

It may be observed that the portfolio being evaluated has a rate of return of 9 per cent p.a., whereas the average portfolio has a rate of return of 8.2 per cent p.a. Thus there is an excess return of 0.8 per cent p.a. of which 0.7 per cent is due to asset allocation. It follows that the return arising from stock selection is 0.8 per cent − 0.7 per cent = 0.1 per cent p.a.

In order to determine the currency contribution to portfolio return when foreign investments are included it is necessary to compare a fully hedged version of the portfolio with a version that is completely unhedged against currency movements. The profit or loss on the forward or futures position that is needed to hedge the portfolio equals the loss or profit on the currency exposure. The currency contribution to portfolio return is the negative of the profit or loss on the forward or futures position that would be needed to hedge the portfolio against currency movements.

7

~

Stock indices and stock index futures

Stock indices

Stock indices are measures of the price performance of stock portfolios which may be seen as representative of a stock market as a whole, or a segment of the market. The better-known indices include the Dow Jones Industrial Average, the Standard and Poor's 100, and the Standard and Poor's 500 in the United States, the Financial Times Stock Exchange 100 and the Financial Times Ordinary in the United Kingdom, the Nikkei Dow in Japan, the DAX in Germany, the CAC 40 in France, and the Hang Seng in Hong Kong. All countries with stock markets would have at least one index, and some countries (in particular the United States) have numerous indices.

This chapter is primarily concerned with the mechanics of the calculation of indices. This is of importance since it determines the comparability of the movements of different indices, and the interpretation that can be put upon a change in a particular index. Indices can be categorised in a number of ways: (i) the number of stocks included (or the proportion of the market of which it is intended to be representative); (ii) the method of weighting the stock prices; and (iii) the nature of the averaging.

The number of stocks can vary from a small number of large company stocks — for example, the Dow Jones Industrial Average and the Financial Times Ordinary are both based on just 30 stocks — to complete coverage of a particular market as provided by the New York Stock Exchange Composite Index. The indices based on a narrow range have the advantage of easy calculation but the disadvantage of being imperfectly representative of the market as a whole.

The contribution of individual stock prices to an index may be unweighted (as in the case of the Financial Times Ordinary Share Index), value-weighted (for example the Financial Times Stock Exchange 100), or price-weighted (such as the Dow Jones Industrial Average).

In the case of unweighted indices an average of daily rates of price change is calculated each day. The product of such averages (that is multiplying them together) since a base date provides the index (possibly after multiplying by 100 or some other base value). This calculation gives all stocks equal influence irrespective of the stock price or market capitalisation (that is, size) of the corporation concerned. To illustrate the calculation of an unweighted index,

Table 7.1 Prices and numbers of
three stocks

Stock	Price	Number
A	50p	10 million
B	100p	10 million
C	200p	5 million

suppose that it is to be based on just three stocks whose prices and numbers issued are as shown in Table 7.1. It is further supposed (a) that stock A rises in price by 15 per cent while the other two prices remain unchanged, and (b) that stock C undergoes a 15 per cent price rise while the other two prices remain constant. Before the price rise the index equals 100.

In the event of a 15 per cent rise in the price of A the new index will be (using arithmetic means):

$$\frac{\text{New value}}{\text{Old value}} \times 100 = \frac{(1.15 + 1 + 1)}{(1 + 1 + 1)} \times 100 = 1.05 \times 100 = 105$$

If the price of C rises by 15 per cent the new index will be:

$$\frac{\text{New value}}{\text{Old value}} \times 100 = \frac{(1 + 1 + 1.15)}{(1 + 1 + 1)} \times 100 = 1.05 \times 100 = 105$$

It can be seen that a 15 per cent rise in either stock price has the same effect on the index despite the fact that C has a higher stock price and relates to a larger company.

Price-weighted indices weight percentage price increases by the initial stock prices. They can be calculated as follows:

Index at time T equals

$$\left(\frac{\text{sum of stock prices at time } T}{\text{number of stocks in the sample}} \right)$$

divided by

$$\left(\frac{\text{sum of stock prices on the base date}}{\text{number of stocks in the sample}} \right)$$

multiplied by 100 (or other base value).

The calculations, using the information in Table 7.1 and 15 per cent price rises for stocks A and C respectively but based on a price-weighted approach, provide the following indices:

(a) $$\frac{\text{New value}}{\text{Old value}} \times 100 = \frac{(57.5p + 100p + 200p)/3}{(50p + 100p + 200p)/3} \times 100$$

$$= 1.0215 \times 100 = 102.15$$

(b) $\dfrac{\text{New value}}{\text{Old value}} \times 100 = \dfrac{(50\text{p} + 100\text{p} + 230\text{p})/3}{(50\text{p} + 100\text{p} + 200\text{p})/3} \times 100$

$$= 1.086 \times 100 \quad = 108.6$$

It can be seen that the impact on the index is four times as great when the price rise is in stock C rather than stock A, this reflects the fact that stock price C is initially four times stock price A. So high-priced stocks have the greatest influence on the index.

Using the same example but calculating a value-weighted index (weighting percentage increases by the market capitalisations of the companies: that is, stock price times number of shares issued) may be based on the formula:

Index at time T equals

$$\left(\frac{\text{sum of the market capitalisations at time } T}{\text{sum of the market capitalisations on the base date}} \right)$$

multiplied by 100 (or other base value).

The sums of the market capitalisations could be divided by the total number of shares issued so that the equation might be interpreted as the average stock price at time T divided by the average stock price on the base date.

A 15 per cent increase in the price of stock A raises the index from 100 to:

$\dfrac{\text{New value}}{\text{Old value}} \times 100 = \dfrac{(\pounds5.75\text{m} + \pounds10\text{m} + \pounds10\text{m})}{(\pounds5\text{m} + \pounds10\text{m} + \pounds10\text{m})} \times 100$

$$= 1.03 \times 100 = 103$$

whereas a 15 per cent increase in the price of stock C raises the index to:

$\dfrac{\text{New value}}{\text{Old value}} \times 100 = \dfrac{(\pounds5\text{m} + \pounds10\text{m} + \pounds11.5\text{m})}{(\pounds5\text{m} + \pounds10\text{m} + \pounds10\text{m})} \times 100$

$$= 1.06 \times 100 = 106.$$

The impact of the rise in stock price C is double that of the rise in stock price A. This reflects the fact that the initial market capitalisation of C (200p × 5 million) is twice that of A (50p × 10 million). When indices are value-weighted, large corporations have the greatest influence.

All the calculations thus far have used arithmetic means. It is interesting to repeat the calculations using geometric means. The computations and resulting indices are as follows.

Unweighted

(a) $\dfrac{\text{New value}}{\text{Old value}} \times 100 = \dfrac{\sqrt[3]{(1.15 \times 1 \times 1)}}{\sqrt[3]{(1 \times 1 \times 1)}} \times 100 = \sqrt[3]{1.15} \times 100$

$$= 104.8$$

(b) $\dfrac{\text{New value}}{\text{Old value}} \times 100 \;=\; \dfrac{\sqrt[3]{(1 \times 1 \times 1.15)}}{\sqrt[3]{(1 \times 1 \times 1)}} \times 100 = \sqrt[3]{1.15} \times 100$

$$= 104.8$$

Price-weighted

(a) $\dfrac{\text{New value}}{\text{Old value}} \times 100 \;=\; \dfrac{\sqrt[3]{(57.5 \times 100 \times 200)}}{\sqrt[3]{(50 \times 100 \times 200)}} \times 100 = 104.8$

(b) $\dfrac{\text{New value}}{\text{Old value}} \times 100 \;=\; \dfrac{\sqrt[3]{(50 \times 100 \times 230)}}{\sqrt[3]{(50 \times 100 \times 200)}} \times 100 \;= 104.8$

Value-weighted

(a) $\dfrac{\text{New value}}{\text{Old value}} \times 100 \;=\; \dfrac{\sqrt[3]{(5.75 \times 10 \times 10)}}{\sqrt[3]{(5 \times 10 \times 10)}} \times 100 = 104.8$

(b) $\dfrac{\text{New value}}{\text{Old value}} \times 100 \;=\; \dfrac{\sqrt[3]{(5 \times 10 \times 11.5)}}{\sqrt[3]{(5 \times 10 \times 10)}} \times 100 = 104.8$

As a consequence of the fact that calculating geometric means involves multiplying values together, all the calculations are equivalent to obtaining an unweighted index. This explains why the unweighted, price-weighted and value-weighted computations produce identical results and why the result is the same irrespective of whether the 15 per cent increase is in the price of stock *A* or the price of stock *B*.

If the value-weighted arithmetic mean is regarded as the most accurate method of ascertaining the index it can be seen that the geometric mean overestimates the effect of rises in the prices of smaller company stocks but underestimates the effect of rises in the stock prices of larger companies. Since large corporations are usually large because of rapid growth in the past it follows that the use of geometric means gives too little weight to the stock prices of rapidly growing companies and too much weight to the stock prices of slow-growth companies. So the use of geometric means underweights stocks whose prices rise rapidly and overweights stocks whose prices increase slowly. In consequence, over the long term, indices based on geometric means tend to understate the true rate of increase in stock prices. The same argument and conclusion applies to indices based on unweighted arithmetic means.

Exercise 7.1

Question
The following information is current:

Stock	Price	Number
A	50p	10 million
B	100p	10 million
C	200p	5 million

Stock indices based on these stocks are currently quoted at 100. Using arithmetic means ascertain the new price-weighted, value-weighted and unweighted indices in the event of a 15 per cent increase in the price of (i) stock A and (ii) stock C. What would the new indices be if geometric means were used?

Answer
Price-weighted

(i) $\dfrac{\text{New value}}{\text{Old value}} = \dfrac{(57.5p + 100p + 200p)/3}{(50p + 100p + 200p)/3} = 1.021$

New index = $100 \times 1.021 = 102.1$

(ii) $\dfrac{\text{New value}}{\text{Old value}} = \dfrac{(50p + 100p + 230p)/3}{(50p + 100p + 200p)/3} = 1.086$

New index = $100 \times 1.086 = 108.6$

Value-weighted

(i) $\dfrac{\text{New value}}{\text{Old value}} = \dfrac{(£5.75m + £10m + £10m)/25m}{(£5m + £10m + £10m)/25m} = 1.03$

New index = $100 \times 1.03 = 103$

(ii) $\dfrac{\text{New value}}{\text{Old value}} = \dfrac{(£5m + £10m + £11.5m)/25m}{(£5m + £10m + £10m)/25m} = 1.06$

New index = $100 \times 1.06 = 106$

Unweighted

(i) $\dfrac{\text{New value}}{\text{Old value}} = \dfrac{(1.15 + 1 + 1)}{(1 + 1 + 1)} = 1.05$

New index = $100 \times 1.05 = 105$

(ii) $\dfrac{\text{New value}}{\text{Old value}} = \dfrac{(1 + 1 + 1.15)}{(1 + 1 + 1)} = 1.05$

New index = $100 \times 1.05 = 105$

Using geometric means

Price-weighted

(i) $$\frac{\text{New value}}{\text{Old value}} = \frac{\sqrt[3]{(57.5 \times 100 \times 200)}}{\sqrt[3]{(50 \times 100 \times 200)}} = \frac{104.8}{100} = 1.048$$

New index $= 100 \times 1.048 = 104.8$

(ii) $$\frac{\text{New value}}{\text{Old value}} = \frac{\sqrt[3]{(50 \times 100 \times 230)}}{\sqrt[3]{(50 \times 100 \times 200)}} = \frac{104.8}{100} = 1.048$$

New index $= 100 \times 1.048 = 104.8$

Value-weighted

(i) $$\frac{\text{New value}}{\text{Old value}} = \frac{\sqrt[3]{(5.75 \times 10 \times 10)}}{\sqrt[3]{(5 \times 10 \times 10)}} = 1.048$$

New index $= 100 \times 1.048 = 104.8$

(ii) $$\frac{\text{New value}}{\text{Old value}} = \frac{\sqrt[3]{(5 \times 10 \times 11.5)}}{\sqrt[3]{(5 \times 10 \times 10)}} = 1.048$$

New index $= 100 \times 1.048 = 104.8$

Unweighted

(i) $$\frac{\text{New value}}{\text{Old value}} = \frac{\sqrt[3]{(1.15 \times 1 \times 1)}}{\sqrt[3]{(1 \times 1 \times 1)}} = \sqrt[3]{1.15} = 1.048$$

New index $= 100 \times 1.048 = 104.8$

(ii) $$\frac{\text{New value}}{\text{Old value}} = \frac{\sqrt[3]{(1 \times 1 \times 1.15)}}{\sqrt[3]{(1 \times 1 \times 1)}} = \sqrt[3]{1.15} = 1.048$$

New index $= 100 \times 1.048 = 104.8$

Financial futures

A financial future is a notional commitment to buy or sell, on a specified future date, a standard quantity of a financial instrument at a price determined in the present (the futures price). It is rare for a futures contract to be used for the exchange of financial instruments. Indeed many contracts have no facility for the exchange of the financial instrument. Instead financial futures markets are independent of the underlying spot market, albeit operating parallel to that market. For instance, currency futures are different instruments to the currencies themselves but currency futures prices move in ways that are related to the movements in currency prices. However, since futures markets are independent of the markets in the underlying instruments this relationship is less than perfect and it is possible for futures prices to exhibit changes that have no parallel in the underlying currency markets.

The main economic function of futures is to provide a means of hedging.

A hedger seeks to reduce an already-existing risk. This risk reduction might be achieved by means of taking a futures position that would tend to show a profit in the event of a loss on the underlying position (and a loss in the case of a profit on the underlying position). For example, a borrower who fears a rise in interest rates could take a position in interest rate futures that would show a profit from a rise in interest rates. So the hedger takes a futures position that is opposite to his or her existing cash market position. Unlike forward contracts, futures typically are not the mechanism for the acquisition of the desired financial instrument. In the case of many futures, including stock index and short-term interest rate futures, there is no facility for acquiring the desired position in the underlying by means of futures. A short-term borrower would not take out a loan via the futures contract; he or she would borrow in the spot money markets. The futures contracts would have protected him or her from an interest rate increase by providing a compensating profit but would be independent of the borrowing itself. The futures would be closed out simultaneously with the borrowing being undertaken, but would have no direct association with the borrowing.

Positions in futures markets can be taken much more quickly and much more cheaply (in terms of transactions costs) than positions in the underlying spot markets. For example, a position in stock index futures can be established within a few minutes (from the time of the decision) at little cost in terms of commissions and bid−ask spreads. The construction of a balanced portfolio of stocks would take much longer and be more costly in terms of commissions and spreads. For these reasons futures markets tend to be more efficient than the underlying spot markets in that futures prices would be quicker to respond to new information. So futures have a second economic function which might be termed price discovery. Futures prices may be indicative of what prices should be in the markets for the underlying instruments. This price discovery function might be particularly important where the underlying spot market is poorly developed or illiquid, as could be the case in countries with poorly developed financial systems or for instruments that are not frequently traded.

The margin system

The margin system is central to futures markets. There are three types of margin: initial margin, maintenance margin, and variation margin. The initial margin is a sum of money to be provided by both the buyer and the seller of a futures contract when they make their transaction. This margin is a small percentage of the face value of the contract (perhaps 1 per cent). The initial margin is subject to variation (by a *clearing house*) and will be dependent upon the volatility of the price of the underlying instrument concerned (initial margins might be as little as 0.1 per cent or as much as 10 per cent of the value of the instrument to which the futures contract relates).

The maintenance margin is the minimum sum of money (or other security) that must remain in a contract holder's margin account with the clearing house. On some futures exchanges this is equal to the initial margin, whereas on others the maintenance margin is less than the initial margin.

Variation margin is payable on a daily basis and reflects futures price movements. It is the means whereby futures profits and losses are realised on a daily basis. Someone whose futures contract shows a loss on a day must pay the amount of the loss to the clearing house by the following morning. Correspondingly, a futures position showing a profit on a day will result in a cash payment to the contract holder's account by the following morning. The process whereby profits and losses are realised on a daily basis via variation margin payments and receipts is known as *marking to market*.

One implication of the margin system is that futures are highly geared investments. For example an initial margin of 1 per cent of the underlying means that the exposure acquired is one hundred times the initial money outlay.

Futures funds

Futures funds are collective investments that operate by means of keeping most of their assets in a liquid form such as short-term bank deposits, whilst the remainder is used to finance the margin requirements of futures trading. The gearing offered by futures provides an opportunity for such funds themselves to be highly geared. The market exposure of a futures fund might be several times the value of the fund. Obviously such highly geared funds are very risky.

Futures funds often contain a wide variety of futures contracts. Multisector funds would not only contain a range of financial futures but also commodity futures. Furthermore the contracts are likely to derive from exchanges in a number of different countries. Such diversification helps to reduce the risk inherent in the futures funds. They may be particularly attractive to fund managers since they are likely to exhibit little or no correlation with the assets (such as stocks and bonds) that constitute the major part of investment portfolios. An asset that has low correlation with the other elements of a portfolio will tend to reduce the risk of the portfolio.

Taking views on market movements can normally be achieved more quickly and cheaply via using futures than by means of the spot instruments. Futures bid—offer spreads and commissions are often much lower than in the spot markets and time need not be spent on deciding between specific securities. It follows that a fund that is likely to shift frequently between sectors would benefit from the use of futures rather than spot market instruments.

Not only do futures allow quick and cheap movement between types of assets, such as equities and gilts, but also between national markets. The time and expense of researching foreign stocks can be avoided by means of using stock index futures relating to the foreign stock markets. Furthermore only margin payments are subject to currency exposure; the bulk of the fund can remain in the home currency.

Futures funds, like 90/10 funds, commonly guarantee that the initial investment is safe (in the sense that this is the minimum repayment at the end of the investment term, which may be several years). In such cases the loss is limited to the interest foregone, and even this loss might be ameliorated by a guaranteed rate of interest. A futures fund might, for example, hold 60 per cent of the original fund on deposit whilst making the remaining 40 per cent available for futures trading. A quarter (for example) of the money available for futures trading might be deposited as margin at any one time.

A futures fund would involve most of the fund being invested in short-term money market assets such as bank deposits or Treasury bills and the remainder being used for the margin requirements arising from futures positions. The futures may relate to a sum of securities equal to the value of the fund, but not necessarily. Futures provide the flexibility to gain exposure to a quantity of assets in excess of the value of the fund, or to take a short position on the underlying instrument.

Hedging with stock index futures

Stock index futures provide no facility for delivery and receipt of stock via exercise of the contract. Stock price movements are matched by compensatory cash flows. Futures contracts are available on many stock indices (frequently the index was created for the purpose of futures trading). Stock indices on which futures are traded include the S & P 100, S & P 500, Nikkei 225, FTSE 100, DAX, CAC 40 and the Hang Seng. There are contracts relating to all the major stock markets. Contract sizes are based on sums of money per index point. So if an S & P 500 contract is based on $500 per index point and the index (in the futures market) stands at 200, then each futures contract relates to 200 × $500 = $100,000 of stock. Similarly, at £25 per index point a FTSE 100 of 2000 (in the FTSE 100 futures market) indicates that each futures contract relates to 2000 × £25 = £50,000 worth of shares.

When using stock index futures to reduce stock market risk the anticipation is that any losses arising from movements in stock prices are offset by gains from parallel movements in futures prices. An investor might be anxious about the possibility that the prices of his or her stock might fall. He or she could reduce the risk of a reduction in the value of their portfolio by taking a position in the futures market that would provide him or her with a gain in the event of a fall in stock prices. In such a case the investor would take a short position in stock index futures contracts. By taking a short position he or she guarantees a notional selling price of a quantity of stock for a specific date in the future. Should stock prices fall and stock index futures behave in a corresponding fashion the notional buying price on that date would be less than the predetermined notional selling price. The investor could close out his or her position in futures by taking a long position in the same number of contracts. The excess of the selling price over the buying price is paid to the investor in cash in the form of variation margin. This gain on the futures contracts is received on a daily basis as the futures price moves (a procedure known as marking to market). Had the prices of stocks risen the investor would have gained from his or her portfolio of equities but lost on futures dealings. In either case the investor has succeeded in reducing the extent to which the value of their portfolio fluctuates.

The use of futures to hedge the risk of a fall in stock prices does not require any alteration of the original portfolio. It is thus preferable to any form of hedging that involves changing the composition of the portfolio: for example, liquidating part of the portfolio.

HYPOTHETICAL EXAMPLES

In Example 7.1 the portfolio holder fears a generalised fall in equity prices and wishes to avoid a fall in the value of his or her portfolio.

Example 7.1

Cash (spot) market	*Futures market*
5 April	
Holds a balanced portfolio of equities valued at £1,000,000 but fears a fall in its value. The current FTSE 100 index is 2000.	Sells twenty June FTSE 100 contracts at a price of 2000 each. He has thus committed himself to the notional sale of £1,000,000 of stock on the June delivery date at the level of equity prices implied by the futures price on 5 April. (£1,000,000 = 20 × 2000 × £25, where each futures contract relates to stock worth £25 per index point hence 2000 × £25.)
10 May	
The FTSE 100 index has fallen to 1900. Correspondingly the value of the portfolio has declined to £950,000.	Closes out the futures position by buying twenty June FTSE 100 contracts at a price of 1900. The notional buying price of each contract is thus 100 below the notional selling price.
Loss on the portfolio = £50,000	Gain from futures trading = £50,000 (20 × 100 × £25)

By 10 May the portfolio holder feels that the fall in equity prices is complete and chooses to close out his or her futures position. Of course this strategy is one that reduces variations in the value of the portfolio holder's assets. If, in Example 7.1, the FTSE 100 index had risen there would have been a cash market gain offset by a futures market loss.

Example 7.2 shows how a long position in futures can be used as a hedge. In this case a fund manager anticipates receipt of £1 million on 10 January and intends to use it to buy a balanced portfolio of UK equities. He fears, one month earlier, that stock prices will rise before the money is received.

Example 7.2

Cash (spot) market   *Futures market*

10 December
Anticipates receipt of £1 million on 10 January. Current FTSE 100 index is 2200. Fears a rise in the index.

Buys eighteen March FTSE futures contracts at a price of 2200. He thereby notionally commits himself to paying £990,000 (18 × 2200 × £25) for stock on a future date.

10 January
The new FTSE 100 index is 2300.

Closes out by selling eighteen March FTSE futures contracts at a price of 2280. He notionally guarantees a receipt of £1,026,000 (18 × 2280 × £25) upon maturity of the contracts.

Requires an additional £45,455 in order to buy the quantity of stock that £1 million would have bought on 10 December.

Profit from futures of £36,000.

In Example 7.2 futures prices did not move precisely in line with the FTSE 100 index and as a result the hedge was imperfect. Another source of hedge imperfection might be differences in the percentage price changes between the hedged portfolio and the FTSE 100 index arising from the portfolio having a beta different from that of the index. This latter source of imperfection can be dealt with by the use of hedge ratios.

HEDGE RATIOS

Hedge ratios become necessary when the volatility of the futures contract is likely to differ from that of the instrument to be hedged. If the instrument to be hedged shows relatively large variations, then it is appropriate to use more futures contracts than in the case of a more stable instrument. It is unlikely that a portfolio of stocks, for which hedging is required, precisely corresponds to the composition of a stock index. It is thus probable that it will show more or less volatility than the index.

The beta factor of a stock is a measure of the extent to which it moves in line with stock prices in general. A balanced portfolio is likely to have a beta factor of about 1. A stock with only half the movement of the market as a whole would have a factor of 0.5 while one with double the degree of change has a factor of 2. The beta factor of a portfolio of stocks is the weighted average of the beta factors of the stocks that constitute the portfolio.

If the calculation indicates a beta factor of 1.2, then the portfolio tends to change by 20 per cent more than the stock index. Hedging the portfolio would require the value of the stock index futures contracts used to exceed the portfolio value by 20 per cent. The relatively large losses (or profits) arising from the high volatility require correspondingly large offsetting profits (or losses) from futures contracts, and this necessitates a relatively large number of futures contracts.

Exercise 7.2

Question
On 1 October a portfolio manager holds the following stocks. The number of shares, prices, and the betas are as follows:

Stock	Shares	Price	Beta
Honeywell	4,000	62⅝	1.20
Deere	8,310	24½	1.05
MCA	4,300	47⅞	0.95
K mart	7,500	32⅛	1.15

The portfolio will be liquidated on 30 November. The portfolio manager believes that the market will rally during October and November and would like to increase the beta to 1.3. The December S & P 500 futures price is 186.50. Construct a transaction that will increase the beta to 1.3. (The futures contract size is $500 per index point.)

Answer
Value of the portfolio

$$\begin{aligned}
&4,000 \times 62.625 \\
+\ &8,310 \times 24.5 \\
+\ &4,300 \times 47.875 \\
+\ &7,500 \times 32.125 \\
&= \$900,895
\end{aligned}$$

Market exposure of the portfolio

$$\begin{aligned}
&(4,000 \times 62.625 \times 1.2) \\
+\ &(8,310 \times 24.5 \times 1.05) \\
+\ &(4,300 \times 47.875 \times 0.95) \\
+\ &(7,500 \times 32.125 \times 1.15) \\
&= \$987,022.25
\end{aligned}$$

Portfolio beta = $987,022.25/$900,895 = 1.096
Additional beta required = 0.204
This amounts to additional market exposure of:

$$\$900,895 \times 0.204 = \$183,782.58$$

Each futures contract provides an exposure of:

$$186.5 \times \$500 = \$93,250.$$

So the number of futures contracts to be bought is:

$$\$183,782.58/\$93,250 = 1.97$$

which approximates to 2 contracts.

Determination of futures prices

Arbitrage is crucial to the establishment of futures prices. Arbitrage can be defined as the pursuit of riskless profits with zero capital outlay (that is, any purchases are made with borrowed money).

The arbitrage that determines short-term interest-rate futures prices is based on forward-forward interest rates. Futures interest rates should show little deviation from the forward-forward rates; a substantial deviation would lead arbitragers to borrow via one of them (futures or forward-forwards) and lend via the other in order to obtain a profit. This arbitrage would reduce the extent of deviation so that the available arbitrage profits would no longer exceed the transactions costs arising from the bid—offer (bid—ask) spreads.

The emphasis here will be on the pricing of stock index futures. One reason for choosing stock index futures is that the arbitrage process leaves considerable scope for other determining factors since transactions costs (and risks) are such that the range of possible prices indicated by arbitrage possibilities is a very wide one. Another reason for choosing stock index futures pricing is the similarity of the principles of stock index futures pricing and government bond futures pricing. They are both based on cash and carry arbitrage.

Cash and carry arbitrage involves either buying in the cash market (stocks or bonds) and selling in the futures market, or selling (short) in the cash market and buying futures. The futures price should be such that there is no opportunity for profit from such a procedure.

If stocks are purchased and futures sold, a financing cost is incurred. Interest must be paid (or foregone) on money used to buy the portfolio of shares. Conversely, the money raised from selling stocks can be put on deposit to earn interest. The shares acquired when buying stock will produce a dividend yield (which constitutes a loss when stock is sold). The absence of arbitrage profits requires the futures price (stock index) to be at a premium (or discount) against the spot stock index so as to compensate for the excess (or shortfall) of the interest rate over the expected rate of dividend yield. So, in the case of buying

141

stock and selling futures, the cost incurred in the form of interest payments must be matched by the sum of expected dividend yield and the capital appreciation guaranteed by the futures premium. The excess of the interest rate over the expected rate of dividend yield is known as the net cost of carry, and this determines the excess of the futures price (stock index) over the spot stock index.

Deviation of the actual futures price (stock index) from the one thus determined could lead to the opportunity for profitable cash and carry arbitrage. If the futures price were higher than the implied (fair) value, buying a portfolio of shares and selling futures should generate a profit. The opposite arbitrage would be suggested by a low futures price. So a high futures stock index would cause arbitragers to sell futures, thereby depressing their prices towards the fair value. A low futures price would lead to buying pressure from arbitragers, which would tend to raise the price towards the fair value.

However, arbitragers must cover their costs (and compensate for any risks) before they show a net profit. When transactions costs (and risks) are taken into account the arbitrage that involves selling futures implies a much higher futures stock index than the arbitrage based on buying futures. Transactions costs include bid−ask spreads on both stocks and futures (although bid−ask spreads on futures are usually extremely small), commissions on the transactions in stocks and futures, and any tax payable (such as stamp duty in the UK). These costs could amount to as much as 2 per cent of the value of the underlying position. In addition to requiring compensation for transactions costs arbitragers may also require a risk premium as compensation for risks incurred. The cash and carry arbitrage is not totally riskless. It requires the establishment of a balanced portfolio of shares simultaneously with acquiring a futures position. Absolute simultaneity is impossible and prices may move adversely while the arbitrage is being constructed. Furthermore the stock portfolio is unlikely to be identical to the portfolio used to calculate the stock index and hence may have a different beta (so that their price movements may not be identical). There may also be interest costs on variation margin payments, and these would be of uncertain amount. So the arbitrage is not entirely riskless and some profit margin may be required to compensate for the risk.

It follows that cash and carry arbitrage does not determine a single unique futures price. There is a fair price based on net cost of carry (interest rate minus expected dividend yield), but arbitrage may not be worthwhile until the futures price has deviated by more than 2 per cent from the fair price. So arbitrage merely serves to keep the futures price (stock index) within a band of values, sometimes referred to as the *no arbitrage* band. The existence of the no arbitrage band has implications for the mechanism of futures pricing and for hedging strategies. As for the determination of futures prices, the no arbitrage band allows trading based on speculation to play a role.

Arbitragers may operate between the futures market and the market for the underlying financial instrument. By doing so, they help to create liquidity in the futures market and dampen excessive divergences between futures prices and the prices of the underlying financial instruments. Therefore, if hedgers sought to take a net long position for a particular delivery month there would be a tendency for the price of the contract to rise. The arbitrager could sell futures and buy equities with a view to subsequently closing both positions and making a profit. Such might be the case if the premium of the futures price over the cash market price gave a return that exceeded the excess of the financing cost of holding equities over the running yield of those equities. Thus tendencies for futures prices to diverge too far from the underlying equity prices would be tempered by arbitrage.

The role of speculators

Speculators (often alternatively referred to as traders) take risk in the anticipation of making profits. They buy if they expect prices to rise and sell if a fall is anticipated. Speculation is vital for the efficiency and stability of financial markets. In the absence of speculators other users, such as hedgers, may be unable to conduct the transactions that they require.

Suppose that hedgers seek to adopt a net short position — that is, the hedgers wanting to sell futures outweigh hedgers wishing to buy so that, in aggregate, hedgers are net sellers. This would tend to reduce futures prices, a situation that provides opportunities for speculators. If the futures price falls below the expected future spot price speculators may buy futures in order to make a profit from a subsequent rise in futures prices towards the expected level. The situation in which a futures price lies below the expected spot price so that the futures price is expected to rise is known as *normal backwardation*.

Conversely, if hedgers are net buyers of futures, then speculators must be induced to be net sellers. To be induced to sell they must expect falling futures prices. This requires the futures price to exceed the expected spot price. This condition is known as *contango*.

So falling prices induce speculators to buy, thereby moderating the falls. Rising futures prices lead to sales by speculators, who would thereby dampen the price rises. So speculation can reduce the extent of price fluctuation and hence render markets more stable. However, price fluctuation would not be eliminated completely. Some deviation of futures prices from the expected levels is required in order to provide the prospective profits that induce speculation. Furthermore the prospective profits, and hence price deviation, must be sufficient to compensate the speculators for their transactions costs — which are usually very low in futures markets, particularly for those who do not need to use brokers — and for the risks incurred.

So the presence of speculators ensures that hedgers are able to buy or sell futures contracts when they need to and that they do not face prices distorted by demand and supply imbalances. Speculators fill any deficiency in demand or supply.

The behaviour of speculators helps to determine where, within the no arbitrage band, the futures price will actually fall. In particular, the actual price would be close to the future spot price expected, on average, by speculators. If it were below this expectation they would buy, thereby pushing the price up, whereas if it were above the expected level they would sell and hence push it down towards the expected price. There would remain some deviation of the futures price from the expected spot price. The direction of deviation would depend upon whether the market exhibited normal backwardation or contango (that is, whether hedgers were net sellers or net buyers). The extent of deviation would be determined by the level of transactions costs and risks for which speculators must be compensated. Anticipated profits must at least provide such compensation and, as a result, small price deviations from expected values may persist because they provide inadequate profit potential.

Exercise 7.3

Question

Three-month interest rates are 11½−11⅜ per cent p.a. The expected rate of dividend yield on the FTSE 100 portfolio over the next three months is 4 per cent p.a. If the current value of the FTSE 100 is 2500, calculate the no arbitrage band of futures prices for contracts maturing in three months on the assumption of:

1. No transactions costs.
2. Bid−offer spreads on stock of 1 per cent, but no other transactions costs.

What risks may be present in a cash and carry arbitrage? How might such risks influence the no arbitrage band of futures prices?

Answer

1. One cash and carry arbitrage would involve:

    (a) buy stock, e.g. £62,500;
    (b) borrow money, £62,500;
    (c) sell one futures contract.

    The cash flows would be:

    (a) financing cost = £62,500 × 0.115 × 0.25 = £1796.88;
    (b) dividend yield = £62,500 × 0.01 = £625.

    The net financing cost is thus £1796.88 − £625 = £1171.88. To match this the futures profit must be £1171.88/£25 index points, i.e. 47 index points. This implies a futures price of 2547.
      The other cash and carry arbitrage involves:

    (a) sell stock, e.g. £62,500;
    (b) deposit proceeds, £62,500;
    (c) buy one futures contract.

    The cash flows would be:

    (a) interest receipts = £62,500 × 0.11375 × 0.25 = £1777.34;
    (b) dividends forgone = £625.

The net receipts are therefore £1777.34 − £625 = £1152.34. To match this the futures loss must be £1152.34/£25 index points, i.e. 46 index points. This implies a futures price of 2546.

So the no arbitrage band would be 2546–2547.

2. There is a bid−offer spread of 1 per cent which on 2500 amounts to 25 index points. So the futures price must deviate by at least 25 index points from its fair value in order that the arbitrage profits cover this 1 per cent cost. Interest flows also need to be recalculated.

One cash and carry arbitrage would involve:

(a) buy stock, e.g. £62,812.5;
(b) borrow money, £62,812.5;
(c) sell one futures contract.

The cash flows would be:

(a) financing cost = £62,812.5 × 0.115 × 0.25 = £1805.86;
(b) dividend yield = £62,500 × 0.01 = £625.

The net financing cost is thus £1805.86 − £625 = £1180.86. To match this the futures profit must be £1180.86/£25 index points, i.e. 47 index points (bearing in mind that the minimum price movement is 0.5 index point). This implies a futures price of 2547.

The other cash and carry arbitrage involves:

(a) sell stock, e.g. £62,187.5;
(b) deposit proceeds, £62,187.5;
(c) buy one futures contract.

The cash flows would be:

(a) interest receipts = £62,187.5 × 0.11375 × 0.25 = £1768.46;
(b) dividends foregone = £625.

The net receipts are therefore £1768.46 − £625 = £1143.46. To match this the futures loss must be £1143.46/£25 index points, i.e. 45.5 index points. This implies a futures price of 2545.5.

So the no arbitrage band would be 2545.5–2547. The 25 index points needed to match the bid−offer spread also needs to be taken into account. Profits from the first arbitrage would accrue only with a futures price above 2547 + 25 = 2572 and the second arbitrage requires a futures price below 2520.5. So the no arbitrage band is 2520.5–2572.

As to the risks present in a cash and carry arbitrage: there is the possibility of adverse market movements while the requisite transactions are taking place (a large number of stock transactions would be involved); the portfolio used is unlikely to be identical to the FTSE 100 portfolio and hence the beta may not be identical to that of the futures contract (with the result that there is a net market exposure); the interest on variation margin cash flows is uncertain both in terms of amount and whether it is positive or negative; and transactions costs at the unwinding stage are unknown since they depend on the final value of the index.

The existence of risk might cause arbitragers to seek higher profits in compensation and this would have the effect of widening the no arbitrage band since greater price deviations would be required to entice arbitrage activity.

Asset reallocation

Stock index and government bond futures can be used to expedite asset reallocation. A fund manager wanting to switch from stocks to government bonds can change the fund's exposure very quickly and at low cost by selling stock index futures and buying government bond futures. This process is much quicker than selling stocks and buying bonds. Having switched the exposure using futures, the fund manager can take time and care over the decisions as to which stocks to sell and which bonds to buy. The futures positions would be lifted as new portfolios are established.

Exercise 7.4

Question
A UK fund manager decides to increase exposure to the US stock market at the expense of UK equity investments. It is desired that £1 million of exposure be reallocated immediately with stock selection (for both sales and purchases) to take place during the following two weeks.

It is March 20 and the current price data includes:

$$
\begin{aligned}
\text{June FTSE 100 futures} &= 2500 \\
\$/£ \text{ exchange rate} &= \$2.00/£1 \\
\text{June S \& P 500} & \\
\text{futures} &= 200.
\end{aligned}
$$

Design a strategy that might be followed and calculate the numbers of futures contracts involved.

Answer
The UK equity exposure is reduced by selling FTSE 100 futures. The US stock exposure is increased by buying S & P 500 futures. The US dollar currency exposure implicit in a US stock holding is obtained by selling sterling currency futures. The futures positions are progressively closed out as the spot market transactions take place.

Numbers of futures contracts

$$
\begin{aligned}
£1,000,000/(£25 \times 2500) &= 16 \text{ FTSE 100 futures contracts} \\
£1,000,000/£62,500 &= 16 \text{ sterling currency futures contracts} \\
\$2,000,000/(\$500 \times 200) &= 20 \text{ S \& P 500 futures contracts.}
\end{aligned}
$$

Appendix: Calculating numbers of stock index futures and options contracts required for hedging

Basis is the difference between a spot (cash market) price and the corresponding futures price. Changes in basis reduce the efficiency of hedging with futures. One source of basis change arises directly from price movements. Futures prices tend to stand at premiums (or discounts) to cash market prices. This relationship between futures and cash prices, which is based on cost of carry, extends to the relationship between changes in futures prices and changes in cash prices. In the absence of a change in cost of carry, a futures premium would entail the extent of movement in the futures price exceeding that of the cash price. This means that basis changes as a result of price changes. The analysis that follows demonstrates that this source of basis change can be eliminated by an appropriate calculation of the number of futures contracts, a calculation that may seem to be counter-intuitive.

To determine the number of contracts when hedging with stock index futures, consider the hypothetical situation in which the FTSE 100 index stands at 2000, the FTSE 100 futures index stands at 2200, and the portfolio to be hedged has a current market value of £550,000 and a beta of one. Two alternatives for the calculation of the requisite number of contracts are (at £25 per index point):

$$\frac{\text{Value of hedged portfolio}}{£25 \times \text{spot index}} = \frac{£550,000}{£25 \times 2000} = 11 \text{ contracts}$$

and

$$\frac{\text{Value of hedged portfolio}}{£25 \times \text{futures index}} = \frac{£550,000}{£25 \times 2200} = 10 \text{ contracts}$$

The effectiveness of these alternatives can be judged in the context of two scenarios: (1) an immediate 10 per cent fall in the market, and (2) the spot index being at 2000 on the futures maturity date. In both cases the portfolio is hedged by a short futures position:

1. The decrease in the value of the portfolio is £55,000. In the absence of any change in interest rates or expected dividend yield the futures index would also exhibit a 10 per cent fall to 1980. So the profit on each futures contract is 220 × £25 = £5,500. At £5,500 per futures contract the £55,000 fall in the value of the portfolio is compensated for by 10 contracts. This suggests that the futures index should be used in the denominator when ascertaining the requisite number of futures contracts.

2. The value of the portfolio remains at £550,000. If futures are held to maturity they should provide an effective increase in the value of the portfolio based on the relationship between the initial spot and futures indices (2200/2000 = 1.1, that is a 10 per cent increase in the value of the portfolio).

The achievement of this outcome requires a futures profit of £55,000. Convergence (to equality between the spot and futures indices on the futures maturity date) implies that the futures index falls by 200 so that the cash flow from each futures contract is 200 × £25 = £5,000. A total cash flow of £55,000 thus requires the use of 11 contracts. This implies that the index to be used in the denominator when calculating the number of futures contracts is the spot index.

The implication of this analysis is that the number of futures contracts to be used depends upon when they are likely to be closed out. If they are likely to be closed out immediately then the futures index should be used in determining the number of contracts. If the futures contracts are to be held to their maturity date the spot index should be used. A closing-out date between these extremes would suggest an index between the spot and futures indices based upon interpolation.

THE NEED FOR LEVERAGE

When closing out takes place immediately after a futures position is established the futures profit or loss includes a futures premium and hence is more than is required to offset cash market movements. The futures coverage thus needs to be leveraged downwards. This is achieved by dividing the exposure by the futures index, which will include the futures premium.

Consider the following data:

$$
\begin{aligned}
\text{Cash exposure} &= \pounds 1{,}000{,}000 \\
\text{FTSE 100 futures price} &= 2500 \\
\text{Current FTSE 100 index} &= 2451 \\
\text{Futures premium} &= 2\%
\end{aligned}
$$

A 100 point fall in the FTSE 100 index would entail a 102 point fall in the futures price. As a result the £40,800 cash market loss would be offset by a profit on:

$$\frac{\pounds 40{,}800}{102 \times \pounds 25} = 16 \text{ futures contracts.}$$

Sixteen futures contracts relate to a current cash exposure of:

$$16 \times 2451 \times \pounds 25 = \pounds 980{,}400.$$

The exposure covered is leveraged down in order to offset the distorting effect of the futures premium.

THE SECURITY MARKET LINE

The illustration that follows uses the *security market line* to derive portfolio values. This section explains the security market line and hence the analysis used in the calculation of portfolio values under various assumptions about the behaviour of the index of market prices.

The security market line is developed from a security pricing model known as the Capital Asset Pricing Model. The expected return on an investment is seen as consisting of the return on risk free assets (such as Treasury bills or bank deposits) plus an additional element to compensate for systematic risk. The greater the systematic risk, the higher the enhancement of return. (Systematic risk is risk common to the market as a whole, as opposed to stock or sector specific risk.)

Two points need to be emphasised. First, that return includes both income flows (such as dividends, coupons, and interest) and capital gains or losses. Second, that when referring to expected returns the relevant definition is that of statistical expectation. Figure 7.1 illustrates the calculation of a statistical expectation.

The equation for the security market line is:

$$E(Ri) = r_f + B[E(Rm) - r_f]$$

where $E(Ri)$ is the expected return on the particular stock or portfolio (stock or portfolio i), r_f is the risk-free rate of return, B is the beta of stock or portfolio i, and $E(Rm)$ is the expected return on the market portfolio (which is a portfolio of shares in every stock with the weighting based on market capitalisation — this might be approximated by a stock index portfolio).

Beta is a measure of systematic risk. The market portfolio would have a beta of 1. A defensive stock would be less volatile than the market (in terms of

---

Statistical expectation

Expected return

= (possible return *A*) × (probability of occurrence)

+ (possible return *B*) × (probability of occurrence)

+ . . . .

+ (possible return *N*) × (probability of occurrence)

Example

The probability of a −4% return is 10%

The probability of a   0% return is 20%

The probability of a +4% return is 40%

The probability of a +8% return is 20%

The probability of a +12% return is 10%

The expected return

= (−4)(0.1) + (0)(0.2) + (4)(0.4) + (8)(0.2) + (12)(0.1) = 4%

Figure 7.1 The calculation of a statistical expectation

systematic risk) and would therefore have a beta less than 1. As a result such a conservative stock would have a relatively low expected return. Conversely, an aggressive stock has a beta greater than 1, indicating greater volatility and hence risk. This additional risk is compensated for by a relatively high expected rate of return. So the security market line indicates that expected investment returns rise with increasing risk. (The non-systematic risk is not compensated for with a higher return since it can be diversified away.)

AN ILLUSTRATION

The merits of using a weighted average of spot and futures prices, rather than the futures price, in ascertaining the appropriate number of futures contracts can be illustrated by the following illustration.

Futures contracts with four months to maturity are to be used to hedge a portfolio over a three-month period. The following information is available:

Value of S & P 500 index	= 200
Value of portfolio	= $10,200,000
Risk-free interest rate	= 10% p.a.
Expected dividend yield on S & P 500	= 4% p.a.
Beta of portfolio	= 1.34

The spot index, interest rate, and expected dividend yield imply a fair futures price of 204 (the futures premium being based on 10 per cent p.a. minus 4 per cent p.a. over four months). If the actual futures price is equal to the fair futures price, then each futures contract would relate to 204 × $500 = $102,000 of stock. Using the futures index in the denominator indicates a requisite number of contracts equal to:

$$1.34 \times (\$10,200,000/\$102,000) = 134$$

whereas using a weighted average of the futures and spot prices would involve a denominator based on an index of 200(0.75) + 204(0.25) = 201. The denominator would thus be 201 × $500 = $100,500 and the implied number of contracts would be:

$$1.34 \times (\$10,200,000/\$100,500) = 136$$

Table 7.A1 shows three possible index values after three months, the corresponding fair futures prices (on the asumption of unchanged interest rates

Table 7.A1

Value of index after 3 months	180.0	200.0	220.0
Fair futures price	180.9	201.0	221.1
Value of portfolio after 3 months	$8,883,180	$10,249,980	$11,616,780

Table 7.A2

Profit (loss) from futures	$1,547,700	$201,000	($1,145,700)
Value of portfolio plus futures	$10,430,880	$10,450,980	$10,471,080

Table 7.A3

Profit (loss) from futures	$1,570,800	$204,000	($1,162,800)
Value of portfolio plus futures	$10,453,980	$10,453,980	$10,453,980

and expected dividend yields), and the portfolio values inclusive of dividend receipts.

Table 7.A2 shows the futures profits (losses) from a short futures position over the hedge period, and the resultant value of portfolio plus futures, when 134 contracts are used.

Table 7.A3 shows the futures profits (losses) and the resultant value of the portfolio and futures combined when 136 futures contracts are used.

The risk-free rate of return on the initial portfolio value would have provided $10,455,000 after three months. It can be seen that using the futures price to determine the number of contracts sold neither completely eliminates risk nor approximates portfolio performance to the risk-free rate of interest. Using an average of the initial spot and futures prices, weighted by the anticipated time to closing out, completely eliminates risk and generates a performance close to that provided by the risk-free rate of interest. (The remaining deviation from the risk-free rate of return arises because multiplication by beta is a procedure which provides only an approximation.)

IMPLICATIONS FOR FIXED HEDGING WITH OPTIONS

Analysis relating to futures should have implications for options. In fact synthetic futures positions can be achieved by combining long and short option positions. Analysis relating to futures should be applicable to synthetic futures and hence the constituent components of synthetic futures. The analysis relating to the determination of the appropriate number of futures contracts is thus applicable to the calculation of the requisite number of option contracts.

AN ILLUSTRATION

A portfolio contains the following stocks:

	Value (£m)	Beta
Bank of Warwick	2	0.8
Grand Neapolitan	4	1.2
Coventry Cement	3	1.3
Midland Brewery	1	0.7

The current FTSE 100 index is 1960, the March FTSE 100 futures price is 2000, and the prices of March 2000 call options and put options are both 100 index points.

The portfolio manager wants (1) to ascertain the appropriate number of futures contracts for completely hedging this portfolio, and (2) to find the number of option contracts that would be required for a fixed hedge of the whole portfolio:

1. Portfolio beta = $(0.2 \times 0.8) + (0.4 \times 1.2) + (0.3 \times 1.3) + (0.1 \times 0.7) = 1.1$

   Size of market exposure is £10 million $\times$ 1.1 = £11 million.

   Assuming the possibility of very early closing out of futures contracts the futures index can be used in the calculation of the requisite number of contracts. So:

   £11,000,000/(2000 $\times$ £25) = £11,000,000/£50,000 = 220.

   Therefore, 220 contracts should be sold. (If the contracts were likely to be held to maturity, then the requisite number of contracts would be £11,000,000/(1960 $\times$ £25) = £11,000,000/£49,000 = 224, to the nearest whole number.)

2. The synthetic futures price is $2000 + 100 - 100 = 2000$.

   If the options are likely to be exercised or sold very early, then the index level of 2000 can be used to calculate the requisite number of put options for a fixed hedge:

   £11,000,000/(2000 $\times$ £10) = £11,000,000/£20,000 = 550.

   (If the options were likely to be held to expiry, then the requisite number of contracts would be £11,000,000/(1960 $\times$ £10) = £11,000,000/£19,600 = 561, to the nearest whole number.)

8

———— ∾ ————

Financially engineered investments

Financial futures, options and swaps can be used to produce a vast range of investment opportunities that are not available (or at least not easily available) from deposits, bonds and equities. This chapter illustrates some out of the huge number of possibilities.

Futures funds

Futures funds are collective investments that operate by means of keeping most of their assets in a liquid form such as short-term bank deposits while the remainder is used to finance the margin requirements of futures trading. The gearing offered by futures provides an opportunity for such funds themselves to be highly geared. The market exposure of a futures fund might be several times the value of the fund. Obviously such highly geared funds are very risky.

Futures funds often contain a wide variety of futures contracts. Multisector funds would not only contain a range of financial futures but also commodity futures. Furthermore the contracts are likely to derive from exchanges in a number of different countries. Such diversification helps to reduce the risk inherent in the futures funds. They may be particularly attractive to fund managers since they are likely to exhibit little or no correlation with the assets (such as stocks and bonds) that constitute the major part of investment portfolios. An asset that has low correlation with the other elements of a portfolio will tend to reduce the risk of the portfolio.

Taking views on market movements can normally be achieved more quickly and cheaply via using futures than by means of the spot instruments. Futures bid—offer spreads and commissions are often much lower than in the spot markets and time need not be spent on deciding between specific securities. It follows that a fund that is likely to shift frequently between sectors would benefit from the use of futures rather than spot instruments.

Not only do futures allow quick and cheap movement between types of assets, such as equities and gilts, but also between national markets. The time and expense of researching foreign stocks can be avoided by means of using stock index futures relating to the foreign stock markets. Furthermore only margin payments are subject to currency exposure; the bulk of the fund can remain in the home currency.

A futures fund would involve most of the fund being invested in short-term money-market assets such as bank deposits or Treasury bills, the remainder being used for the margin requirements arising from futures positions. The futures may relate to a sum of securities equal to the value of the fund, but not necessarily. Futures provide the flexibility to gain exposure to a quantity of assets in excess of the value of the fund, or to take a short position on the underlying instrument.

THE MARGIN SYSTEM

The margin system is central to futures markets. There are three types of margin: initial margin, maintenance margin, and variation margin. The *initial margin* is a sum of money to be provided by both the buyer and the seller of a futures contract when they make their transaction. This is a small percentage of the face value of the contract (perhaps 1 per cent). The initial margin is subject to variation (by a clearing house) and will be dependent upon the volatility of the price of the underlying instrument concerned. (Initial margins might be as little as 0.1 per cent or as much as 10 per cent of the value of the instrument to which the futures contract relates and are returnable deposits.)

The *maintenance margin* is the minimum sum of money (or other security) that must remain in a contract holder's margin account with the clearing house. On some futures exchanges this is equal to the initial margin, whereas on others the maintenance margin is less than the initial margin.

Variation margin is payable on a daily basis and reflects futures price movements. It is the means whereby futures profits and losses are realised on a daily basis. Someone whose futures contract shows a loss on a day must pay the amount of the loss to the clearing house by the following morning. Correspondingly, a futures position showing a profit on a day will result in a cash payment to the contract holder's account by the following morning. The process whereby profits and losses are realised on a daily basis via variation margin payments and receipts is known as *marking to market*.

One implication of the margin system is that futures are highly geared investments. For example, an initial margin of 1 per cent of the underlying means that the exposure acquired is one hundred times the initial money outlay.

Types of futures funds

BULL FUTURES FUND

The money in the fund is held on deposit (or in other money market instruments) whilst stock index futures are purchased. The value of the stock underlying the futures may match the sum on deposit (which includes the margin balance).

BEAR FUTURES FUND

Similar to the bull futures fund except that stock index futures are sold rather than bought. This provides profits from a falling market but losses from a rising market.

GEARED BULL FUTURES FUND

Similar to the bull futures fund except that the value of stock underlying the futures contracts exceeds the sum on deposit. This provides more than proportionate profits from market rises, but a heavy fall in the market could reduce the fund to zero.

GEARED BULL FUTURES FUND WITH DOWNSIDE PROTECTION

This is similar to the geared bull futures fund except that there is disaster insurance in the form of heavily out-of-the-money put options. For example, the purchase of put options with a strike price 20 per cent below the current market index would prevent the fund from losing more than 40 per cent of its value (the 40 per cent is based on a 2 to 1 ratio between the futures and the deposits).

CONTROLLED-RISK INDEX FUND

This might be looked upon as a fund that uses derivatives to reduce downside risk at the cost of sacrificing some upside potential. It is a useful vehicle for demonstrating that even within a class of strategy there is a tremendous variety of different structures and hence different payoff profiles. One possible structure is illustrated by Figure 8.1.

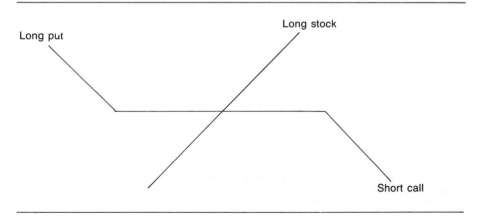

Figure 8.1 One possible structure for a controlled-risk index fund

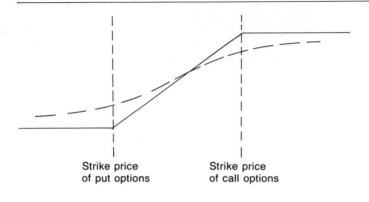

Strike price
of put options

Strike price
of call options

Figure 8.2 Payoff profile resulting from the structure in Figure 8.1

The investor holds a portfolio of stock together with a cylinder. The cylinder involves buying a put option with a low strike price whilst selling (writing) a call option with a high strike price. The put option provides some protection against a fall in the market but the call option attenuates the profit potential from a rise in stock prices.

Figure 8.2 illustrates the payoff profile that arises from the structure of Figure 8.1. The unbroken line shows the possible outcomes at the expiry date of the options. The broken line shows the profit or loss at different stock indices prior to the expiry date of the options. The profile of Figure 8.2 is obtained by adding together the profits and losses on the stock and options of Figure 8.1 (this includes, in the case of the prior-to-expiry profile, taking account of the time value of the options).

If options are held to expiry the result is the prevention of a fall in the value of the portfolio below a minimum value at the cost of sacrificing possible gains above a maximum level. If one considers the position before the option expiry date (shown by the broken-line profile), the effect of the cylinder can be seen to be that of moderating the market movements. This structure can be varied in a number of ways:

1. The stock index may coincide with one of the strike prices rather than falling between the option strike prices.
2. The value of stock underlying the options need not match the value of the stock held in the portfolio.
3. The put options and call options need not be in equal numbers.
4. A futures position (or synthetic futures position) may be held instead of a portfolio of shares.
5. More than two option strike prices may be used.

This list of variations is far from exhaustive but hopefully gives a feel for the range of alternatives available.

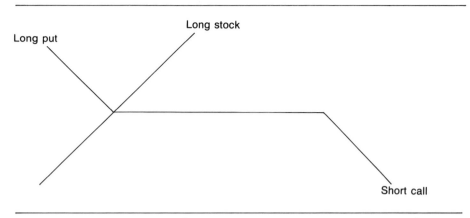

Figure 8.3 Lower strike price coincides with actual stock index

Figure 8.3 illustrates a case in which the lower strike price coincides with the actual stock index. (A close alternative is for the lower strike price to coincide with the futures stock index.)

A fund manager with a mildly bullish view might choose to write a number of call options that exceeds the number of put options purchased. This could have the result that there is a net premium receipt to add to the portfolio dividend yield so as to produce a high-yield fund. However, this risks losses in the event of a substantial market rise if it involves writing call options that relate to a quantity of stock in excess of that held in the portfolio. Diagrammatically the result could be as shown in Figure 8.4.

The profile depicted by Figure 8.4 is that of a call ratio spread. To avoid the risks arising above the higher strike price while preserving the ability to be a net recipient of option premiums, the fund manager could match the number of short calls to the size of the portfolio while buying a smaller number of put options. Such a strategy would lessen the downside protection of the put options.

A fund manager may seek to remove the unlimited loss potential of the call

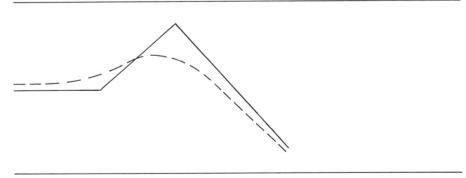

Figure 8.4 Profile of a call ratio spread

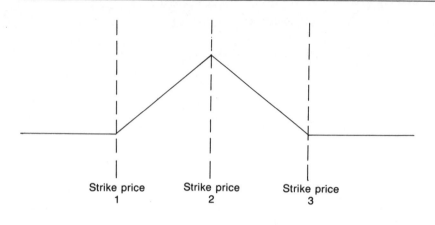

Figure 8.5 Buying call options at a third strike price: profile of a butterfly

ratio spread in Figure 8.4 by means of buying call options at a third, higher, strike price. The result might be as depicted in Figure 8.5. This profile is that of a butterfly. Strike price 1 is the put option strike price (and also the stock index). Strike price 2 is the strike price of the written calls. Calls are bought at strike price 3.

Instead of holding a portfolio of stocks the investor could buy stock index

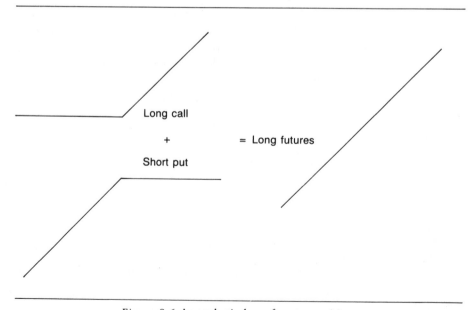

Figure 8.6 A synthetic long futures position

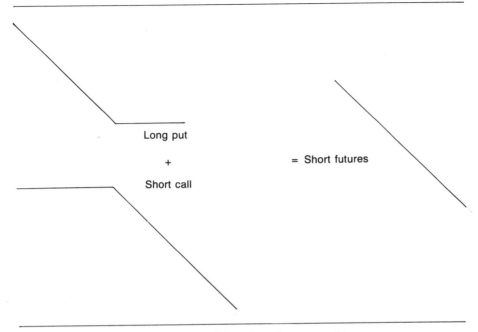

Figure 8.7 A synthetic short futures position

futures (or synthetic stock index futures) while holding the fund in the form of deposits (or other short-term money market instruments). In such a case the fund would consist entirely of bank deposits and derivatives (options and/or futures). It is worth noting that the use of derivatives allows for a short position in the underlying portfolio (by selling futures). Such a short position would profit from a falling stock market while losing from a rising one.

Synthetic futures are created by combining long and short option positions. A synthetic long futures position would be created by buying a call option and selling a put option with the same strike price and expiry date. A synthetic short futures position involves buying the put and writing the call. These constructions are illustrated by Figures 8.6 and 8.7.

An investor could choose to create synthetic futures positions while holding the fund in the form of deposits instead of holding stock. Arbitrage would tend to ensure that the synthetic futures price is close to the actual futures price (otherwise arbitragers could profit by buying the cheaper and selling the dearer). Cash and carry arbitrage would tend to maintain a close relationship between the stock index and the futures price (index). If investors hold futures or synthetic futures it does not mean that stocks are not being held. The stocks themselves would be held by arbitragers who simultaneously buy stocks and sell futures (to the investors), a process known as cash and carry arbitrage. The investor using futures or synthetic futures has an indirect exposure to the stocks themselves.

PARTICIPATING FORWARDS

A participating forward may be held in conjunction with bank deposits as an investment strategy, or could be used in combination with a portfolio. A participating forward involves buying and selling options at the same strike price but in different numbers. For example, a number of out-of-the-money call options might be bought, with this purchase being financed by writing a smaller number of in-the-money put options (out-of-the-money options tend to be cheaper than in-the-money-options). The payoff profile from this participating forward is shown in Figure 8.8.

Since the long calls outnumber the short puts the potential for profit from stock price rises exceeds the possible losses from market falls. It must be realised that the strike price in this case will be above the spot price, so there would be a loss in a stable market. An investor may choose to limit the loss potential by buying out-of-the-money puts. Finally, it is possible to construct participating forwards with in-the-money calls and out-of-the-money puts and/or short calls and long puts.

COVERED WRITING (VERY HIGH INCOME FUNDS)

These funds involve writing call options against the stock portfolio that is being held. The premium receipts from writing the options provide an addition to the stock dividends in producing an income yield for the investor. A drawback with such a strategy is that the potential to profit from rising stock prices is largely lost, since profits on the portfolio would be offset by losses on the short

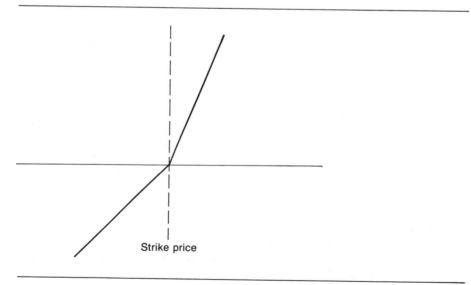

Strike price

Figure 8.8 Payoff profile from a participating forward

call. Indeed there is a danger that the capital value of the fund will fall over time because market declines might be locked in by written call options at the lower market prices (a downward ratchet effect).

Some investors might write puts as well as calls against a portfolio of stocks. While this considerably enhances the income yield from the fund it adds to the risks. A falling market leads to losses from the put options as well as from the portfolio. To limit this loss potential, out-of-the-money put options might be purchased.

Removing or enhancing exposures

ISOLATING STOCK SELECTION

A fund manager may want to isolate the firm or sector specific exposure (if the expertise or opportunity is in stock selection) or to isolate the market exposure (if the expertise or perceived opportunity is in market timing). In order to isolate the stock selection dimension the investor might remove market exposure by the use of a short position in stock index futures. The calculation of the appropriate number of futures contracts to sell will involve ascertaining the market exposure of the stock portfolio. The market exposure of the stock portfolio is not the same as its market value. Market value needs to be adjusted by the stock betas. A high-beta stock will tend to display disproportionately high responsiveness to overall market movements. Conversely, stocks with betas of less than one will tend to be less volatile than the market as a whole. (The stock market taken as a whole would have a beta of one, and stock index portfolios such as the S & P 500 are often treated as having betas equal to one.) Table 8.1 shows hypothetical stock betas and the corresponding market exposures, which are calculated by multiplying the market values of the stocks by the betas.

Having ascertained that the market exposure of the portfolio is $2,097,875, it is necessary to find the market exposure of a stock index futures contract. If the S & P 500 futures are to be used and the S & P 500 index stands at 450, then each futures contract would relate to 450 × $500 = $225,000 of stock. (The use of the spot index is more appropriate than the futures index if the stock is to be held to or beyond the futures maturity date.) The requisite number

Table 8.1 Hypothetical stock betas and the corresponding market exposures

Stock	Value of shares ($)	Stock beta	Market exposure ($)
Aetna Life	531,250	1.1	584,375
American Express	600,000	1.2	720,000
Bethlehem Steel	432,500	1.0	432,500
Boeing	451,250	0.8	361,000
			2,097,875

of futures contracts would be $2,097,875/$225,000 = 9.32$ contracts. This rounds down to 9 contracts. (Given the uncertainties relating to the measurement and stability of stock betas, rounding down would normally be preferred to rounding up.) Although this technique of selling stock index futures in order to neutralise the general market exposure of a specific stock portfolio is not perfect (due to the imperfect reliability of betas and the inability to trade fractions of futures contracts), it can remove most of the market exposure of a portfolio and thereby allow an investor to take positions on the performance of individual stocks or sectors relative to the market as a whole. Looking for stocks that will outperform the market is the speciality of the stock pickers.

Exercise 8.1

Question

An investor has the following portfolio:

	Number of shares	Share price (p)	Share beta
Bank of Coventry	20,000	300	0.9
Coventry Motors	30,000	100	1.5
Nuneaton Manufacturing	10,000	600	1.3
Cheylesmore Stores	25,000	300	0.8

It is 15 February and the March FTSE futures price is 3000.

1. How can the investor hedge the portfolio with futures? How might the investor hedge against a fall in the value of the portfolio whilst preserving the ability to benefit from a rise in share prices?
2. What factors might reduce the effectiveness of the measures taken in (1)?

Answer

1. Calculate the market exposure of the portfolio by summing the market exposures of individual stocks (market exposure = number of shares × share price × beta):

$$20,000 \times 300p \times 0.9 = 5.4 \text{ m}$$
$$30,000 \times 100p \times 1.5 = 4.5 \text{ m}$$
$$10,000 \times 600p \times 1.3 = 7.8 \text{ m}$$
$$25,000 \times 300p \times 0.8 = \underline{6.0 \text{ m}}$$
$$23.7 \text{ m}$$

The total market exposure is 23,700,000p (i.e. £237,000). The market exposure provided by one futures contract is:

$$3,000 \times £25 = £75,000$$

Hedging the portfolio with futures would involve selling:

$$£237,000/£75,000 = 3.16 \text{ contracts.}$$

Since futures contracts are indivisible this would indicate 3 contracts.

The investor could hedge against a fall in the value of the portfolio whilst preserving the ability to benefit from a rise in share prices by buying FTSE 100 put options. Each option relates to £10 × the current FTSE 100 index. The current FTSE 100 index is likely to be close to the futures index of 3000. So each option contract relates to approximately 3000 × £10 = £30,000 of stock. The requisite number of put option contracts to be bought is therefore:

£237,000/£30,000 = 7.9

Since contracts are indivisible, 8 contracts would be bought. A strike price of 3000 would be appropriate.

2. Factors that could reduce hedge effectiveness include basis risk, the indivisibility of contracts, instability of beta, and the cost of option contracts.

ISOLATING MARKET EXPOSURE

The specialist in market timing may wish to avoid exposure to non-systematic risk. In other words, the intention may be to gain market exposure whilst avoiding the risk that the stocks bought may underperform the market. Such an investor could obtain market exposure by buying stock index futures while keeping the investment fund on deposit, in either the home or the foreign currency. If the inclination is to take no view (and no risks) on currency movements, or if a bearish view is taken on the foreign currency, then the deposit (or investment in low risk securities such as Treasury bills) would be in the home currency.

In effect the fund manager is creating a futures fund. The market value the stocks underlying the stock index futures bought might be matched to the sum on deposit. If the S & P 500 stands at 450 so that each futures contract reflects 450 × $500 = $225,000 of stock, then one futures contract would be bought for every $225,000 held on deposit. Note that if the deposit is held in a currency other than US dollars, currency fluctuations will remove the one-to-one relationship between the value of the deposit and the value of the stocks underlying the futures. So constant monitoring and rebalancing (that is, changing the number of futures contracts held) may be necessary. Stock market movements would entail no such need for rebalancing since variation margin cash flows would tend to keep the size of the deposits in line with the value of stock underlying the futures contracts. For example, a rise in the market and hence futures prices would generate variation margin receipts that can be added to the deposit, so the deposit grows as the market rises.

Options funds

An options fund is characterised by upside exposure to a stock index (or other underlying price) together with a lower limit to the value of the fund. This profile of returns can be achieved in two main ways (see Figure 8.9). One is the fiduciary call (another name for 90/10 fund) which involves investment in risk-free assets

---

1. *Fiduciary call (90/10)*   Investment in risk-free assets to provide the guaranteed sum plus purchase of call options to give upside exposure.
2. *Protective put*   Equity investment to provide upside exposure. Purchase of put options plus investment in risk-free assets to produce the guaranteed sum.

   (a) $M = X(1+r)^T$
       $N = (V-X)/C$

   (b) $M = X(1+r)^T + NK$
       $N = (V-X)/(S+P)$

   where M = guaranteed minimum fund value, X = investment in risk-free assets, r is the interest rate on risk-free assets, T is the maturity of the fund, N is the number of options, V is the initial value of the fund, C is the price of a call option, K is the strike price, P is the price of a put option, S is the value of stock relating to one option.

Figure 8.9 Alternative means of constructing options funds

and call options. The risk-free assets, such as Treasury bills, provide the guaranteed minimum value while the call options provide the upside exposure to the stock market.

The other main approach is that of the protective put. This consists of a holding of stock to give the upside exposure together with put options that guarantee a minimum value of that shareholding. Protective put strategies (sometimes referred to as portfolio insurance) also tend to involve some investment in riskless assets in order to guarantee the minimum value. The minimum value is ensured by a combination of an investment in assets such as Treasury bills, or bank deposits, and a lowest possible value of the shareholding based on the strike price of the put options.

The fiduciary call (90/10) approach involves calculating the present value of the guaranteed sum and investing it in risk-free assets. This generates the minimum value upon maturity of the fund. The remainder is used to buy call options. The cost of the downside protection is reduced profit on the upside. Potential returns from a rising stock market are less than would be obtained if the entire fund were to be invested in shares. The proportion of market returns accruing to the fund in the event of a market rise is dependent upon the guaranteed minimum value and the strike price of the options. A greater guaranteed sum requires relatively substantial investment in risk-free assets and hence relatively low expenditure on options. This would entail a low potential to profit from a market rise. Acceptance of a high option strike price, and hence high market index beyond which market exposure begins, involves cheaper options and hence a greater number that can be purchased for a given money outlay. So a high strike price allows the fund to obtain a higher proportion of the stock market returns above the strike price.

An options fund created using the protective put approach also involves the trade-offs between the proportion of a market rise that is obtained, the guaranteed minimum value, and the index level at which exposure begins.

However, since the guaranteed minimum value is provided from two sources — the investment in risk-free assets, and a shareholding combined with put options — it is necessary to use simultaneous equations to calculate the amounts of the constituent components.

If M is the guaranteed minimum value, X is the amount to be invested in risk-free assets, K is the option strike price, r is the interest rate on risk-free assets, T is the maturity of the fund and N is the number of put options (which matches the amount of stock purchased), then:

$$M = X(1 + r)^T + NK$$

that is, the guaranteed minimum fund value equals the maturity value of the investment in risk-free assets plus the minimum value of the shareholding guaranteed by the put options.

The value of N can be calculated as:

$$N = (V - X)/(S + P)$$

where V is the value of the fund, S is the value of stock covered by one option, and P is the price of a put option. N is thus the number of combinations of stock and put option that can be purchased after X has been allocated to the purchase of risk-free assets.

The two equations can be simultaneously solved for X and N. In this way the amount to be invested in risk-free assets can be ascertained together with the number of matched combinations of stock and put option.

Exercise 8.2

Question
The FTSE 100 stands at 3000. Two-year European style at-the-money call options are priced at 600 and the corresponding put options are priced at 250. The two-year risk-free interest rate is 10 per cent p.a. How might a fund manager construct an options fund that guarantees the return of the initial £1 million at the end of a two-year period while providing upside exposure to the FTSE 100 index? What proportion of the return on the FTSE 100 portfolio would be obtained?

Answer
If the fiduciary call approach were to be used the sum to be invested in risk-free assets would be £1,000,000/$(1.1)^2$ = £826,446 which leaves £1,000,000 − £826,446 = £173,554 to be used to buy call options. The number of call options that could be purchased is £173,554/£6,000 = 28.9 (29 to nearest whole number).

The number of units of the FTSE 100 that could be bought if a unit equals £10 per index point (corresponding to the option size) would be £1,000,000/£30,000 = 33.33. The option fund would obtain (29/33.33) × 100 per cent = 87 per cent of the capital appreciation of the FTSE 100 portfolio but would receive none of the dividend return.

If the protective put approach were to be used it is necessary to solve the equations:

$$M = X(1 + r)^T + NK$$
$$N = (V - X)/(S + P)$$

for X and N when M = £1,000,000, r = 0.1, T = 2, K = 3000 × £10, V = £1,000,000, S = £30,000, and P = 250 × £10:

$$£1,000,000 = X \cdot (1.1)^2 + N \cdot £30,000$$
$$N = (£1,000,000 - X)/£32,500$$

so:

$$£1,000,000 = X \cdot (1.1)^2 + (£1,000,000 - X) \, £30,000/£32,500$$
$$£1,000,000 - £923,077 = X \cdot (1.21 - 0.923077)$$
$$X = £76,923/0.286923$$
$$X = £268,096$$
$$N = (£1,000,000 - £268,096)/£32,500 = 22.52$$

Ignoring the problem of the indivisibility of option contracts, the strategy would appear to involve a deposit of £268,096, the purchase of stock to the value of £30,000 × 22.52 = £675,603 and the purchase of 22.52 put options at £2,500 per contract. In practice the number of put options bought would be 22 or 23. The proportion of the return on the FTSE 100 portfolio that would be obtained would be (£675,603/£1,000,000) × 100% = 67.56 per cent.

VARIATIONS ON THE THEME

An options fund need not necessarily be bullish. It is possible to create funds that profit in the event of a market decline. In the case of a fiduciary (i.e. 90/10) strategy this would involve an investment in risk-free assets plus a purchase of put options. The alternative would be a short position in stock (selling borrowed stock) and the purchase of calls as a protective strategy (against a rise in the market).

Taking a short position in stock is not always possible. An alternative would involve a short position in stock index futures, which would be accomplished much more easily. Indeed options funds that require long stock positions may, as an alternative, use stock index futures in order to obtain the market exposure.

Another variation might be to use vertical spreads in combination with an investment in risk-free assets. Vertical bull spreads involve buying call options at a low strike price and writing an equal number of calls at a high strike price (they could also be constructed using put options). The lower net cost of the option position allows the number of vertical spreads to exceed the number of options that could alternatively be bought. As a result, upside capture would be enhanced as far as the higher strike price. However, there would be no further gains from stock market rises beyond the higher strike price.

COSTS OF OPTIONS FUNDS

When considering the costs of options funds it is appropriate to view it from two perspectives: that of the constructor of the fund, and that of the investor in the fund. Costs also need to be measured against the two alternative benchmarks: full investment in stocks, and total investment in risk-free assets such as Treasury bills or bank deposits with a maturity matching that of the options fund. A further dichotomy is between the costs involved in the fiduciary call and the protective put approaches.

From the point of view of the creator of the fund the cost of a fiduciary call compared to total investment in risk-free assets is the call option premiums, whereas the cost of a protective put relative to the risk-free assets is the option premium plus the net income flow foregone (excess of interest rate over expected dividend yield). For the costs to be identical the call price must equal the put price plus interest on risk-free assets minus expected dividends, which would be the case if put—call parity holds.

Again from the perspective of fund construction but using complete investment in stocks as the alternative, the cost of a protective put would be the option premium, whereas the cost of a fiduciary call would encompass the net expected income flow as well as the option premium. Compared with an investment in stocks the fiduciary call approach provides interest income while foregoing dividend receipts; as a result the cost amounts to the call premiums plus dividends foregone minus interest receipts. If the cost of the protective put and that of the fiduciary call are to be equal then the put price must equal the call price minus the excess of prospective interest receipts over expected dividends. As before, this would be the case if put—call parity holds.

From the point of view of the investor in the fund the distinction between the fiduciary call and protective put approaches is of no concern — indeed the investor may not even know which has been used. The investor has a profile of possible returns from the fund which entails some exposure to upward movements in stock prices together with a guaranteed minimum fund value at maturity; whether this arises from a fiduciary call or protective put is of no significance to the investor.

An investor in the fund is interested in how the fund compares with the alternatives of investment in risk-free assets and of investment in stocks. When comparing an options fund with risk-free assets the potential to profit from a rising stock market is obtained at the cost of a reduced interest return on the investment. Upside exposure and interest return would be inversely related; more of one involves less of the other. When comparing the payoffs from an options fund with those from investment in stocks, the protection against stock price falls below a particular level is obtained at the cost of foregoing dividend receipts and perhaps obtaining less than the full benefit of market rises. For example, the fund may provide just 80 per cent of market rises above the guaranteed minimum level.

SOME POINTS RELATING TO FIDUCIARY CALL (90/10) FUNDS

These funds provide security together with upside exposure. As with other funds, increased profit potential is obtained at the cost of increased risk. The greater the proportion of the fund in options, the lower is the capital certainty. Raising the proportion of the fund that is used to buy options will raise the delta of the fund (the delta being the relationship between changes in the value of the fund and changes in the prices of the stocks that underlie the options). The proportion of the fund in options can be raised either by buying a greater number of options or by buying deeper in-the-money (or fewer out-of-the-money) options, either way the delta of the fund would be increased.

If the wish is to obtain exposure to the stock market in general rather than specific stocks, then stock index options would be better than options on individual stocks. Such an approach spreads the risk, so that adverse developments that are specific to particular stocks can be diluted (and offset by favourable developments in other stocks). The avoidance of stock-specific risk reduces option premiums. Volatility is an important determinant of option premiums. Since a stock index avoids the risks that are specific to individual stocks (and bears only the general market risk that is common to all stocks), it tends to be less volatile than individual stock prices. Consequently, option premiums for stock index options tend to be lower than those for individual stocks. This is a good reason for using stock index options rather than individual stock options.

Finally, it might be noted that 90/10 funds provide a means of reducing the currency risk that normally accompanies investment in overseas stock markets. A fund that is 90 per cent invested in sterling deposits and 10 per cent invested in US options has considerably less exposure to the risk of a fall in the value of the US dollar than a fund that is 100 per cent invested in US stocks, although they might have identical exposures to the US stock market.

Immunisation with bond futures

Interest rate risk on bond portfolios may be reduced by the following means:

1. *Dedicated portfolios* The prospective cash flows from the assets held correspond to the future cash flow requirements in both amount and timing. For example, the future payments to pensioners from an annuity fund might be synchronised with the coupon and redemption receipts from the bonds that constitute the fund. Such a dedicated portfolio is difficult to construct.
2. *Maturity matching* The maturities of the bonds in the portfolio match the times at which cash flows will be required. This avoids the price risk from interest rate changes but is subject to reinvestment risk (the rate of interest on invested coupon receipts is uncertain).
3. *Duration matching* The modified duration of the assets matches the time at which a cash flow will be required. Bond price changes tend to offset variations in returns from reinvested coupons. So both the bond price risk of interest rate changes and the reinvestment risk are substantially reduced. Immunisation by duration matching is less effective if the slope of the yield

curve changes. Not only is duration matching a very effective means of immunising a bond portfolio, it may also be the easiest. The ease of the strategy arises from the facility of using bond futures to achieve the requisite adjustment. Any discrepancy between the duration of the liabilities (prospective cash outflows) and the duration of the assets can be removed by taking an offsetting position in bond futures.

CALCULATING MODIFIED DURATION

The calculation of modified duration involves the calculation of Macauley's duration and then a modification step. Macauley's duration is the average period of time to the cash flows where each time is weighted by the contribution of its cash flow to the fair value of the bond. Macauley's duration is converted to modified duration by dividing by $(1 + r/n)$ where r is the redemption yield and n the number of coupon payments per year.

Such calculations are illustrated by the following example of a Treasury bond with two years to final maturity and which has just paid its six-monthly coupon of $6. The yield curve is assumed to be flat at 10 percent p.a.

The cash flows to be received are:

After 0.5 of a year	$6
After 1 year	$6
After 1.5 years	$6
After 2 years	$106

A six-month interest rate of 10 per cent p.a. means that 5 per cent is yielded each six months. The period is six months and the rate of discount is 5 per cent so the fair price of the bond is calculated as:

$$P = \$6/(1.05) + \$6/(1.05)^2 + \$6/(1.05)^3 + \$106/(1.05)^4$$
$$= \$5.71 + \$5.44 + \$5.18 + \$87.21$$
$$= \$103.54$$

Macauley's duration is calculated as:

$$D = (\$5.71/\$103.54)(0.5) + (\$5.44/\$103.54)(1) + (\$5.18/\$103.54)(1.5)$$
$$+ (\$87.21/\$103.54)(2)$$
$$= 0.0276 + 0.0525 + 0.075 + 1.6846$$
$$= 1.84 \text{ years (to 2 decimal places).}$$

Modified duration $= D/(1 + r/n)$. Since the redemption yield is 0.1 and there are 2 coupon payments per year, modified duration

$$= 1.84/(1.05)$$
$$= 1.75 \text{ years (to 2 decimal places).}$$

Modified duration allows the calculation of the percentage change in the bond price arising from a change in the redemption yield, as shown by the following equation:

$$\%\Delta P = - M \times \Delta r$$

where

$\%\Delta P$ = percentage change in the bond price
M = modified duration
Δr = change in the redemption yield

The minus sign arises from the inverse relationship between bond prices and yields. Exercise 8.3 further illustrates the calculation of modified duration and also shows how it can be used to forecast bond price movements resulting from interest rate changes.

Exercise 8.3

Question
It is 24 November 1992. Treasury 12 per cent 1994 (which has just paid a coupon) has a final maturity date of 24 May 1994. The yield curve is flat at 8 per cent p.a. Calculate (i) the duration, and (ii) the modified duration, of the gilt.

What capital gain or loss would arise from a holding of £1 million nominal of this gilt in the event of a ¼ per cent p.a. fall in interest rates (throughout the length of the yield curve). Comment on the accuracy of this estimate of capital gain or loss.

Answer
The price of the bond would be:

B = £6/(1.04) + £6/(1.04)² + £106/(1.04)³
  = £5.77 + £5.55 + £94.23
  = £105.55

The duration of the bond would be:

$$D = \left(\frac{£5.77}{£105.55}\right) 0.5 + \left(\frac{£5.55}{£105.55}\right) + \left(\frac{£94.23}{£105.55}\right) 1.5$$

= 0.0273 + 0.0526 + 1.3391 = 1.419
= 1.42 years (to 2 decimal places)

The modified duration would be:

M = 1.419/1.04 = 1.3644
  = 1.36 years (to 2 decimal places)

The value of £1 million nominal of the gilt would be:

£1,000,000 × £105.55/£100 = £1,055,500

The capital gain would be calculated from:

% rise in bond price = modified duration × change in redemption yield
                = 1.36 × 0.25 = 0.34%

So the capital gain would be 0.0034 × £1,055,500 = £3,588.7. Hence the new value of the bonds would be £1,055,500 + £3,588.7 = £1,059,088.7. It is to be noted that £6/(1.03875) + £6/(1.03875)^2 + £106/(1.03875)^3 = £5.7762 + £5.5607 + £94.5742 = £105.9111.

Hence according to the discount model the new value of the bonds would be £1,059,111. So the modified duration approach predicts the new value of the bonds very closely — the error is less than £23.

Modified duration does not provide a precisely accurate answer since it assumes a linear price–yield relationship, whereas the relationship is actually convex.

Price factors and the cheapest to deliver

Before the examination of the application of bond futures to the manipulation of the duration of a portfolio, the reader will be reminded of the concepts of price factors and the cheapest-to-deliver bond.

Price factors bring bonds on to a common basis with bond futures contracts. For example, in the case of LIFFE Long Gilt contracts, the futures price is based on a notional gilt with a 9 per cent coupon. By assuming a 9 per cent p.a. redemption yield the notional gilt is priced at £100. Gilts with other coupons will have different prices when the 9 per cent p.a. redemption yield is assumed. For example, a 12 per cent coupon gilt might have a value of £125. In that case the 12 per cent coupon gilt might be said to have a price factor of £125/100 = 1.25. The use of price factors makes it possible for bonds with different coupons and maturities to be rendered comparable to one another and to the notional gilt on which the futures contract is based. (Note that the method of calculating price factors varies between exchanges; this example was intended merely as a means of providing an intuitive feel for the principles involved.)

The seller of a futures contract has the choice as to which bond to deliver. The receipts for the bond (the invoice amount) are based on the futures settlement price and the price factor of the bond. This invoice amount normally differs from the market price of the bond. The seller would choose to deliver the bond whose market price is furthest below the invoice amount, or least far above it. This is the cheapest-to-deliver bond.

The futures price would tend to reflect the price behaviour of the cheapest-to-deliver bond. This is because the relationship between the futures price and the price of the underlying bond is determined by cash and carry arbitrage. Long cash and carry arbitrage involves buying bonds and simultaneously selling futures. The bonds that would be chosen would be the cheapest to deliver. Thus the cash and carry arbitrage links the futures price with the price of the cheapest-to-deliver bond.

ADJUSTING PORTFOLIO DURATION WITH FUTURES

The volatility of a bond portfolio may be measured as the change in portfolio value arising from a basis point change in yield. This can be obtained by

---

Bond portfolio immunisation

Interest rate risk on bond portfolios may be reduced by means of duration matching. The modified duration of the portfolio matches the time at which the cash flow will be required. Bond futures can be used to achieve duration matching.

Volatilities

1. Measure the volatility of the portfolio

    = modified duration × portfolio value × 0.0001

    i.e. volatility is the change in portfolio value from one basis point change in yield.

2. Calculate portfolio volatility when modified duration is at the desired level.

    = desired modified duration × portfolio value × 0.0001.

3. Measure the volatility of a futures contract. This requires calculation of the volatility of the cheapest-to-deliver bond per £50,000 nominal (the size of the gilt futures contract) and division of this volatility by the price factor of the cheapest-to-deliver bond.

4. Divide the difference between volatilities 1 and 2 by volatility 3. This gives the number of bond futures contracts to be bought or sold.

Figure 8.10 Bond portfolio immunisation using futures

multiplying the modified duration by the value of the portfolio and by 0.0001 (the decimal of 1 basis point). Since multiplying the modified duration by the yield change gives the percentage change in the value of the portfolio, further multiplying by the value of the portfolio provides the change in money terms (see Figure 8.10).

Suppose that the portfolio has a duration of 15 years, a redemption yield of 8 per cent p.a., a value of £10 million, and that coupons are semiannual. Then portfolio volatility can be calculated as:

$$\frac{15}{1.04} \times £10 \text{ m} \times 0.0001 = £14,423$$

(1.04 is used since the redemption yield has to be divided by the number of coupon payments per year). So an interest rate change of 0.01 per cent p.a. (1 basis point) is expected to result in the portfolio value changing by £14,423.

Suppose that the portfolio manager seeks to reduce the portfolio duration to ten years, then the desired volatility is given by:

$$\frac{10}{1.04} \times £10 \text{ m} \times 0.0001 = £9,615.$$

So portfolio volatility needs to be reduced by £14,423 − £9,615 = £4,808. The desired one-third reduction in duration entails a one-third reduction in volatility.

The next step is to measure the volatility of a futures contract. This entails calculating the volatility of the cheapest-to-deliver bond and then dividing by its price factor. Suppose that the cheapest-to-deliver has a duration of 12 years, a redemption yield of 8 per cent p.a., a price of £110 (i.e. £55,000 per £50,000 nominal), and pays coupons twice a year. Then for £50,000 nominal (the size of the long gilt futures contract):

$$\frac{12}{1.04} \times £55,000 \times 0.0001 = £63.46.$$

If the cheapest-to-deliver has a price factor of 0.9875, then the volatility of a futures contract is calculated as £63.46/0.9875 = £64.26. So, in order to reduce the portfolio volatility by £4,808 it is necessary to sell £4,808/£64.26 = 74.8 contracts. Since futures contracts are indivisible, either 74 or 75 contracts would be sold in order to reduce the portfolio duration from 15 to 10 years.

Such a reduction in portfolio duration could be seen as a partial hedge, and a bond portfolio manager seeking to fully hedge the portfolio could be regarded as aiming to achieve a duration of zero. Exercise 8.4 provides an example of complete hedging.

Exercise 8.4

Question
A bank buys £10 million nominal of Treasury 12½ per cent 2012. This gilt has a price factor of 1.302615, a duration of 8.6 years, and a price of £96¾. This purchase is financed by the issue of certificates of deposit. The cheapest-to-deliver gilt is Exchequer 12 per cent 2010 whose price factor is 1.238401 with a duration of 8.3 years and a price of £95⁵/₁₆. Both gilts have a redemption yield of 13 per cent p.a. How might the holding of gilts be hedged (assuming that the certificates of deposit have negligible duration)?

Answer

$$\frac{£10,000,000}{£50,000} \times 1.238401 \times \frac{8.6}{8.3} \times \frac{96.75}{95.3125} = 260.469$$

The risk of a fall in gilt prices can be hedged by the sale of 260 or 261 gilt futures contracts. The reader may note that the calculation is based on dividing the volatility of the gilt portfolio by the volatility of a futures contract, and the terms based on redemption yields cancel out since the redemption yields are equal.

SOME CAVEATS

A bond portfolio manager using duration-based immunisation needs to be aware of the need for frequent rebalancing for three reasons. First, modified duration declines more slowly than term to maturity. So the passage of a year will reduce modified duration by less than a year. Modified duration would then exceed the investment horizon. Second, the price–yield relationship for bonds is convex (as pointed out in Exercise 8.3). So modified duration changes as interest rates rise or fall. Third, changes in the slope of the yield curve will affect duration. Finally, when using futures, attention needs to be paid to the significance of interest on variation margin cash flows. There may be a need to take account of this by factoring down the number of futures contracts, either by tailing or by use of variation margin leverage.

Using swaps

CURRENCY SWAPS

A currency swap may be carried out by direct negotiation between the counter-parties or by means of a bank acting as intermediary and effectively becoming the counterparty to each participant. Figure 8.11 illustrates the latter case. Borrower A acquired a sterling liability and sold the sterling raised for dollars in order to acquire assets in the US. Borrower B, facing easier access to the US capital market than the UK one, borrowed dollars and sold them in order to purchase assets in the UK. Both borrowers have an exchange rate exposure, having assets in one currency and liabilities in another. Borrower A would find that, in the event of a strengthening of the pound against the dollar, both the interest payments and the sum to be repaid at maturity rise in dollar value. Conversely, Borrower B is vulnerable to a strengthening of the dollar.

They enter the swap agreements depicted by Figure 8.11. Borrower A simulates a dollar liability whilst Borrower B simulates a sterling liability. This is a achieved by means of Borrower A undertaking to meet the interest and principal payments on Borrower B's dollar liability by making the dollar payments to Borrower B via the bank, whilst Borrower B makes a similar commitment to service Borrower A's sterling debt. The bank operates as counterparty to both, and Borrowers A and B need not even know the other's identity. Borrower A remains the debtor of Lender A, similarly for Borrower B and Lender B. The lenders may not know of the swap.

The bank runs the risk of losses arising from default by one of the parties.

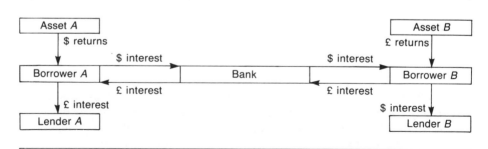

Figure 8.11 Currency swap with a bank as intermediary

If, for example, the dollar strengthens against sterling, the bank will be gaining from its transaction with Borrower A but losing with B. Normally these gains and losses would cancel each other out, but if A were to renege on its obligation, the bank would be left with its loss-making commitments to B. The bank is committed to paying both interest and principal in the relatively strong dollar whilst receiving the same in the weakened sterling.

Swaps allow advantage to be taken of the relatively advantageous terms that some borrowers might obtain in particular markets. In Figure 8.11 Borrower A may be able to borrow sterling more cheaply than Borrower B while Borrower B obtains a lower rate of interest than A when borrowing dollars. It is mutually advantageous for both to borrow in their more favourable market and then exchange both the currencies borrowed — in practice, they may buy the desired currency in the spot market rather than exchanging currencies with each other, the effect is the same — and the liabilities acquired. Swaps may arise from different motives and need not involve an exchange of spot currency; there may merely be an agreement to service each other's debt.

POSITION TAKING

If borrowers expect that the currency in which their liability is denominated is likely to appreciate they may swap into a currency that they expect to depreciate. If the expected exchange rate movements occur they may subsequently reverse the swap in order to lock in the fall in the value of the liability caused by the exchange rate depreciation.

Figure 8.12 illustrates the case of a borrower with a sterling liability and Deutschmark assets. A borrows sterling which is used to buy Deutschmarks for the purpose of investment in Deutschmark-denominated assets. Following a depreciation of sterling against the Deutschmark, A decides to lock in the gain by swapping the sterling liability for a Deutschmark one. This liability is less than would have been incurred if Deutschmarks had originally been borrowed to finance the acquisition of the Deutschmark asset.

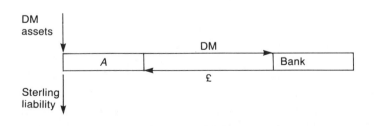

Figure 8.12 Locking in a currency gain

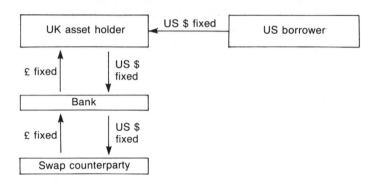

Figure 8.13 An asset-based currency swap

ASSET-BASED CURRENCY SWAPS

Although swaps are typically exchanges of liabilities, the technique can also be used for assets. Figure 8.13 illustrates the situation in which the UK holder of a US-dollar bond fears a depreciation of the US dollar against sterling and decides to swap the dollar asset into a sterling asset. The bondholder receives a flow of interest receipts plus the payment of principal at maturity in US dollars from the US issuer of the bond. Fearing a fall in the value of the dollar the bondholder swaps into a sterling asset agreeing to pay interest and principal in dollars in return for sterling receipts. The swap counterparty is not necessarily transacting an asset-based swap; either assets or liabilities could be being swapped.

ASSET-BASED INTEREST RATE SWAPS

An interest rate swap could be used by a fixed rate bondholder to gain from a rise in interest rates. Figure 8.14 depicts the situation in which the holder of a bond with a coupon yield of 12 per cent p.a. feels that interest rates, now at 10 per cent p.a. for maturities matching the remaining term of the bond, are likely to rise. He swaps into a floating rate asset in order to profit from a rise in interest rates.

The investor originally buys an undated bond for £1 million at 12 per cent p.a. When the interest rate on undated debt falls to 10 per cent p.a. the value of the bond rises to £1.2 million. By swapping the fixed coupon yield of £120,000 p.a. for LIBOR + 1 per cent on £1.2 million, the lender obtains the opportunity to profit from a rise in interest rates. The lender could reverse the swap (by entering another swap) subsequent to a rise in interest rates to fix a rate on £1.2 million, so that at the end of the operation the annual receipts are in excess of £120,000 p.a.

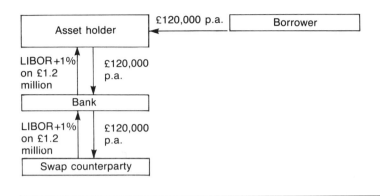

Figure 8.14 An asset-based interest rate swap

EQUITY SWAPS

An equity swap involves an agreement to exchange the returns on a stock index portfolio for a flow of interest payments. Such swaps could be arranged for any of the major stock indices, for example the S & P 500, FTSE 100, Nikkei 225, CAC 40, DAX. Figure 8.15 illustrates an equity swap.

Investor A has a balanced portfolio of French stocks but is bearish about the French stock market. As an alternative to selling the portfolio the investor could enter an equity swap. The swap illustrated by Figure 8.15 would be suitable if the investor were bullish on the US dollar and US dollar interest rates.

Investor B might be an American fund manager who wants an exposure to the French stock market but does not have the expertise to evaluate alternative French stocks. By entering the equity swap of Figure 8.15 the American fund

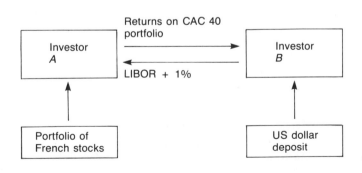

Figure 8.15 An equity swap

manager simulates a balanced investment in French stocks without getting involved in the analysis of individual French stocks.

The implications of implicit options in constant ratio funds

Option positions can be replicated by positions in the underlying instrument or the corresponding futures. The positions in the underlying or futures should provide the same profit/loss outcome as the option being replicated. The amount of the underlying or futures should reflect the option delta. For example, an option on £1 million of the underlying with a delta of 0.7 would tend to give the same profit or loss as £700,000 of the underlying (which has a delta of 1). A small price move in the underlying should provide the same profit/loss outcome on £700,000 with a delta of 1 as on £1 million with a delta of 0.7. Replication of a call with futures is illustrated by Figure 8.16 and replication of a short call with the underlying stock is demonstrated by Exercise 8.5.

Such replication will involve cash flows. Replicating long option positions involves buying when the price of the underlying rises and selling when it falls. This is because a rise in the price of the underlying causes an increase in delta

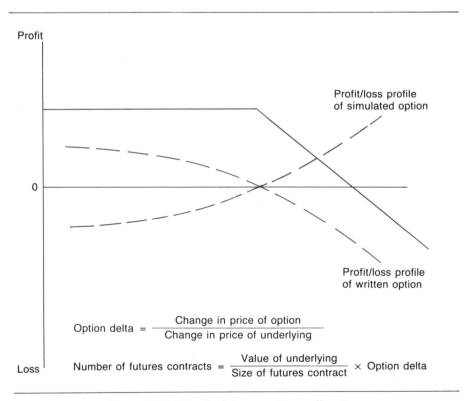

Figure 8.16 Delta hedging a written call option

178

and hence the need to buy more of the underlying (or futures). Conversely, a fall in price lowers delta and necessitates selling. Buying high and selling low entails a net cash outflow. The theoretical time value of the option equals the expected losses from such transactions. So replicating long option positions results in losses that correspond to the time value of the replicated option. (Specifically this is the time value resulting from volatility of the price of the underlying rather than from financing costs.) Conversely the replication of short option positions would be expected to provide profits that correspond to the time (volatility) value.

Exercise 8.5

Question
An equity options trader sells an at-the-money call option on 1,000 shares of the equity of XYZ plc for a 28-day period. The trade is hedged in the equity market using delta-weighted hedging until 7 days before expiry, when the position is closed by buying back a similar call in the market. Assuming that the trader always deals at the market's price, and neglecting the funding of interim cash flows, calculate the net profit or loss on the transaction, given the following information about the underlying share price and the option's delta:

Week	Share price(p)		Option price (p)		Option delta	Days remaining
	Bid	Offer	Bid	Offer		
1	98.5	101.5	2.5	4.0	0.54	28
2	103.5	106.5	5.5	7.0	0.78	21
3	105.5	108.5	6.5	8.0	0.89	14
4	108.5	111.5	9.5	11.0	1.00	7

Answer
Week 1. Sell call option for £25. Buy 540 shares at £101.5 = £548.10
Week 2. Buy 240 shares at £1.065 = £255.60
Week 3. Buy 110 shares at £1.085 = £119.35
At close. Buy call option for £110. Sell 890 shares at £1.085 = £965.65
Net loss: £25 − £548.10 − £255.60 − £119.35 − £110 + £965.65 = £42.40

The analysis will consider three constant ratio funds: (i) 50 per cent in equities and 50 per cent in short term deposits; (ii) 50 per cent in equities and 50 per cent in bonds with a positive correlation of returns; and (iii) 50 per cent in equities and 50 per cent in bonds with a negative correlation of returns. The funds are rebalanced to the 50 per cent split once a year.

1. Suppose that the fund has just been rebalanced and that over the following five years the rate of return on equities is constant at 8 per cent p.a. and the rate of interest on deposits is constant at 4 per cent p.a. What is the overall rate of return on the fund? What would the rate of return have been in the absence of rebalancing over the five-year period?

Suppose that the fund initially consists of £100 in equities and £100 on deposit. The progress of the fund is as follows:

Year	Initial value (£)		Value after return (£)		Value after rebalancing (£)	
	Equities	Deposit	Equities	Deposit	Equities	Deposit
1	100.00	100.00	108.00	104.00	106.00	106.00
2	106.00	106.00	114.48	110.24	112.36	112.36
3	112.36	112.36	121.35	116.84	119.10	119.10
4	119.10	119.10	128.63	123.87	126.25	126.25
5	126.25	126.25	136.35	131.30	133.82	133.82

The total fund value after five years is:

$$£133.82 + £133.82 = £267.64$$

In the absence of rebalancing the fund value would have been:

$$£100(1.08)^5 + £100(1.04)^5 = £268.60$$

2. What fund values would have emerged if deposits had consistently yielded 4 per cent p.a. while equities yielded 28, − 12, 28, − 12 and 15.8 per cent in successive years? (Note that these equity yields provide the same average compound rate of return as a constant 8 per cent p.a.)

Year	Initial value (£)		Value after return (£)		Value after rebalancing (£)	
	Equities	Deposit	Equities	Deposit	Equities	Deposit
1	100.00	100.00	128.00	104.00	116.00	116.00
2	116.00	116.00	112.64	120.64	116.64	116.64
3	116.64	116.64	149.30	121.31	135.30	135.30
4	135.30	135.30	119.07	140.71	129.89	129.89
5	129.89	129.89	150.41	135.09	142.75	142.75

The total value of the fund after five years is £285.50. In the absence of rebalancing the fund value would have been £100 (1.28) (0.88) (1.28) (0.88) (1.158) + £100(1.04)^5 = £268.59.

There is a dynamic replication of a short call option position. Rising stock prices lead to a sale of shares, producing a decline in delta; falling share prices lead to buying, thereby raising the delta of the implicit option. The implicit option sale should enhance returns, with the enhancement rising with share price volatility and the length of time for which the investment is made.

The difference between the fund values of £267.64 in (1) and £285.50 in (2) represents the time value of the implicit short option. In (1) there is zero volatility of returns on equities whereas in (2) there is a non-zero volatility. It will be seen from (3) that an increase in the volatility of equity returns causes an increase in the time value of the implicit option and hence a further enhancement of the return on the fund.

3. Carry out (2) with equity returns of 56, − 24, 56, − 24, and 4.5 per cent in successive years. (These equity returns provide the same average compound rate as in (1) and (2)).

Year	Initial value (£)		Value after return (£)		Value after rebalancing (£)	
	Equities	Deposit	Equities	Deposit	Equities	Deposit
1	100.00	100.00	156.00	104.00	130.00	130.00
2	130.00	130.00	98.80	135.20	117.00	117.00
3	117.00	117.00	182.52	140.61	161.56	161.56
4	161.56	161.56	122.79	168.02	145.41	145.41
5	145.41	145.41	151.95	151.22	151.59	151.59

The total value of the fund after five years is £303.17. This compares to £268.59 without rebalancing and £293.87 with 100 per cent investment in equities.

4. Carry out (3) but instead of the deposit use an investment in bonds with returns of 28, − 12, 28, − 12, and −4.1 per cent. (The average compound rate of return on bonds is thus the same as that produced by a constant 4 per cent p.a.)

Year	Initial value (£)		Value after return (£)		Value after rebalancing (£)	
	Equities	Deposit	Equities	Deposit	Equities	Deposit
1	100.00	100.00	156.00	128.00	142.00	142.00
2	142.00	142.00	107.92	124.96	116.44	116.44
3	116.44	116.44	181.65	149.04	165.34	165.34
4	165.34	165.34	125.66	145.50	135.58	135.58
5	135.58	135.58	141.68	130.02	127.85	127.85

The total fund value after five years would be £255.69. In the absence of rebalancing, the fund value would have been £268.59. The implicit short call on the equities is accompanied by an implicit long call on the bonds. The enhancement from the short option is offset by the implicit payment of an option premium.

5. Carry out (4) but with bond returns of − 12, 28, − 12, 28, and 4.1 per cent (again producing an average compound rate of return equal to that from a constant 4 per cent p.a.).

Year	Initial value (£)		Value after return (£)		Value after rebalancing (£)	
	Equities	Deposit	Equities	Deposit	Equities	Deposit
1	100.00	100.00	156.00	88.00	122.00	122.00
2	122.00	122.00	92.72	156.16	124.44	124.44
3	124.44	124.44	194.13	109.51	151.82	151.82
4	151.82	151.82	115.38	194.33	154.86	154.86
5	154.86	154.86	161.82	148.51	155.17	155.17

The total fund value after five years would be £310.33. In the absence of rebalancing, the fund value would have been £268.59. In this case both equities and bonds are subject to a 'buy low, sell high' strategy so that there are implicit short options on both equities and bonds, and hence yield enhancements on both corresponding to the option premiums.

CONCLUSIONS

When using a fixed ratio between equities and deposits total fund returns are greater when the volatility of equity returns rises. This is consistent with the yield enhancement from the implicit sale of an option rising with increased volatility, as would be expected given the relationship between option prices and the volatility of the underlying instrument.

When comparing fixed ratio strategies it can be seen that if bond returns negatively correlate with equity returns, then combining equities with bonds provides the highest returns, whereas if bond returns positively correlate with equity returns, then combining equities with deposits is the superior strategy. Empirically, bond returns tend to positively correlate with equity returns, whereas returns on deposits tend to have a lower (possibly even negative) correlation with equity returns. Such observations suggest the superiority of equity−deposit funds over equity−bond funds.

This superiority of equity−deposit funds could be overturned if bond returns, on average, sufficiently exceeded returns on deposits. This implies that higher correlation with equity returns should be compensated for with higher expected returns on bonds. Such an inference is consistent with the increased expected returns required to compensate for increased systematic risk (usually measured by beta) in the Capital Asset Pricing Model.

9

——— ∾ ———

Concluding remarks

The reader will now be aware of the vast variety of financial investments available. However, financial investments are only one part of the investment picture. Other types of investment are important, and in the early years of a person's working life may be far more important.

Property, especially residential property, is an important form of non-financial investment. Although buying a home may generate some capital gains the main return from such an investment is in the form of having somewhere to live. In other words, the returns are primarily of a non-financial nature. Furthermore the cost of the property may not be entirely monetary. Besides paying a sum of money for their home many people spend time and effort in improving the property and, in so doing, enhance its market value. The addition to the monetary value of a property due to the work of its residents is sometimes referred to as 'sweat equity'.

Other forms of non-financial investment might include businesses. The investment might include purchase of property, stocks of materials, and equipment. The 'sweat equity' is likely to be considerable. Some people invest in the form of antiques, paintings, stamps, or coins. In these cases, much of the return would be in the form of the pleasure that the owner obtains from them.

A form of investment that is frequently overlooked is the investment in human capital. The acquisition of expertise and skills enhances earnings potential. The present value of such enhanced earnings can be so large that it exceeds all other forms of investment put together.

So far all investments discussed have been individual investments. There are also communal or public investments. Roads, parks, non-private schools, non-private hospitals, defence establishments, and other government property ultimately belong to the residents of the country and constitute part of the investment portfolio of those residents. It must also be remembered, however, that government debt is really taxpayers' debt.

Glossary

Acceptance   By accepting a bill issued by a company a bank guarantees that it will be honoured.

Accrued interest   The interest earned since the last payment on a bond. This amount is paid to a seller of a bond.

Aggressive stocks   Stocks which have betas greater than one.

American depository receipt (ADR)   When dealing in many of the big UK shares, American investors don't deal in London. Instead shares are left on deposit with US banks, while investors trade in ADRs, which effectively give them the right to those shares should they want them.

American style options   Options that can be exercised prior to expiration.

Annuities   Funds that provide annual income, generally for retirement and most often for the life of the annuitant (the person who owns the annuity).

Arbitrage   Exploiting price anomalies for profit. For example, if prices for the same item differ between locations, the item may be bought relatively cheaply and sold at a higher price. Pure arbitrage involves no risk and no use of the arbitrager's own capital.

Asked price   The price at which an investor can buy. (Also known as **offer price**.)

Asset allocation   The attempt to find a mix of asset classes (stocks, bonds, real estate, etc.) that best meets the needs of the investor.

At best   An order to a stockbroker to deal at the best possible price rather than at a limit, getting the highest selling price or finding the lowest buying price.

Attainable set   All possible portfolios that can be made from a given universe of securities.

Back-end load   (also called a *redemption fee*, an *exit fee*, or *deferred sales charge*)   A fee paid upon the sale of mutual fund shares.

Bank bill   A bill of exchange accepted by a bank.

Basis point $1/_{100}$th of 1 per cent.

Basket trade   The trade on entire portfolios of securities at one time.

Bear   Someone who expects a fall in the prices of instruments such as stocks and bonds.

Bearer bond   A bond that is not registered in a name. The rights to coupons and principal accrue to the holder.

Bed & breakfast   Market practice of selling securities and buying them back to establish a profit or loss for *capital gains tax* purposes.

Beta   A measure of the responsiveness of the price of an individual stock to movements in stock prices as a whole.

Bid price   The price at which an investor can sell to a market maker.

Bid rate   The rate of interest at which an investor can deposit money.

Big Bang The decontrol of London financial markets in 1986, which, among other things, permitted foreign ownership of British brokerage firms.

Bill of exchange A document which commits one company to pay a specific sum of money to another on a particular date.

Blue-chip High-quality, financially strong companies which are leaders in industries and which have been viable over some years.

Bond A security sold in order to raise capital. Bonds normally provide the buyer with an income flow plus the return of the initial capital on the maturity date of the bond.

Broker An intermediary that buys or sells on behalf of an investor or other client.

Broker-dealer A broker that can deal on their own account as well as acting as an agent for clients.

Bull Someone who expects a rise in the price of a financial instrument.

Bulldog bonds United Kingdom sterling-denominated bonds issued by non-British entities.

Call money A bank loan repayable on demand.

Call option The right to buy a financial instrument at a specific price during a period of time (or at a point in time).

Call provision The call provision of a bond allows the issuer to pay off the bond prior to maturity.

Capital gain (or loss) The change in value of an investment.

Capital Asset Pricing Model (CAPM) A theory that suggests that the excess expected return on a security (excess over that on risk-free assets such as Treasury bills) is positively related to the systematic risk of the security. Given the systematic risk, it can be used to estimate the required rate of return to be used as the discount rate in the Dividend Discount Model.

Capitalisation issue Exactly the same as a scrip issue, that is, a free issue of shares to shareholders in proportion to their existing holding. They become no richer as a result, the issue being just a bookkeeping exercise.

Cash and carry Arbitrage determines the relationship between the price of an underlying instrument (e.g. government bonds or a stock index portfolio) and futures contracts on the instrument. Long cash and carry arbitrage involves buying the instrument (with borrowed money) and simultaneously selling futures. Short cash and carry arbitrage involves short selling the instrument (and depositing the receipts) whilst buying futures.

Certificate of deposit (CD) A negotiable instrument issued by a bank in return for a deposit. The maturity is normally short (e.g. three months).

Chartists Technical analysts who believe that they can predict future price movements by analysing trends in past movements, hence their reliance upon charts.

Circuit breaker Price change limits and trading halts aimed at curbing the extent of price fluctuation.

Clearing house An institution that settles mutual indebtedness between organisations or which records trades. (In the case of futures and options the clearing house may also become the counterparty to contract holders.)

Closely held shares Insider-owned shares.

Closing price The price at the close of the market.

Commercial bill A bill issued by an organisation other than a government.

Commercial paper Unsecured notes issued by companies for short-term borrowing.

Commission The fee charged by brokers for security transactions.

Compound rate of return The average rate of return on an investment held for more than one period. It involves interest on interest.

Glossary

Conflicts of interest Actions taken on one's own behalf at the possible expense of a customer, as when an account executive owns a sizeable position in a particular security and issues an advisory to customers to buy that security.

Constant growth model (Gordon model) A special case of the dividend discount model in which expected growth in dividends is assumed to be constant.

Contrarian An approach to investing by buying into a market decline and selling into a market advance.

Conversion premium The price of a convertible security minus the conversion value, frequently expressed as a percentage of the latter.

Conversion price The face value of a convertible security divided by the conversion ratio.

Conversion ratio The number of shares of stock for each convertible security.

Conversion value The market price of a convertible security if converted now. The conversion value equals the conversion ratio times the market price of the stock (share price).

Convertible (bond) A bond that can be converted into a specified number of shares of stock at a point, or points, in time.

Convexity As a numerical measure, convexity gives the difference between the actual percentage change in bond value due to a yield change and the approximate percentage change in bond value as measured by modified duration.

Correlation A statistical measure of the relationship between two variables. For example, if two values tend to move up and down together they would exhibit positive correlation. If they tend to move in opposite directions they are negatively correlated. The coefficient of correlation has a maximum value of 1 and a minimum value of -1.

Coupon An interest payment on a bond or note.

Covered call Covered call writers own the underlying stock and write calls.

Cross-hedging The use of a futures on one underlying as a 'near substitute' for the asset that one really wishes to hedge.

Cum Latin for 'with', so that a share quoted as 'cum' something will carry with it the rights to the forthcoming dividend, scrip issue, rights issue or whatever. If quoted 'ex' it will not carry those rights.

Cumulative Describing instruments in which, if a specified payment is missed, it must be made up before dividends may be paid to shareholders.

Currency account Bank account in a foreign currency.

Cyclical stocks Companies whose earnings fluctuate with the business cycle.

Cylinder A long cylinder is constructed by buying a call option at a high strike price and writing a put option at a low strike price. A short cylinder involves buying a low strike price put and writing a high strike price call.

Day order A limit order that is good only for the day in which it is placed.

Debt ratio The proportion of long-term debt to total capital.

Default risk The risk that a security cannot make its fixed payments.

Delta The change in the price of an option due to a one point change in the price of the stock underlying the option.

Deregulation Reduction in government control.

Derivative securities (options, forwards, futures, swaps) The transfer of actual investments, such as stocks, bonds, real estate, and currencies, in the future.

Direct quotation Quotation of an exchange rate in terms of a number of units of the domestic currency per unit of the foreign currency.

Discount (1) Amount by which the current price falls below the final redemption value of a security. (2) Amount by which the forward price of a currency falls below its spot price.

Discount rate   The rate of interest used to convert a future value into a present value.

Disintermediation   Flows of funds between borrowers and lenders (e.g. by bond sales) that do not involve the money passing through financial intermediaries such as banks.

Diversifiable risk   Non-market or non-systematic risk that can be reduced through portfolio diversification.

Dividend cover   The number of times the net dividend could have been paid from a company's earnings attributable to its shareholders.

Dividend discount model (DDM)   A valuation model in which the value of a share of common stock is defined as the present value of the dividends that can be expected from the share over the share's lifetime or horizon, which may be assumed to be infinite.

Dividend yield   The annual cash dividend divided by the current price of the stock.

Dividends   The payments by a company to its shareholders (owners of ordinary shares or common stock).

Dow Jones Industrial Average   An American stock index consisting of 30 industrial stocks.

Drop-lock bond   A floating rate bond which automatically becomes a fixed rate bond in the event of interest rates falling below a particular level.

Dual-currency bonds   Bonds that pay interest in one currency and principal in another.

Dual-listed stock   Stock that is listed on more than one exchange.

Duration   The duration of a bond (without callability, putability, or convertibility features) is defined as the weighted average time until the bond's cash flows, where the weights are the percentage of the cash flow's present value of the total (present) value of the bond.

Dynamic portfolio insurance   An insurance that protects most of the return on the portfolio by quickly pulling money out of asset markets that are performing poorly and putting it into markets that are performing well.

Earnings   Net profit after tax due to holders of ordinary shares but not necessarily paid out to them. Earnings are usually expressed as so many pence per share.

Earnings yield   A company's annual earnings per share, expressed as a percent of the share's market price.

ECU (European Currency Unit)   A basket currency comprising sums of the currencies of the members of the European Monetary System (EMS).

Efficient frontier   A description referring to all possible Markowitz-efficient portfolios giving an optimal trade-off between risk and return.

Efficient market hypothesis (EMH)   A view that asset prices respond quickly to new information and that all relevant information is incorporated into security prices by the time it reaches the investing public. (See also **semi-strong form**, **strong form** and **weak form**.)

Equities   Ordinary shares (common stock) whose owners take the main risks and who are entitled to those profits left over after all prior charges have been met. They represent part ownership of a company.

Equity   A representation of ownership in a business.

Eurobonds   Bonds issued in any currency but offered to investors in a number of countries by an international syndicate of underwriters.

Eurocurrency   Deposits and loans denominated in a currency other than that of the country in which the deposit is held or loan made.

Eurodollars   US dollars held on deposit in a bank or bank branch outside the United States.

European-style options   Options that cannot be exercised prior to the expiration time.

Glossary

Ex The opposite to cum, ex means 'without'. A price quoted 'ex dividend' will not carry the right to the current dividend. Similarly shares which are ex rights, or ex scrip will exclude the rights to such distributions.

Ex-dividend With reference to a stock, ex-dividend means that any one who acquires that stock at the time will not receive the declared dividend.

Ex-rights day The day on which the stock begins to trade without rights.

Exchange rate risk The risk associated with a foreign investment in that the exchange rate may move against the investor.

Execution The implementation of an order to purchase or sell a security.

Exercise price The price at which the holder of an option has the right to buy or sell (alternatively known as the **strike price**).

Expected rate of return The rate of return expected by investors.

Expiration date The last day on which an option agreement still holds.

Extendible bond A bond that may be extended for a longer period at the holder's option, possibly at a higher interest rate.

Fill-or-kill order A limit order for immediate execution. If it is not immediately executed it is withdrawn.

Financial future The notional right to buy or sell a standard quantity of a financial instrument on a specific future date at a price determined at the time of buying or selling the futures contract.

Fixed annuities Annuities that guarantee a set amount of money each year and, as such, are subject to erosion by inflation.

Fixed income investment An investment, such as a bond, that pays a stated amount of money per period.

Fixed-mix funds Asset allocation mutual funds that divide their assets on a specified basis. (Also known as *constant ratio funds*.)

Floating rate notes (FRNs) Relatively long-dated securities, but the interest payment amount is determined periodically at a prevailing money-market rate.

Flotation The issue of shares of stock in a company for the first time.

Forward Agreement to exchange financial instruments on a future date (e.g. forward currency).

Forward—forward Agreement on the future exchange of financial instruments that will mature on a more distant date (e.g. forward—forward interest rates).

Forward rate agreement (FRA) Notional agreement to deposit or borrow on a specific future date at an interest rate determined in the present (a form of interest rate future).

Front-end load A sales fee paid for the purchase of mutual fund shares.

FTSE-A All Share Index Value weighted index of approximately 700 stocks traded on the International Stock Exchange in London.

FTSE Eurotrack 100 Value weighted index of 100 European stocks (excluding UK stocks).

FTSE Mid 250 Value weighted index of 250 UK stocks (the 101st to the 350th in terms of size).

FTSE 100 Financial Times — Stock Exchange 100. A value-weighted index of the top 100 UK stocks.

Fundamental analysis Ascertaining the appropriate prices of securities by analysing economic data.

Futures contract An obligation to buy or sell an 'underlying' investment or commodity at a given price on a specified future date.

Gearing Expressed as a percentage, gearing usually refers to the extent of a company's indebtedness, being the ratio of all its borrowings to its share capital.

Gilt   Gilt-edged security. A British government bond.

Good-till-cancelled order (or **open order**)   An order that remains on the books until it is cancelled.

Hard currency   A currency that is convertible into major currencies such as the US dollar through the currency markets.

Hedge   A transaction undertaken in order to reduce an existing risk.

Immunisation   The elimination of interest rate risk in a fixed-income portfolio.

Index-linked gilts   UK Government bonds on which both the level of interest paid, and the final redemption payment, are linked to the increase in the retail price index.

Indirect quotation   Quotation of an exchange rate in terms of the number of units of foreign currency per unit of domestic currency.

Industry risk   Risk associated with a particular industry.

Inflation risk   The same as purchasing power risk.

Information risk   The risk that other investors may not recognize an investment's true worth.

Information trade   A trade made by an active manager and based upon information concerning the security.

Inside information   Information about a company that is not available to the general public.

Insider trading   Trading on inside information.

Institutional investor   An institution that invests money on behalf of a number of smaller investors (e.g. pension fund, insurance fund, mutual fund).

Interbank market   The market in which banks lend to, and borrow from, one another.

Interest rate parity relationship   The equilibrium relationship between the spot and forward exchange rates and the interest rates associated with the two currencies.

Interest rate risk   The risk of price change in fixed income investments due to changes in market interest rates.

Intermediary   An institution that takes deposits and uses the receipts to make loans.

In-the-money   A reference to calls whose underlying asset value is above the exercise price or put options whose underlying asset value is below the exercise price.

Intrinsic value   The gross profit available from the immediate exercise of an (American-style) option.

Investment trust   A quoted company whose business is to invest, mainly in other shares, for the benefit of its own shareholders. It differs from a unit trust in being a 'closed-end fund' and in having its own shares quoted on the Stock Exchange. (A type of mutual fund.)

Junk bond   Corporate bond with high risk of default and corresponding high yield.

Kerb market   Unofficial market, often operating outside the normal trading hours of the official market.

LIBOR (London Interbank Offered Rate)   The rate of interest at which major banks in London will lend to each other. (It is the borrowing rate as opposed to the deposit rate which is LIBID.)

Limit order   An order to a stockbroker which only permits a deal to be done if it is possible to execute at a certain price or better.

Liquidation   The sale of an asset.

Liquidity   Assets that are either in the form of money or can be easily converted into money.

Liquidity risk   The risk that an investment may not be convertible into cash at the full current market value.

Glossary

Liquidity premium   The additional return generally paid to investors for sacrificing the liquidity of their investment.

Listed security   One that is traded on an organised exchange.

Long   Someone holding shares is said to be long in them.

Manipulation   The activity of a person or a pool of people that is designed to make the price of a security behave in a manner that is different from that caused by supply and demand forces.

Manipulation risk   The risk that the investment could be part of fraudulent manipulation.

Market efficiency   The tendency for security prices to reflect economic information fully.

Market maker   A dealer who publishes bid and ask prices on certain securities and is committed to trade at those prices. It is thus ensured that a market always exists in those securities.

Market order   An order placed at the market price.

Market portfolio   A portfolio that contains all securities in proportion to their relative market value.

Market price   The price at which a security currently trades.

Market risk   Non-diversifiable or systematic risk that affects the entire market.

Market timing   A reference to attempts to move capital in and out of various markets to maximise participation in bullish movements.

Markowitz-efficient   A Markowitz-efficient portfolio means that there is no other portfolio that has both a higher expected return and less risk as measured by standard deviation.

Maturity   Period to the redemption of a financial claim.

Momentum   For example momentum of earnings measures the 'growth in the growth rate' of earnings.

Money broker   As a broker in the interbank market, a money broker brings together banks wishing to lend and those wishing to borrow. There are also money brokers in currencies and eurobonds.

Negative yield curve   Short-term interest rates higher than long-term ones.

Net asset value (NAV)   The value of all assets held by a mutual fund divided by the number of shares outstanding.

New York Stock Exchange (NYSE) composite index   A stock index based on the entire NYSE and value-weighted.

No arbitrage band   A range of futures prices within which no profits are available from arbitrage (e.g. from cash and carry arbitrage). If the futures price moves outside the band it becomes possible to make arbitrage profits. The arbitrage would tend to move the futures price back into the band.

Noise trades   Trades that occur as a result of emotional impulses.

Noise trading   The trading activity of all those without sound fundamental information.

Nominal rate of return   The rate of return that is not adjusted for inflation.

Nominal value   The face value or par value of a security as opposed to its market value.

Nominee   Shares can be registered in a nominee name, rather than the real one, if they are being managed on behalf of someone else (also known as **street name**).

Normal distribution   The distribution of the probabilities of alternative values of a variable (e.g. a price). It has a bell-shaped form indicating high probabilities of values near the average and low probability of extreme values.

Note   An instrument recording a promise to pay sums of money in the future. Similar to bonds but typically of shorter maturity.

Offer price   The price at which an investor can buy. (Also known as **asked price**.)

Introduction to financial investment

Offer rate   The rate of interest at which money can be borrowed.

Offshore banking   Banking facilities in locations that offer a very favourable tax environment. Typically the country in which the bank is registered is not that in which the actual banking operations are undertaken.

Open interest   The number of outstanding contracts in a futures market.

Open market operations   Dealings in the money markets by a central bank for the purpose of influencing the liquidity of financial institutions and/or controlling interest rates.

Option   The right to buy or sell at a specific price during a time period (or at a point in time). Can also be a right to borrow or lend at a particular interest rate.

Out-of-the-money   A reference to call options whose stock price is below the exercise price or put options whose stock price is above the exercise price.

Over the counter (OTC)   Tailor-made instruments, as opposed to the standardised exchange-traded ones.

Oversubscription   An offer of shares or other securities to the investing public is oversubscribed when the number of shares applied for exceeds the number available. This can lead to the scaling down of applications, their placing in a ballot or even their rejection.

Par value   The value of a bond at maturity, also known as *face value*, or **nominal value**.

Partly paid   Securities on which only part of the full cost has been paid, with a further call or calls due to be paid by holders at a future date.

Political risk   Risk associated with foreign investments due to political instability in the country or region.

Portfolio   An investor's collection of assets.

Portfolio insurance   Strategies used to protect a portfolio in the event of a market downturn.

Portfolio rate of return   The rate of return on an entire portfolio of investments.

Positive yield curve   Long-term interest rates higher than short-term ones.

Preference shares   Shares on which a fixed level of dividend is paid, providing the money is available. They rank in the pecking order below debentures and loan stock but above ordinary shares (common stock), with dividends paid before holders of ordinary equity get their money.

Premium   (1) Price of an option. (2) Amount by which the forward price of a currency exceeds its spot price. (3) Excess of a futures value over the spot value.

Price/earnings (P/E) ratio   The current price of the stock divided by the company's last reported annual earnings per share.

Primary market   The market for newly raised capital.

Principal   (1) Someone buying or selling on their own account rather than as an agent for a client. (2) The sum of money repayable at the maturity of a bond or other debt instrument.

Private placement   The sale of an entire issue of securities to one or a few investors.

Program trading   The trading of entire portfolios or baskets of stock at one time, often in conjunction with derivative instruments.

Purchasing power risk   The risk that inflation may diminish the purchasing power of the funds.

Put bonds   Put bonds limit buyer risk by obligating the issuer to buy the bond if the price falls below a certain level.

Put option   The right to sell an instrument at a particular price during a time period (or on a specific date).

Glossary

Raider An investor who attempts to take over another company without the co-operation of the target company.

Random walk hypothesis The theory that price changes will be random if they rationally reflect available economic information.

Rate of return The return on an investment stated as a percentage of the amount invested.

Real rate of return The inflation-adjusted rate of return.

Redemption date The date when fixed-interest stocks, such as gilts and debentures, are redeemed, usually at their par value.

Redemption yield The yield on a fixed-interest stock which takes into account the annual benefit to be gained as the stock climbs towards its redemption price. If the stock stands above its redemption price, the redemption yield will be lower than the running yield.

Repo Sale and repurchase agreement. The sale of short-term securities with a simultaneous commitment to buy them back at a later date. A means of short-term borrowing.

Retractable bonds Bonds that may be redeemed, at the holder's option, on a specified date prior to expiration.

Return on investment (ROI) The net income divided by total capital, where total capital is debt plus equity.

Return on equity (ROE) Net income (total earnings) divided by equity.

Return to volatility ratio (Treynor measure) Measures the ratio of average excess returns to portfolio beta.

Reward to variability ratio (Sharpe measure) Measures the return to the investor above the riskless rate due to taking on the uncertainty of a portfolio of risky securities rather than Treasury bills. It is calculated as the ratio of average 'excess returns' to portfolio standard deviation, where excess returns is the difference between portfolio returns and Treasury bill yields or 'riskless' returns.

Rights issue An issue of new shares to shareholders, generally at a discount to the current market price, with the number of shares offered being in proportion to the shareholder's existing holding.

Risk-free investment An investment that is virtually free of risk, such as a short-term Treasury bill.

Risk management Controlling the level of financial risk to which an investment is exposed (e.g. by hedging).

Round-trip commission Often used in commodities and futures, it involves paying the purchase and sales commissions up front.

Running yield Alternatively known as the *flat yield*, or *interest yield*, or *current yield*, this is the annual rate of return offered by the interest or dividend on a stock or bond.

Samurai bonds Yen-denominated bonds issued in Japan by non-Japanese issuers.

Secondary market A market in which already-existing securities are bought and sold. Distinct from the primary market in which newly issued securities are sold.

Securitisation (1) The aggregating of existing assets such as mortgages so as to use them as backing for bond issues; effectively selling a bundle of existing assets. (2) Sale of bills or bonds as an alternative to borrowing from banks.

Security A medium of investment (e.g. stocks, bonds, bills).

Security market line (SML) Shows where individual securities lie on a graph, charting their market risk and return.

Semi-strong form (of the efficient market hypothesis) This form of the hypothesis maintains that the market is efficient with respect to all publicly available information.

Settlement The actual transfer of the security from seller to buyer.

Share An instrument denoting part ownership of the equity of a company. Alternatively known as a **stock**.

Short position In a futures contract, a short position is the legally binding agreement to deliver.

Short selling Selling borrowed stock.

Signalling theory A theory stating that companies may signal information through the use of dividends, etc., rather than announce it, partly because a signal has greater credibility.

Sinking fund Provisions in a bond's indenture which help guarantee that the bond will be repaid at maturity. The indenture specifies that a certain amount of the firm's earnings are put aside each year for this purpose.

Small firm effect A reference to anomalous findings that the purchase of the shares of smaller capitalisation companies produced stronger portfolio performance.

Sovereign risk Risk of expropriation of assets held in a foreign country.

Special drawing rights (SDRs) A form of international money issued by the International Monetary Fund.

Specialist The market maker on some exchanges.

Specific risk Risk beyond market and industry risk that relates to the specific investment being undertaken.

Speculation Buying or selling with a view to making profits from price changes.

Spot price Current price as opposed to forward or futures price.

Spread The excess of the asked (offer) price or interest rate over the bid price or interest rate. It is the market-maker's or banker's margin.

Stag Someone who applies for a new issue of shares, intending to sell them almost immediately in order to make a quick profit.

Standard deviation A measure of the extent to which a set of values (forming a normal distribution) are dispersed around their average (mean). Often used as a measure of price volatility.

Statistical arbitrage A type of program trading where a relatively small but well-diversified basket of stocks that is correlated with the stock index is used instead of buying the market.

Stock Most commonly used to denote shares representing ownership of the equity of a firm (common stock, ordinary shares). However, it is sometimes treated as synonymous with bonds.

Stock dividends Extra shares of stock, based upon the number already owned.

Stock exchange Market for the trading of stocks and bonds.

Stock index A measure of the average value of stock prices at a point in time (e.g. S & P 500, FTSE 100, Nikkei Dow, DAX, CAC 40, Hang Seng).

Stock split Similar to a stock dividend in that the shareholder will be given a certain number of new shares for every share owned.

Stop loss order An order to sell shares once the price of the stock falls to a certain level.

Straddle The simultaneous long position of a put and call on the same stock with the same expiration date and striking price. (A short straddle involves short positions in both put and call options.)

Strangle A put and a call with different strike prices but the same expiration (the options are either both long or both short).

Strap The purchase of two calls and a put.

Street name A reference to registration of customer's securities in the name of the brokerage firm.

Glossary

Striking price   The contract exercise price of an option.

Strip   The purchase of two puts and a call.

Strong form (of the efficient market hypothesis)   This form of the hypothesis maintains that all information of any kind, including non-public inside information, is already reflected in any security price that we see.

Swap   (1) An agreement by two parties to service one another's debts. (2) A simultaneous spot purchase (or sale) and forward sale (or purchase), that is, buying for one point in time and selling for another.

Tap stock   Government securities of which only part of the issue has so far been sold to the public, the rest being let out on to the market as the government, through its agents, sees fit.

Tax rate risk   The risk that tax rates may change, resulting in a loss of after-tax return.

Tax shelter   An investment whose primary purpose is the reduction of taxes rather than a return from the investment per se.

Technical analysis   Prediction of price movements based on the proposition that markets have their own internal momentum independent of economic events. Chartism is a form of technical analysis that uses charts and graphs of past price movements to forecast future price behaviour.

Tender   An issue of securities in which investors must bid a maximum price at which they are willing to subscribe. When the striking price is fixed, all those tendering at that level or above will receive shares.

Time value   The time value of an option is the amount by which the value of an option exceeds its intrinsic value.

Tombstone   A reference to an advertisement for a public issue of bonds that contains the names of all the members of the selling syndicate.

Treasury bill   A debt instrument issued by the central government for raising short-term finance.

Treasury bond   A debt instrument issued by the central government for raising long-term finance.

Treasury stock   Stock that has been bought back by the company and held in the Treasury.

Turnover   In the brokerage business, turnover refers to the volume of buying and selling.

Undated   Government securities which have no fixed date set for repayment.

Underlying   The instrument upon which a futures or option contract is based. Underlying instruments include stocks, bonds, interest rates, stock indices and currencies.

Underwriter   Someone who undertakes to subscribe for all or part of an issue of securities if it is not wholly taken up by the public, in return for which an underwriting commission is paid. The underwriter will pass on this commitment to sub-underwriters such as banks, insurance companies and pension funds, and they will also receive commission.

Unit trust   A trust formed to manage a portfolio on behalf of the holders of its units. Each unit-holder's stake in that trust is in direct proportion to the number of units he or she holds. The value of units depends, not upon supply or demand, but upon the value of the portfolio. (An open-ended mutual fund.)

Unsecured loan stock   A fixed-interest stock issued by a company, but which is not secured by any of its assets.

Value-weighted   Refers to an index whose components are weighted by the value of the stock.

Variable annuities   Annuities that pay an amount of money each year which is determined by the market performance of funds invested.

Volatility of return A measure of the degree of fluctuation over time, often measured by standard deviation.

Warrant A long-term option giving the holder the right to subscribe for a stock (or other instrument) at a specific price during a period of time.

Weak form (of the efficient market hypothesis) This form of the hypothesis maintains that the market is efficient with respect to information in historical security prices.

White knight A friendly acquirer of a company faced with a hostile takeover.

White squires Used to prevent hostile takeovers by holding large blocks of a company's shares in their friendly hands.

Wholesale market The market for deposits and loans in which each transaction involves a large sum of money. It is largely an interbank market.

Yankee bond A bond issued in the United States by a company outside the United States, but denominated in US dollars.

Yield For traded securities the yield is the interest or the dividend divided by the present price, measured as a percentage.

Yield curve Shows the relationship between time to maturity and yield to maturity.

Yield curve options OTC options traded on the difference between the yields on Treasury securities of different times to maturity.

Yield gap The difference between the average yield on long-dated gilts and that on equities.

Zero-coupon bond A bond that pays no interest or coupon. The return to the holder arises from the bond being sold at a discount to its redemption value at maturity.

Zero sum game The activity in which the profits of some are matched by the losses of others so that there is no net gain. Attempts by fund managers to outperform an index may be an example.

Index

Index

Index

Index

Shareholder's equity, definition 15
Shareholding value, hedging using put
    options 73–4
Shares,
  preference 52–3
  preferred 52
  see also Stocks
Sharpe measure 126
Simple returns 4
Standard deviation 18
Statistical expectation 18
Stock,
  required rate of return 44–5
  see also Stock valuation
Stock Exchange Automated Quotation
  (SEAQ) 58
Stock exchanges 55–8
  functions 55–6
  national 57
  over the counter 57
  regional 57, 58
  types 57–8
Stock index futures 16–18
  hedging 135, 137–41, 147–52
  pricing 141–3
Stock index options 168
  determination of strike price 90–1
Stock index warrant 87
Stock indices 129–34
Stock leverage 15
Stock markets,
  global trading 58
  primary markets 56–7

secondary markets 56–7
trading systems 58–61
  order-driven system 59, 60–1
  quote-driven system 58–9
Stock valuation 43–9
  discounting cash flows 43–4
  discounting future dividends 44–9
Subordinated debt 28
Swaps 174–8
  asset-based interest rate swaps 176–7
  currency 174–6
  equity swaps 177–8
Synthetic futures 159
Systematic risk 6–7
  reduction using portfolio diversification
    19–21

Tax rate risk 6, 7
Technical analysis 53–4
Third-party warrants 87
Tokyo Stock Exchange 61
Treasury bills 2–3, 26

Undated bonds 27
Unit trusts 120–2

Warrants 86–7
With-profits funds 122–4

Yield curve 36–42

Zero coupon bonds 2, 32